Contents

Appendix

Plates

Figures

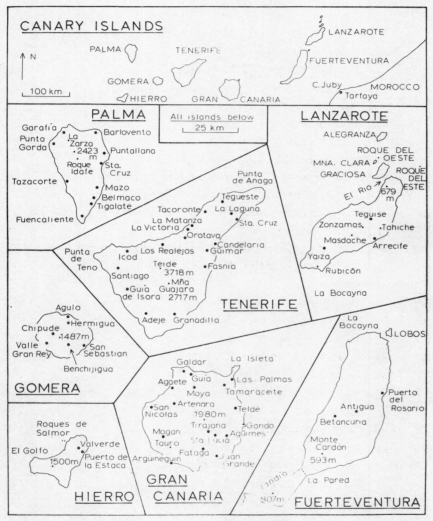

Figure 1   *Map of the Canary Islands*

Introduction

The ancient people of the Canaries have long been of interest to Europeans. This first took the form of slave-catching raids, soon followed by full-scale invasions and then colonization. Once the islanders had as a result disappeared as a recognizable people, the Europeans romanticized them and then made them the subjects of scholarship. In the last two decades there has been much scientific investigation into the Canaries' past. This interest has been one of the stimuli to island consciousness — secondary to the greater influences of the archipelago's economic problems and of Spanish regionalism — to the point where a few even support an independence movement claiming to represent the disappeared ancient people. CAMDEN P.L.

It should be said at once that this book combines several aims. History is alive to the degree to which it throws light on the present. The conquest and near-extermination of the simple shepherds of the Canaries was the first stage in the European colonial cycle now approaching its end. The sophisticated stratagems used throughout the world in the following centuries can be seen in crude incipient form in the invasions of the Canaries — as can the aftermaths of slavery and degradation under the colonial power. Not that parallels are limited to the past: in Brazil, for example, the original inhabitants are at present subject to similar physical and cultural assault. The reader interested in these matters should find the present book useful in assessing the ethnic aspect of the present Canary independence movement, though to say this is in no way to support its aims and tactics, alien to almost the entire archipelago population.

Of course, the legendary ancient people are equally of great interest for their peculiar culture and because of the complex problems they present to archaeologists. Above all, perhaps, by their welcoming and forgiving behaviour towards strangers and invaders — perhaps one of the touchstones of social maturity — in this clearly surpassing the conquerors and settlers, as even the early chroniclers noted. This has been a characteristic of many 'primitive' societies, in the majority also disappeared. In fact, treating the evolution of the Canary Islanders either as an academic exercise or as entertaining folklore is less rewarding than a consideration of their place in the development of human behaviour and society.

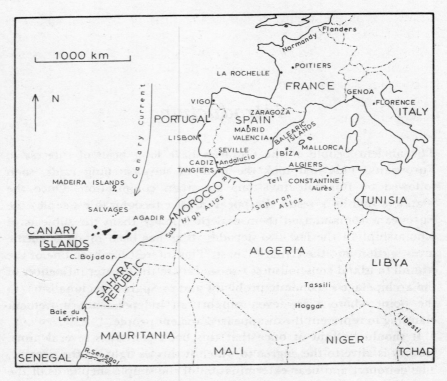

Figure 2   *Map of N. W. Africa and W. Europe*

Reliable and informative major sources begin about the time of Christ with the narrative by explorers sent out by Juba II, king of Roman Mauretania. The next information comes from a description of the raids by Niccoloso da Recco in 1341. The most valuable MSS are those of the French invaders, Gadifer de la Salle and Jean de Bethencourt, 1402-5. In the middle of the same century came the notes of two men passing through the Canaries on Portuguese slaving expeditions to W. Africa: Gil Eannes de Azurara, 1443, and Ca da Mosto, 1455. The Spanish conquests at the end of the fifteenth century are best known from works compiled later, though there are useful notes in writers such as Bernáldez, 1479, Sedēno, 1484, and Gómez Escudero, 1494. The best of the detailed works are those by the Dominican Alonso de Espinosa, c. 1558 (published 1594, Tenerife only), the Italian fortifications engineer Leonardo Torriani, c. 1590, and the Franciscan Juan de Abreu y Galindo, c. 1600 (published 1632). The early writers, no less than the later, drew upon their predecessors; however, they do often disagree in detail and even in major aspects, suggesting that, understandably, each had only a partial knowledge of the varied island cultures. Romantic works, like that of Antonio de Viana, 1604, cannot be considered trustworthy.

Late in the eighteenth century came José de Viera y Clavijo's thorough history of the conquests (1772). The only major source-book in English, that of George Glas, was published in 1764; it made some interesting observations, for example over the origins of the ancient tongue, but is known primarily for its inclusion of Abreu y Galindo's work, the only form in which this is known.

The nineteenth century saw three scholars at work in the Canaries. Sabine Berthelot, Gregorio Chil y Naranjo and René Verneau each made excellent syntheses, including observations on their own period, these now ethnological material. Verneau can be seen as the first of the line of modern field-workers: painstakingly and often in dangerous conditions, he collected physical and cultural material and data from the pre-conquest sites. Inevitably, much archipelago material went to France; Verneau founded the Institut de Paléontologie Humaine (Paris).

Interest in the Canaries' inscriptions began with the recognition a century ago of those on Hierro's Julan lava-flows. The opening in 1879 of El Museo Canario by Chil brought together a huge collection of skeletal material, resulting in an emphasis on physical anthropology throughout the first half of the twentieth century; the major study was by Ernest Hooton, 1925. John Abercromby summarized the pottery and the language, 1914–17. Domenik Wölfel also studied the ancient tongue, 1940. The Civil War brought many more German and Austrian scholars to the archipelago. Unlike Verneau, however, the academics of the early twentieth century rarely ventured into the field so that, their theories once out-dated, their work offers little of interest.

Between 1926–68, Elías Serra Rafols held the history chair at La Laguna University, Tenerife, publishing many early MSS and reconstructing blank periods in the Canaries' past; his students have continued this work, in particular throwing light on island slavery. In 1924 Serra's department first published *Revista de Historia* (now *de Canaria*). About a decade later *El Museo Canario* appeared on Gran Canaria, published by the Las Palmas museum. In 1933, Serra launched *Fontes Rerum Canariarum*, devoted to original documents and archives. A new phase of activity began at La Laguna, in 1968, with the opening of the Department of Archaeology, Prehistory and Ethnology; the first professor, Manuel Pellicer y Catalán, brought a much-needed re-appraisal and new approach to Canary archaeology, together with the first — yet essential — understanding of NW African prehistory. An initial project has been to map the archipelago sites, the publication of this work under way at the time of writing.

Late in the 1950s, Frederick Zeuner began an invigorating and varied series of field and laboratory studies, leading a group from

London University; his death left the work incomplete. Simultaneously there was renewed investigation into the physical anthropology. The wide-ranging approach of Miguel Fusté Ara was also interrupted by his death, in 1966. The invaluable work of Ilse Schwidetsky now covers two decades.

In this century, full-length works of archaeological synthesis have been few: Diego on Tenerife (1968), the present author on Fuerteventura (1973), Hernández Pérez on Palma (1977). A detailed prehistory of the whole archipelago has never before been written. Yet much new evidence has become available in the last two decades; archaeology has itself also evolved. The same can be said of the study of the historical period — and of the now-increasing freedom, in Spain, to discuss matters hitherto unacceptable to the establishment. There seems thus to be a need for a three-part synthesis: the prehistoric period, the conquest, the developments of the last half-millenium.

Since the Civil War, archaeology has been controlled by the state, in a pyramidal structure lying across Spain with its apex in Madrid. Thus, in 1943 a Comisaria Provincial de Arqueología was established in each of the Canaries' two provinces. The first commissars were Luís Diego Cuscoy (Tenerife) and Sebastián Jiménez Sánchez (Gran Canaria), respectively with Serra and Juan Alvarez Delgado as their 'zone' delegates. Alvarez has since published works on linguistics. As the only authorized excavators, the two commissars dominated Canary archaeology for a quarter of a century. In the eastern province, for example, over 400 sites were investigated, according to the commissar himself. About 1968 the *comisarias* were taken over by the Inspección General de Excavaciones Arqueológicas, this under the immediate control of the Museo Arqueológico de Madrid. Jiménez retired early in the 1970s, Diego continues at work. The new wave of young and increasingly-scientific workers has strongly criticized the official archaeologists for inadequate techniques, conservation and publication, alleging also (eg Cruz) that the full material and records have never been made available for general study. On Gomera, for example, 50 sites have been investigated without a single detailed report.

From 1945 the centralized organization led to publication of Canary sites in the new official journals of Madrid. But, also in 1945, the Gran Canaria Cabildo, the island's council, brought out the *Anuario de Estudios Atlánticos*, still the best journal on Canary prehistory. In addition to these and to the journals and monographs put out by the Museo Canario and Laguna University, studies will be found in the major national publications and, due to the Canaries' perennial fascination for foreign workers, in numerous European journals. Indeed, in 1970, the Canary Institute was founded in Austria by Herbert Nowak, publishing *Almogaren*; this is almost entirely in German, without abstracts in Spanish or other languages.

In 1958 Diego established the excellent Sta. Cruz Museum, under the Tenerife Cabildo. This museum has published several important monographs and also the proceedings of the fifth Panafrican Congress on Prehistory (1963). Diego's own numerous publications provide clear summaries of the available information on the western Canaries. The present author acknowledges the help of Luís Diego Cuscoy and his staff. Investigators will also find material in the run-down Museo Cosmológico of Sta. Cruz de la Palma and, of course, in the main ethnology collections of Madrid, Paris and London. The enormous and notorious collection unscientifically pillaged from the sites of the adjacent Sahara by Hector Vásquez, commander of the Spanish army of occupation of the 1950s, is now in the Tenerife Museum and thus available for comparison with the ancient Canary culture.

The conservation of field monuments depends both on physical preservation and on the education of the public. Gran Canaria is easily the richest in interesting sites. The earliest conservation was perhaps that of the Cueva Pintada (Gáldar) in 1970, followed by that of the nearby common granary of Valerón (Cuesta de Silva) and of the Cuatro Puertas complex, a religious site, on the east (south of Telde). Appalling official destruction, with *folklórico* reconstruction, has recently taken place at the important site of La Fortaleza de Sta. Lucia (central mountains); the probable scene of the last encounter between islanders and *conquistadores* in 1483, it has played its part in the 1978 celebrations of the founding, five hundred years ago, of Las Palmas, the invaders' first fortress. The unique Gáldar tombs, used as rubbish dumps by the neighbourhood, have only a noticeboard as protection. It is however the inscriptions, notably those of Balos (S.E.), which, by the graffiti obliterating the prehistoric engravings, will permanently record the vandalism amongst the present society. The major inscription sites of Palma (Belmaco, La Zarza) and of Hierro (Julan) have suffered in the same way; where possible the rock faces have been broken off and removed. One museum director, with clear sorrow, said to the author: '*Es un país de bárbaros*', a phrase perhaps not heard from a Spaniard since before the conquest.

The 1970s have seen two revolutions in Canary archaeology. The old school held dogmatically to various beliefs. First, in a 'respectable' antiquity and ancestry for the original islanders, their arrival long placed around 3000 BC and their origins in the non-African Mediterranean. The anthropologists have always kept pace with the archaeologists, adjusting their charges, Procrustes-wise, to fit the current theories. The advent of radiocarbon assay has produced date after date within the last two thousand years. The famous 'megalithic'

tomb of La Guancha (Gáldar) has given a date of eleventh century
AD. The reaction, as elsewhere, was not acceptance and adjustment
but disbelief and a frantic search for reasons upon which to reject the
archipelago's first firm dating evidence. Soon, however, the early
immigrants were quietly moved down into the second millennium. At
first the assays were carried out in N. Europe but recently they have
been the work of the Rocosolana Institute of Physical Chemistry,
Madrid.

Early in the seventies, Pellicer, having come in fresh with no entrenched hypothesis to defend, proposed that the first immigration
occurred in the middle of the first millennium BC, basing himself upon
his two earliest C14 dates from Arena Cave (Tenerife). However, the
only associated material appears to be the bones of giant lizards and
charcoal (in a volcanic island); confirmation is needed that these dates
apply to human occupation and, in particular, to the major immigration (Juba's expeditionaries certainly found traces of earlier
occupation). Also in the early 1970s, and integrating the carbon
datings into the mass of physical, cultural and historical evidence, the
present author proposed (1973) that the major immigration occurred
early in the Christian era. It must be remembered that the Azores,
Madeira and C Verd archipelagos were all empty when discovered by
Europeans at the end of the Middle Ages. One might thus in fact see
the Canaries as populated comparatively early even by the present
writer's dating. Had the immigrants been a seafaring people they
would have soon reached the other groups — a peculiar impulse can be
expected to have caused the movement to the Canaries and, as will be
seen, there is a feasible theory.

The other storm in the archipelago has been over stratification. It
had always been said that there was none in the Canaries, not even in
the postulated 5000 years of occupation. This justified the rapid and
indiscriminate clearance of dwelling and burial sites as if they were
single-level occupations. The young archaeologists of the seventies,
working on Tenerife and Palma, have found stratification . . .
initially labelled as exceptional by the other workers, this stratification or, rather, the recognition and recording of it, will now
be standard practice. One of the main handicaps to progress in
Canary prehistory, the absence of a sound relative chronology, could
soon be eliminated as a result.

It is to be hoped that scientific research, in both prehistory and
history, will not be limited to the three main islands. In prehistory
there are further new techniques to be tried in the Canaries. Damp
caves could yield pottery for thermoluminescence dating and pollen
for the reconstruction of the flora and climate sequences and, through
these, strengthen the chronological framework for the prehistoric

culture. The raised shore-lines are too early to be related to man's occupation but, other than by Zeuner, no attempt has been made to use the lava-flows, themselves dateable by various methods; the frequency of volcanic outpourings can be gauged from those recorded in the historical period (summarized in Chapter I).

It can be seen that there are grounds for optimism. New workers are coming in at last, armed with modern techniques and freeing themselves from the hoary creeds of past scholars. Modern Spain, slowly becoming more liberal, should provide a fertile environment for their researches and for the full development and discussion of their conclusions.

1a Bentayga Rock, sacred place and fortress (Gran Canaria)

b *Almogaren* with libation pit, Bentayga

2a The King's Cave massif (Gran Canaria)

b Side-chambers and floor-pits, King's Cave

3a Lava-field cemetery, Arteara (Gran Canaria)

b Individual tumulus, Arteara

4a Common granary, Cuesta de Silva (Gran Canaria)

b Three large tombs, Gáldar (Gran Canaria)

c Tiering, El Agujero tumulus, Gáldar

5a The engraved outcrop, Bco. de Balos (Gran Canaria)

b Engraved horses and men, Bco. de Balos

6a Idafe, sacred rock (Palma)

b Rock engravings, La Zarcita (Palma)

7a Obsidian blocks on rim of Teide crater (Tenerife)

b Prehistoric working-floor on inner slope of Teide crater

8a Shepherds' burial cave, Llano de Maja (Tenerife)

b Fortified rock, Sta. Lucia (Gran Canaria)

9a El Golfo, with tree plantation (Hierro)

b Roques de Salmor, habitat of giant lizard (Hierro)

c El Golfo, with natural woodland (Hierro)

10a Site of sacred water-tree, with cisterns (Hierro)

b Looking down on the Julan *tagoror* (Hierro)

11a Stream in laurel forest, El Cedro (Gomera)

b Torre del Conde, c.1450, San Sebastián (Gomera)

C pour ce que iadis souloit on mecire
en eserpt les bonnes cheualeries q̃
les princes er les conquereurs souloiēt
faire ainsi que on treuue es anstens
hystoires voulons nous cp̃ faire mā
cion de lenpunse que gaditer de la
sale et berlencourt cheualiers nez du royaume de france
lun poitruin du pais de rouastoys lautre noumt du pais de caux

12 The French invaders in their ship, 1402

13a Graciosa, across El Río, from Lanzarote

b Craters and lava-field (Lanzarote)

14 The first European capitals: Teguise on Lanzarote (a) and
Betancuria on Fuerteventura (b)

15a Coat of arms of early settlers (Palma)

b Independence movement graffiti, Las Palmas (Gran Canaria)

16 Modern communal round-up, Fuerteventura

PART ONE
HABITAT

CHAPTER ONE

Geology, Topography, Climate, Flora and Fauna

The first human beings to reach the Canaries would have found the archipelago a pleasant and reasonably easy place to live. Only the terrain, much of it an alternation of knife-edged ridges and precipitous ravines, may have seemed hostile; nevertheless, the island rock both held many natural caves and was soft enough for lasting, even-temperatured dwellings to be cut into it; and, in turn, the difficult terrain was to defend the islanders against invasion. The wide range of climate and vegetation, available within such small land-masses, would have allowed migration, from daily to seasonal, between crop and pasture lands; both wild vegetable foods and shellfish would have been available in quantity. If there was little to hunt, other than birds and giant lizards, there were also no predators. Available raw materials for making artefacts were headed by the hard woods of the juniper and of well-matured Canary pines; stone tools could be made from the obsidian of Tenerife and the basalts, trachytes and phonolites of the whole archipelago; there were the volcanic soils for pottery. A major drawback, perhaps influential in the conquest of the islands, was the absence of metallic ores. Taken overall, the Canaries did merit their ancient title of the 'Fortunate Isles'. CAMDEN P.L.

GEOLOGY

The last decade has seen intensive research using modern techniques, beyond that in any other field of Canary enquiry, resulting in the rapid growth of knowledge and speculation. Schmincke's recent summary is the basis for the following brief description.

The global plate-tectonics hypothesis proposes that new crust is being steadily produced at mid-ocean rifts, then moving outwards. The Canaries stand on a zone of sea-floor estimated to have been thrown up by the Mid-Atlantic Rift between 180–155 mya (million years ago), in the middle of the Jurassic period. Sedimentary rocks of Cretaceous age (136–65 mya) are visible on some of the islands. There is debate over the opening date of the basalt outpourings, the 'shield' vulcanism, which now form the greater part of each island; one cause of the outpourings may have been the melting of the sub-Canary mantle as part of the continuing plate-tectonics in the region. Schmincke keeps to a minimum dating, of mid-Tertiary (35 mya). Table 1 summarizes the potassium-argon dates so far obtained for these formations, showing an overall E.–W. trend from older to younger across the archipelago. Most islands then underwent a few million years' erosion closed by the latest series of eruptions; the table summarizes available datings for these and also gives the dates of the most recent vulcanism in each island. The latter datings on Gran Canaria and Hierro are by radiocarbon assay on pine-wood covered by eruptions.

| | Shield | | Post- | Latest |
	Majority of dates	Isolated dates	shield vulcanism	eruptions (AD)
F	17–12	22,4	2	A few thousand years ago
L	11–5	20	7–1	1730–6, 1824
GC	16–10	2	13–0	Post-1550 BC
T	7–5	17,2	9–4	15th C, 1704–6, 1798, 1909
G	12–8	7–3	6–0	Early Pliocene?
H	6–0	—	1–0	Post-1000 BC
P	—	—	2–0	1585, 1646, 1677, 1712, 1949, 1971

Table 1: *Potassium-argon (mya) and other dates(AD) of vulcanism, by island*

This view of developments is in conflict with the hypothesis of the older school led by Hausen (eg his 1966 paper, to the 1963 Panafrican Conference on Prehistory). This holds that the Canaries are underlain by continental crust and were once joined to Africa, perhaps as a great cape: a continuous basalt tableland forming a micro-continent has been dissected by fracturing to form the present archipelago. But Schimincke's study of Gran Canaria concludes that the island was built up as a separate volcanic structure, an evolution he considers likely for all islands to the west; again, he finds no field evidence for the older school's tableland-dissecting 'faults'. The new workers of the last decade have however generally accepted a continental basement for the two eastern Canaries but Schmincke at least now feels unequivocal evidence is still needed.

Rejection of the micro-continent theory will be unacceptable to believers in the Atlantis myth who, remarks Schmincke, may be better rewarded by a study of the island of Santorini, in the Aegean. However, there have been changes in the land–sea relationship, around the Canaries, during Quaternary time. Major factors have been the variations in world sea-level; the individual reaction of each island to the build-up of its volcanic load and, conversely, to the lightening of this by erosion; the structure of the underlying crust. Zeuner summarized the now-raised shorelines. The most recent — and thus potentially of archaeological interest — are at about 16m, 8m and 4m above present sea-level (Monastirian, respectively Main, Late and Epi-), each with the *Strombus* mollusc as fossil indicator. The first two are last interglacial in age, the third dates to the first interstadial of the last glaciation. Elsewhere in the world these raised beaches have yielded human relics ranging from Middle to Upper Palaeolithic in culture — but in the Canaries they appear to have had no contemporary occupation.

The landscape which has resulted from the volcanic deposits now varies with the age of each island. The ridge and ravine topography (Pl. 2a, 8b) is present on all islands but the scale increases westwards, especially when compared to the area of the island. Thus the diverse Fuerteventura has undergone so much erosion and deposition that it now holds vast plains of red alluvium or white sand; the central cordillera is low and rounded but the Jandía peninsula has a steeper topography and the widespread groups of very late Pleistocene volcanic cones, surrounded by their multi-coloured lava wastes, *malpaíses* or badlands, are strikingly fresh in aspect. Lanzarote and its islets also have these formations, with the northern Fámara massif (Pl. 13a), the highest zone, paralleling the Jandía peninsula, but a feeling of greater youth is given by the Timanfaya zone (Pl. 13b), its vulcanism still smouldering close to the surface. The red, blue and lilac cinders reach 60°C at 10cm depth, 240°C at 60cm; food can be cooked, with long-handled equipment, in mere holes in the ground.

The other five islands have less varied deposits but are built on a vaster scale. Gran Canaria and Gomera are roughly circular landmasses split by radial canyons; the larger has low coastal lands around the east and in the north-west, with extensive dunes covering the southern tip, but the lesser island has no flat land of any extent. Tenerife consists of a major cone, Teide (Pl. 7, 8a), joined by a long ridge to a complex of lesser peaks, the Anaga mountains in the north east; the crater is 15 km across its N.E.–S.W. axis, the rim peaks reaching 2717m on Montaña Guajara; the island has a large plain in the southern corner.

	F	L	GC	T	G	P	H
Maximum height (metres)	807	670	1949	3718	1487	2426	1501
Area (sq kms)	1764	841	1444	2025	361	629	256

Table 2: *Height and area statistics*

The two youngest islands have distinctive morphologies. Hierro may simply be half a crater of Teide dimensions, now open to the north as El Golfo precipice (Pl. 9ac); similarly eroded volcanoes have been seen in the Jandía, Fámara (Pl. 13a) and Anaga coastal massifs. Hierro has a steep coastline and is also studded and patched with small cones and lava-fields (Pl. 10a) but there is flat ground in the highlands. Palma can be described as a hexagonal land-mass with its southern side extended into an undulating, tapering spine. The northern massif holds a gigantic erosion hollow, known as the Caldera de Taburiente although not in fact a crater; the rim stands generally at around 2000m, with the island's highest point, Roque de los Muchachos, on the north-west arc; some 6–7 km across, the bowl of this *cirque* holds a labyrinth of narrow gorges, soft collapsing ridges and equally unwelcoming pinnacles of hard rock (Pl. 6a). The formation is breached in the south-west by the Barranco de las Angustias, its drainage channel. Palma's southern spine, above 1000m almost to the tip, ends with the archipelago's most recent volcano, Teneguía (1971).

A mountain-dweller, asked the distance to another part of his island, will reply in terms of time and, perhaps, load. Distance on the map is of little consequence — the factors are the heights to be climbed and the nature of the route. Peculiar responses to these, examined later, include the powerful whistled language, the vaulting poles and various features of the pastoralism. The monotonous and rapidly-eroding coasts (Pl. 4b) generally lacking attractive habitation sites, appear to have played a comparatively-minor part in the early people's lives. The mountains provided food and shelter and, perhaps, by their uncompromising splendour, a stimulus towards that upright speculative character recorded in the chronicles.

CLIMATE

The islands' climate depends not only upon local height and exposure direction but upon shifts to the archipelago of the weather conditions of adjoining major regions. The prevailing N.–N.E. trade winds, part of the Atlantic anticyclones, bring down cooler air in the summer; in winter the Atlantic depressions appear as winds from the N.W.–S.W. sector, bringing rain and the rare stormy weather. There are periods when a hot dry dust-laden wind blows from the Sahara, its local intensity varying with distance from the African coast. Storms in the tropics can reach the archipelago. The day-night heating and cooling of the islands and the sea bring powerful cross-contour winds.

Air temperature is below that average for the islands' latitude, due not only to the action of the trade wind but also to that of the ocean. Of importance in assessing early immigration into the islands, the

Height a.s.l. (metres)	Zone within island	Type of climate
Above 2500	Teide crater	Sub-Alpine
2500–1500	North & South	Dry temperate (continental)
1500–1000	North South	Humid temperate Dry ,,
1000–600	North South & all of Lanz. & Fuert.	Humid sub-temp. (Mediterranean) Semi-arid sub-temp. (dry Med.)
600–250	North South & all of Lanz. & Fuert.	Humid sub-tropical Semi-arid sub-tropical (dry Med.)
250–0	North South & all of Lanz. & Fuert.	Dry sub-tropical Arid sub-tropical to semi-desert

Table 3: *Climate against topography, according to Fernandopullé*

steady Canary Current—the 38°–20°N. arc of the clockwise N. Atlantic drift—brings down cool water from the north (Fig. 2). Secondly, the trades-induced displacement of the sea's surface, south-westwards from the Saharan coast—an element in the Canary Current's motive force—results in a compensatory upwelling there of deep cold water. Thus the archipelago sea has a surface temperature no higher than 18°C in February and 21.5°C in July. Air temperature extremes recorded in the islands have been 44°C in Gran Canaria (Gando, sea-level, July) and –16°C in Tenerife (Las Cañadas, c. 2000m, February), to contrast the coast with the mountains again.

Averages	J	F	M	A	M	J	J	A	S	O	N	D
Las Palmas GC) (sea-level)	18	18	18	19	20	21	22	24	24	23	21	20
Izaña (Ten.) (2367m)	4	4	5	7	9	13	17	17	13	9	6	4

Table 4: *Air temperatures (monthly, °C)*

Rainfall is irregular from year to year and often catastrophic when it does come, reaching 300mm a day in the wet zones and 150mm in the dry areas; rain occurs on 20–100 days a year according to region; the wettest areas are the N.W.–N.E. sectors at 750–1500m, these receiving the precipitation from the trades. The two eastern islands are mostly too low to receive rain from these winds. Faunal evidence of the Canaries' increasing dessication may be the recent disappearance of a slug (*Limax*) and an ant species (*Antophora*) from Fuerteventura, the former just surviving, in the east, in a spring on lanzarote and the latter now no nearer than N. Tenerife. The E.-W. rainfall means for 1949–67 were Fuerteventura 147mm, Lanzarote 135mm, Gran Canaria 325mm, Tenerife 420mm, Gomera 410mm, Palma 586mm, Hierro 410mm (Fernandopullé). Snowfalls regularly occur above 1700m, reaching a metre in depth.

Averages (mm)	Total, year	J	F	M	A	M	J	J	A	S	O	N	D
F (Los Estancos)	151	11	27	9	7	0	0	0	0	13	9	40	35
L (Arrecife)	156	28	16	12	6	0	0	0	0	8	11	35	40
GC (Las Palmas)	194	36	23	13	15	3	1	1	2	4	24	39	33
T (Sta. Cruz)	244	29	36	25	15	8	1	0	0	2	28	51	50
P (Sta. Cruz)	544	88	68	58	24	11	3	1	2	16	78	106	94

Table 5: *Monthly rainfall at sea-level (E.-W.), after Font Tullot*

Humidity at sea-level in Gran Canaria ranges between 69–73 (Las Palmas) but is no higher than 24–57 in the heights of Tenerife (Izaña, 2367m). Cloud is statistically sparse over the archipelago (May–October averaging a little over 2 oktas, with double this during November–April, at Sta. Cruz de Tenerife), as are coastal fogs. Cloud is experienced most intensively in the northerly middle-height zones, frequently engulfed in wet cloud; this phenomenon has been influential in human and plant colonization. Conversely, evaporation is adversely high on the southern slopes. The only permanent streams nowadays are in the Bco. de las Angustias (Palma) and El Cedro (Pl. 11a, on Gomera).

According to Font Tullot, the seasons are not evenly distributed through the twelve months. Summer, rainless, cloudy on the trade-wind flanks, with occasional Saharan days, runs from late May into October; autumn then lasts only to mid-December, a period of heavy rain, polar air and the occasional tropical storm; winter, running to mid-March, brings a lesser rainfall with temperate-region storms, though minimum cloud means increased sunshine; a short spring, ending in late May, with varied characterless weather, leads into yet another long summer.

Only the most important aspects of the varied and complex Canary climate have been noted. For greater detail the reader is referred to Fernandopullé, Font Tullot and Huetz de Lemps.

VEGETATION

In the Tertiary period a body of water known as the Tethys Sea covered the present Mediterranean Basin and reached to the Caucasus and the Himalayas. The approach of the Pleistocene ice to the north and of desertification to the south brought to an end the Tethys flora, other than in a few favoured places, above all in the Canaries; not only was their climate buffered but its wide range would have meant that, though most habitats would have shifted position, they would always have remained available somewhere within the islands. The Miocene-Pliocene flora of the Tethys Sea now found as fossils around the Mediterranean but still living in the Canaries is led by the dragon (*Dracaena draco*) and the trees of the laurel forest (*Laurus azorica*, *Ocotea foetens*, *Persea indica*, *Apollonias barbusana*), seen in Pl. 11a (El Cedro, Gomera). Gran Canaria has produced early Pliocene fossils of bamboo and palm as well as laurel species; the evidence is in the form of trees, dolomitized or as casts, and of leaf impressions. On Tenerife a mid-Quaternary puzzolanic deposit has yielded a leaf possibly of a laurel-forest species, *Viburnum*.

Three further aspects demonstrate the great antiquity of the Canary flora. Nineteen genera now exist only in the Canaries. Many species have their only other colonies or close relatives far away, implying long separation. Examples are the Canary pine (*Pinus canariensis*, Pl. 6a, 10b), once part of a pine forest reaching to the Himalayas, the location of its nearest living relative (*P. roxburghii*); the *Canarina* genus (species only in the Canaries and E. Africa); *Euphorbia canariensis* and the Canary *Echium* genus (relatives in S. Africa). Yet others fall within the continental drift theory, being seen as flora of the Gondwanaland block, broken up in the Cretaceous period: *Bystropogon canariensis* and *Drusa glandulosa* have their nearest relatives in the Americas. Finally the chromosome counts of the Canary flora show it much less evolved than that of the rest of the world, with three diploids to one polyploid (compared, for example, to the Algerian Sahara, 2:1; Great Britain around 1:1; Iceland 1:2; Spitzbergen 1:3).

There is little information on the evolution of the Canary vegetation up to the time of the European immigration. Nor has study yet been made of the food-yielding wild species available to the prehistoric people; amongst the trees, for example, were *Visnea mocanera*, *Arbutus canariensis*, *Myrica faya*, *Phoenix canariensis*, *Pinus canariensis*. The first conquistadores reported woods down to the shores, with associated 'running streams'. The pines were enormous; the European *colons* on Tenerife found a single tree would provide enough planks to roof a church. Subsequent unrestrained clearance for fuel, roofing and cultivation, has reduced Gran Canaria's laurel forest by 99% and that of Tenerife by over 90% (Bramwell 1974b). Kämmer has compared Hierro's actual vegetation cover with that likely without man: treeless 28% against 15%, juniper scrub 1%–8%, laurel forest 11%–34%, pine forest 10%–43%, the presumably cleared 50% having gone to intensive (19%) and non-intensive (27%) agriculture, settlement (3%) and re-afforestation (1%). Fire has very recently devastated the northern pine zone of Palma. The primitive laurel forest survives in the five western islands (though almost extinct in Gran Canaria) and there are pine woods in Hierro, Palma, Tenerife and Gran Canaria. Many ancient species of the flora will soon be extinct. Re-afforestation has been variably successful (Pl. 9a).

The current position (Bramwell 1976) is that the archipelago has 1600–1700 species, 470 being endemic and 110 limited to the immediate Atlantic islands (Macaronesian); the other 1100 are mainly Mediterranean natives and introduced weeds and aliens. According to Kunkel, there are also 1300 cultivated species. The following simplified zonation must be read in conjunction with the sections on topography and climate:

a) Hot, dry coastal region, to a maximum of 600m: characterized by xerophytes, such as the euphorbias and *Kleinia neriifolia*. Cultivation requires irrigation.

b) Transitional, notably with junipers and tree heaths; Mediterranean aspect.

c) The middle level with fairly dense laurel forest, of 40 species, if wet enough (to 1300m) or open pine woods otherwise (to 1900m). Cultivation without irrigation.

d) The high zone, cold and drier, with open scrub (eg *Spartocytisus supranubius*, Pl. 7b, 8a, common). Above 2600m, a sub-Alpine violet.

A long line of botanists has made general studies of the Canary flora: Masson, Humboldt, Smith, von Buch, Webb, Murray, Pitard, Proust, Burchard, Lems, Sventenius. The reader in search of a thorough field-guide will now find this in Bramwell's book (1974a). Detailed studies could begin with the bibliographies given in Kunkel's 1976 collection of papers.

FAUNA

In turn, the immigration and distribution of the fauna must be considered against the background of the topography, climate and vegetation. If the earliest flora stemmed from that around the Tethys Sea, did the fauna of those shores also reach the Canaries? Schmincke's view of the geology requires both flora and fauna to be transported by the winds and by birds, by the ocean currents and on drift-wood. However, the *Meteor* soundings showed 8000m of sediments in the channel between Fuerteventura and Gran Canaria, interpretable as an erosion cycle of continental proportions — prior to the separation of the eastern islands from Africa, therefore. This separation of Fuerteventura and Lanzarote by a strait from the continental coast, all three aligned N.N.E.–S.S.W., has been put down to the forces which caused the similarly-oriented fractures, dykes and chains of volcanoes, of various ages, within the two islands.

An interesting range of fossil fauna has now been found in the Canary Islands but is still inadequately described and researched, for example in its relationship to the Tethys fauna. The earliest finds are foraminifera in the Cretaceous sediments of Fuerteventura. Marine fossils are common in the archipelago's raised shorelines, starting in the Miocene. Lanzarote calcarenites have yielded ostrich eggs of Miocene or Pliocene age.

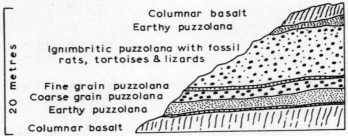

Figure 3   *Volcanic sequence with fossil animals, Tenerife*

The Canary vulcanism (Fig. 3) entombed and burnt alive various giant species of turtle or tortoise, rat and lizard; there is also a mouse and the phalanx of an unknown vertebrate. Klemmer refers to skinks being found in the tuffs, probably of Pleistocene age. The turtle or tortoise (*Testudo burchadii*), its body 80cm long, is known from Tenerife's pumice flows, perhaps late Pliocene; eggs appropriate to it have also been discovered there. The giant rats are found in quantity in puzzolanic levels, some caught in their holes; the latter also sheltered snails (*Helix*). The rat fossils fall within the last million years though the species is felt to have probably arrived with the other Tertiary fauna. Klemmer notes a fossil mouse, *Canariomys bravoi*.

Table 6 summarizes the confused and obviously overlapping information on the lizards, on which interest has in fact always centered. Hierro was perhaps Pliny's 'Lagarteria'. This island's giant lizards were for long known only in the Roques de Salmor (Pl. 9b), at the north-east limit of El Golfo; recently dying out there, they have just been rediscovered elsewhere in Hierro. A good specimen of this ferocious armoured species can be seen in the museum on Palma; Klemmer says that of Tenerife also holds examples (Fig. 4 is drawn from Fernández's plate). All the living lacertids have a faint squeak.

Lacerta sp.	Notes	Authority
L. goliath *L. maxima*	Fossils, Tenerife, up to 1m 50cm, Tertiary	Zeuner & Bravo
L. simonyi	Living, Hierro	Zeuner & Bravo
simonyi	Living, Tenerife (different from Hierro's)	Fernández
L. simonyi	Extinct, in Hierro to 1930s, up to 80cm. Like *L.s. stehlini* but row of broad yellow spots along sides of head and body	Klemmer
L. simonyi stehlini	Living, Gran Canaria (all heights), up to 80cm, brown with yellowish tint	Klemmer
L. galloti	Living, H, G, P, T (to 3200m), up to 35cm. Each is subspecies (Bannerman)	Klemmer
L. atlantica	Living, L, F, up to 24cm long	Klemmer

Table 6: *Fossil and living lizards*

Recent archaeological excavation (Pellicer 1971b, 1976) in the cave of La Arena (Bco. Hondo, Tenerife) has produced lizard remains dating back 2500 years (see Appendix Two for the Canaries' radiocarbon datings); the species were *L. goliath, maxima, simonyi s., simonyi stehlini*. This may be the first time that island excavators have preserved the remains of the wild fauna found on the sites.

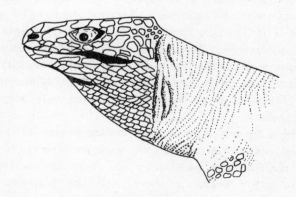

Figure 4   *Head of giant lizard* (Lacerta simonyi), *Hierro*

Species (maximum size)	F	L	GC	T	G	P	H
Lacertids—see Table 6	X	X	X	X	X	X	X
Tarentola delalandii (2 sub-spp), gecko			X	X	X	X	X
T. mauritanica	X	X					
Chalcides viridianus, skink (12cm)				X	X		X
C. sexlineatus (12cm)			X				
C. ocelatus occidentalis (25cm)	X	X					
Hyla meridionalis, tree frog, bright green (55mm)	X	X	X	X	X	X	X
Rana perezi, marsh frog, olive (150mm)	?	?	X	X	X	X	X
Bufo b., common toad?							
Rana temporaria, common frog?							

Table 7: *Reptiles and amphibians*

Table 7 is based on Klemmer's work. Half the species are endemic and, apart from the commoner gecko, all are related to the W. Mediterranean rather than Macaronesian (Atlantic islands) fauna.

The smaller fauna has evolved along lines parallel to those of the vegetation. An earwig (*Anataelia canariensis*) has its nearest relative in China (Zeuner & Bravo). Many species have been evolving in insular isolation; the Carabid beetles include twelve endemic genera, for example (Fernández). Other species may be more recent arrivals, such as the water-fleas, since they are related to those of nearby Africa (Roben).

Bacallado lists sixty resident bird species (F 35, L 36, GC 45, T 53, G 39, P 39, H 31), a part of the Macaronesian fauna; three only are endemic and four more are limited to the Atlantic islands. Many, however, have been classed as sub-species; Bannerman considered 42 (out of 61 residents) to be endemic and a further ten to be peculiar to Macaronesia. The Tertiary immigration is known to have included the ostrich (?always flightless), from its fossil eggs; peculiarly endangered birds such as the Teide finch (*Fringilla teydea*) probably accompanied it. The birds are now closest to the S. European range. There are 156 visiting birds, two-thirds making only 'occasional' or 'rare' appearances.

Finally, the mammals. The dark-brown monk seal (*Monachus m.*), over 2m long, sometimes reaches the eastern islands. It was once common on the shores of Isla Lobos, the crater-islet off N.E. Fuerteventura, probably breeding there, but the European slavers, conquerors and settlers hunted it to extinction there; tame, the seal could be clubbed to death. *Lobo marino* is an old Castillian term for 'seal'. Protected as it nears world-wide disappearance, the monk seal has its last colony on the Sahara coast to the south-east of the Canaries.

Living land-mammals are limited to rats, mice and bats (? species still unrecorded), the S. European variety of rabbit, a hedgehog and a pig. A cave once excavated near Guía de Isora (Tenerife) held a level made up of thousands of bat skeletons, not identified; the cave was called El Campanario, the belfry. The hedgehog perhaps occurs on all islands; Bannerman gave that of Fuerteventura the status of sub-species as *Erinaceus algirus caniculus*, since it is lighter in colour, probably due to its desert habitat, than W. Mediterranean and Moroccan species. The pig roamed the laurel woods of Gomera until some 20 years ago, according to Herrera, then being cleared to help preserve the woodland; it was between the wild and domestic varieties in shape, with a sharp pointed snout and long body averaging 70 kilos in an adult male; it ate bracken roots and laurel berries. Quite possibly both the hedgehog and the 'wild' pig began as domesticated species; the former is bred for eating in the Balearics whilst the Canary people until recently let at least their goats range freely, regularly holding communal round-ups (Pl. 16).

In summary, the interesting Canary fauna is mostly invisible to all but the specialist, out of self-preservation — the rest is extinct. The signs in the Teide national park (Pl. 7, 8a) say 'Do not take away the rocks or pick the plants, they are unique' — but silence is maintained over the effectively unrestrained shooting of the last birds, due to the power of the hunting interests. Equally, the fauna diminishes as a result of agricultural poisons, urban spread and tourism development. Worst of all, though, is probably the average islander's lack of interest in conserving the Canaries' vulnerable biotope, paralleling the vandalism against the prehistoric sites. Unless this changes, the efforts of a few individuals and group, even when backed by preservation orders and laws, will be of little avail.

PART TWO

IMMIGRATION

CHAPTER TWO
Prehistoric Navigation and the African Continent

To reconstruct the first major human immigration into the islands is to enter at once into the main polemic of Canary prehistory, the origins and date of arrival of the ancient people. This chapter will look at each of the most obvious source-regions, noting the main pieces of evidence for or against them as the original homeland of the Canary Islanders. The bulk of the detailed evidence will be laid out in the nine subsequent chapters.

Canary archaeology has not produced any recognized remains of pre-conquest boats. Some of the rock-engravings (eg Fig. 9, Bco. de Balos, Gran Canaria) can be interpreted as sails, as the ribbed hulls of ships or as benches of rowers — but it would be odd if such stylization were the only way used to represent vessels. An eighth-century dug-out coffin on Gran Canaria (Agaete) shows the islanders could have made dug-out canoes. Serra (1957) said that the bones of fish in the pre-conquest occupation deposits were limited to inshore species; as will be seen in Chapter 9, this is in accordance with the several known fishing techniques.

The early chronicles show craft existed in the fifteenth century at least. The French conquerors of 1402–5 referred to Gran Canaria islanders who came out alongside to barter in a *batel*, a word also used for one of their own ship's boats. Torriani (1590) described how, on the same island, the ancient people had 'made boats from the dragon tree, entirely dug out, and then put in stone ballast, and navigated with oars and a palm sail around the coasts of the island; they also used to cross to Tenerife and Fuerteventura on raids'. The chroniclers concur that the Canary Islanders were excellent swimmers — so they were not afraid of the sea.

Further evidence (Abreu) can be inferred from the reaction of the most remote island to the appearance of the French conquerors' boat. The Hierro people of the fourteenth century had a prophet called Yore: on his death-bed he forecast that, when his body had turned to dust, 'their god Eraoranzan would come to them in white houses on the water; and advised them not to resist or fly from him, but to adore him, because he was to come to do them good'. In time, 'seeing the ships approach with their white sails swelling on the surface of the waves, they . . . went to the cave where Yore was buried, and there found his bones crumbled to dust; upon which they ran joyfully to the shore to receive their god Eraoranzan'. Of the meeting and, as an early chronicler might say, of what became of these simple islanders, more later.

Gran Canaria alone, then, may have had boats, likely to have come into use not long before the conquest. The idea, even the first craft, may well have originated with Spaniards captured (1340s) or ship-wrecked (1382) on the island. This would explain the craft's recognition, mentioned not long after, as a *batel*, like their own ship's boat, by the French. However, no matter what their origins, the described vessels would hardly have encouraged a major human immigration, with animals, seed and valued possessions, to set out on a first crossing of at least a hundred kilometres. The obvious inference is that, lacking a seafaring tradition, the first islanders arrived in ships belonging to a different people.

THE ADJACENT AFRICAN COAST

The heights of Fuerteventura can be seen, on a good day, from the region of Cape Juby on the Sahara coast (Fig. 1). Here again there is no evidence for or against pre-medieval navigation (Mercer 1976). The earliest descriptions coincide with the period of European in-vasion of the Canaries. About 1450 the Portuguese on Arguin Island (now N. Mauritania) recorded that the coastal fishermen, good swimmers, had wooden 'canoes' and, naked, three or four to a craft, apparently used their legs as paddles; that the main southern set-tlement of Gran Canaria should be called Arguineguín does suggest a link with this region. Ca da Mosto (1455) wrote that 'The first time they saw sails . . . they believed they were great sea-birds . . . when the sails were lowered . . . that they were fishes. Others . . . that they were phantoms that went by night'. The Venetian explained that the Africans could not understand the caravels' speed; and these always raided in the dark.

Half a century later, Valentim Fernandes said that the only coastal craft of the Western Sahara were rafts of corded tree-trunks, propelled by pieces of wood used oar-wise at the back, the water half-way up the crew's legs. A century further on, about 1600, Pory (translator of Leo Africanus) wrote 'They go to sea in certaine small boats they call *Almadies*'; this work — and perhaps the unknown craft — stems from the Arab immigration into the Western Sahara, on a large scale in the late medieval period.

The focus of slaving and conquest moved gradually southwards from 1600, away from the understandably fierce Saharan tribes and their dangerous and barren coastline. Detailed narratives by shipwrecked and ransomed mariners do not mention boats—and, when the desert became gradually accessible to Europeans, there were no boats to be seen (Robin). The immediate shores of Africa thus do not seem particularly likely to have provided the boats needed for the first main immigration to the Canaries. The next chapters will show there was some physical and cultural overlap between the two regions but, as will be seen, it is hard to separate this from the broad resemblance of the ancient Canary culture to that of proto-historic N.W. Africa in general.

NAVIGATION FROM EUROPE

Northern vessels sailing to the Canaries could not easily have returned home. It was not until the rudder was invented at the end of the medieval period—and, together with the map and the compass, led to the effective genocide of the Canary people—that it would have been possible to have tacked to and fro back up against the prevailing trade wind. The one-way Canary Current (Fig. 2) usually helped by the wind, would certainly have taken drifting vessels from N. Europe and Iberia to the archipelago. Yet this can hardly have brought the main immigration. All islands were populated; it would be necessary to suppose that the vessel or vessels happened to be carrying women, goats, pigs, sheep, dogs and grain; and that the knowledge of building such large ships was subsequently lost. It will be shown that there is little similarity between the physiques and cultures of the islanders and those of ancient Europe.

N.W. AFRICA SINCE THE ARAB INVASION

The first Arabs reached Morocco about 680AD. Their vessels are thought to have ventured but rarely down the Atlantic coast; again, the current and the wind would have taken any drifting vessels to the archipelago. Arab influences, too slight to support an immigration theory, have been seen in one island—once again Gran Canaria. Numerals, but oddly only a few, such as *arba*, four; other words such as *almogaren*, temple, *acoran*, god; artefacts such as *agadir*, granary, and fired-clay stamps comparable to those used to seal Maghreb grain stores; the geometric decoration of the dwelling interiors, pottery and other household objects; some of this pottery's believed imitation of metal vessels. These characteristics could be due to trade and Islamic proselytization; on the other hand, only the first two groups are clearly Arab . . . and the date of their arrival and extent of their use is unknown. The religious conversion of the animist Berbers of N.W. Africa began as soon as the Arabs reached their region—and from the eighth century there were Moslem Berbers carrying both trade and Islam southwards down the coast of the W. Sahara. The speech of the Berbers of N.W. Africa only gradually changed to Arabic, a process still of course incomplete today, so that, if there was in fact contact with the Canary Islanders—speakers of a Berber-affinity tongue, as will be seen—the two peoples could have understood each other right up to the time of the European conquest of the islands.

The level of contact appears slight. For example, the pottery was imitative (if related in fact) rather than made with a knowledge of continental techniques, notably of glazing. Trade would have brought in iron tools but none have ever been found in pre-conquest contexts— at the most the use of a metal tool on an artefact has sometimes been suspected. Nor did any such contact lead to the making and use of boats. Further, any Arab influence is necessarily later than the seventh century—but a third of the Canaries' C14 dates fall into the previous few hundred years. The conscientious Arab historian Ibn Khaldun, writing in the middle of the fourteenth century, described four ab-ducted islanders sold in the Maghreb: it seems that these did not speak Arabic and that the Canaries were still not well known to the Arabs. The Arab contribution is thus likely to have been both limited and late—and thus of little importance to the major problem.

N.W. AFRICA DURING THE ROMAN OCCUPATION

There seems to be no detailed evidence on prehistoric navigation around the Maghreb coasts. The Phoenician expeditionaries, though they passed through the Canaries, left no record of having colonized them. Much was written about the Atlantic islands by the classical historians of two thousand years ago. However, one may feel, with Glas, that the often-quoted accounts 'are so indistinct and confused, that one is at a loss to know which of them they describe'. He accepted that the ancients knew them all, from Madeira to the Cape Verds, but 'confounded them together under the common name of the Fortunate Islands'.

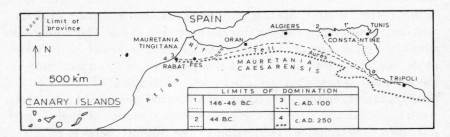

Figure 5   *Map of Roman Africa*

The only coherent classical account of the Canary Islands, that in Pliny, was taken from a description by the expedition sent by Juba II; he reigned over the Roman protectorate of Mauretania (Fig. 5), this including the region of the present Morocco. Juba's long dominion lasted from 29BC to about 20AD. The expedition left a detailed description of an endemic Canary plant, *Euphorbia canariensis* (now the *cardón*); the whole family has since been named by botanists after the king's physician, Euphorbus. According to the report, this comparatively-enlightened expedition — botanizing as well, perhaps, as slaving — found that the Canaries were then uninhabited. However, two islands bore signs of past human occupation: 'Canaria' had 'traces of buildings', 'Junonia' had 'a small temple built of a single stone'. If this lack of inhabitants seems unlikely at this date, it must be recalled that the Azores, Madeira and Cape Verds were all still unoccupied when relocated by Europeans at the end of the middle ages. The traces of huts are to be ascribed to the survivors of vessels brought by the current and wind and to early adventurers whose voyages never became preserved in history. The focus is thus beginning to narrow — if one accepts Juba's account, not obviously less reliable than the hypotheses of archaeologists concerned to give a 'respectable' age to the island's prehistoric people.

Next, an aspect which has been astonishingly ignored: the earliest dateable artefacts in the archipelago are a series of Roman amphoras, some identical to an Athenian type of the third century AD. At least fifteen of these pots have been found, together with fragments. They all come from shallow waters and have been located, since 1964, by the growing number of underwater enthusiasts diving in the Canaries. Unfortunately Garciá y Bellido's valuable study could only cover half a dozen of the amphoras, some having been collected by or sold to tourists, being then lost to archaeology. However, it seems that many are known to be still on the sea-bed, awaiting recovery.

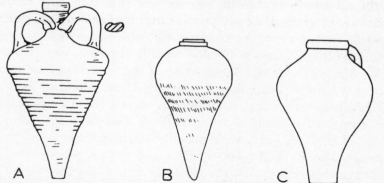

A   B   C

Figure 6   *Roman amphorae: Graciosa (a, 65cm), Lanzarote (b, 30cm), Tenerife (c, 30cm)*

There appear to be at least four types. The Athenian form has been found twice (Fig. 6a) off Graciosa, the small island north of Lanzarote; these amphoras, stuck in the deck, would have held food for the crew, rather than cargo. An example of a second type has been found off Arrecife, Lanzarote's harbour (Fig. 6b); this pot has Iberian-Provence parallels, dated late-Roman by Borges but perhaps fifteenth-sixteenth century AD according to García. A third variety has been recovered to the north of Guadamojete Point and, twice, off San Andrés (Fig. 6c), both Tenerife; it appears unstudied. Gran Canaria is said to have produced an amphora—off Las Palmas— which was 'more globular' in shape than the other forms. Fragments of unknown type appear to have been found in the past off S. Tenerife and Lanzarote. There may then be amphoras off all islands—the westerly three have little shallow water and are probably less explored. It is to be hoped that, before the location of the first wreck, of no matter what period, the authorities will have prepared themselves for scientific underwater archaeology, rather than allow collectors to disappear again—as on land also—with the best material.

It is clear, then, that Roman vessels came to the Canaries. The amphoras cannot belong to Juba's men since the pots are clearly at least two centuries later. So far only one other possible Roman characteristic has been suggested, the *soliferreum*, a distinctive lance (Tenerife at least: Fig. 19ab); it is also said to occur in black Africa but other links with this region are sparse. A study of the reports and remains of Roman N. Africa might well locate further influences.

Mauretania, still including the present Morocco, was made into a Roman province in AD 42 (Fig. 5). The Romans' harsh attitudes over matters such as taxes provoked the subjected Berbers to repeated revolts; raids from the regions of the *insoumis* were also frequent. In AD 100, for example, there had to be a punitive expedition against the Teda of the Tibesti mountains, deep in the Sahara. Banishment, a common Roman punishment, was one way of dealing with rebellious tribes . . . and Juba II's description of the uninhabited Canaries, then the south-west corner of the known world, would have been to hand.

Now the first Europeans to leave records of verbal contact with the islanders, the French of 1402–5, wrote of the Gomerans that 'they say there that a great prince for no crime put them into exile there, and had their tongues cut out'. Additionally, on this island the people have always used a finger-aided articulated whistled language, unique in the world (Classe)—and quite possibly originally developed by men without tongues. Their women-folk would not necessarily have been similarly mutilated, so that the people's normal language would have continued alongside the whistled speech. Carrying several kilometres, this is nowadays only used in special circumstances—for communicating across Gomera's vast ravines. Evidence will be produced of unusually developed whistled communication, in the past, in other islands, though it may have fallen short of speech. Similar topographies occur in many parts of the world — but not in association with whistled languages. One might also wonder whether certain matriarchal aspects of Canary society, notably on Palma (the women were said to be braver than the men) and Lanzarote (polyandry) might not have resulted from a 'founder effect', the mutilation of the men of the first population. The only other immigration story recorded in the Canaries by the early chroniclers was from Tenerife: the Guanches believed they were descended from 60 settlers at Icod.

There is one further aspect. The author's hypothesis in no way rests on this — were it the only evidence of its kind it would be treated as the speculation of a late-medieval scholar with his thoughts in the classical period. Abreu's history (1600) included the following passage:

'Among the books of a library that was in the cathedral of Sta. Ana, in Canaria, there was one, so much disfigured and torn that it wanted both the beginning and the end; it treated of the Romans, and gave an account, that when Africa was a Roman province, the natives of Mauretania rebelled, and killed their Presidents and Governors; upon which the senate, resolving to punish and make a severe example of the rebels, sent a powerful army into Mauretania, which vanquished and reduced them again to obedience: soon after, the ringleaders of the rebellion were put to death; and the tongues of the common sort, and of their wives and children (?), were cut out, and then they were all put on board vessels, with some grain and cattle, and transported to the Canary Islands.'

Even if only an early speculation, it will do as a summary of the present writer's preferred theory. The Canaries would by no means be the only islands in the world to be first populated by deported convicts.

Finally, the radiocarbon datings. Of the first 30 assays, only the two from Arena Cave (Tenerife) are earlier than the Roman period in N.W. Africa. Though those of Arena Cave may well stem from human occupation, in spite of the lack of clear human relics, it would take some further datings or other unequivocal evidence of the same age (first-sixth century BC) to put the main immigration further back than the first centuries AD.

In summary, it is suggested that the major colonization was by tribes deported by the Romans from the interior of the Maghreb. These would of course lack a knowledge of sea-going boats and, especially, of their construction. The next nine chapters will show that it is with this region at that period that the physiques and culture of the first islanders can, taken overall, be best matched. In Part Three, a separate chapter will be devoted to a comparison with the physical anthropology of the late prehistoric inhabitants of N.W. Africa, but in Part Four, on the ancient islanders' culture, comparisons will be made piecemeal within each section, the subjects being less complex and extensive.

THE PROBLEM OF SECONDARY IMMIGRATION

Up to five 'waves' of incomers have been proposed by archaeologists. The evidence is not drawn from archipelago field-work but is the result of the ancient preference, still fashionable in the Canaries, for the immigration of people rather than of ideas or of the development of one or both within the archipelago. The ancient islanders and their culture have been divided into immigrations and periods on the basis of dubiously-comparable events elsewhere.

The only field evidence so far available falls into four groups: the physical types and their distribution, the burial forms, the painted artefacts (Gran Canaria only) and the little stratification at last being recorded. At present all four aspects are subject to different interpretations, involving assumptions and omissions. Until there is more solid material, it is really premature to do more than note, in the appropriate sections, the most feasible of the various workers' conclusions over each aspect. Clearer evidence should be produced by the new generation of Canary archaeologists.

PART THREE

PHYSICAL ANTHROPOLOGY, PAST AND PRESENT

CHAPTER THREE

Skeleton

There are three forms of evidence. The skeletal material of the caves and tumuli, that of the former sometimes mummified. The general impressions made by the living islanders on chroniclers and travellers between the fourteenth century and the present. The physiques of the present islanders. This and the next chapter will summarize the first and third groups of material, using data prepared by the anthropologists of the last hundred years. The haphazard notes of observers over the last half-millennium are valueless in a complex subject requiring large-scale evidence; secondly, their observations were coloured by an inaccurate or, at best, selective idea of the ancient islanders' physical appearance.

It has already been said that the anthropologists fall into three groups: the nineteenth-century scholars (Berthelot, Verneau); the early twentieth-century academics (Hooton, Fischer, Tamagnini, Falkenburger); the recent workers (Fusté 1958–66, Schwidetsky 1956 to the present). If these two chapters are based most immediately on the data of the last two anthropologists, there is of course a general debt to all those who have contributed to the long period of investigations.

The two chapters follow a broad pattern. Each aspect is treated first for the pre-conquest people, then for the modern islanders. Within these treatments there will be breakdowns into islands, into regions within islands and, for the ancient material, into type of burial. However, three groups of problems need to be borne in mind when interpretating the data of these two chapters.

The first group consists itself of three long-standing difficulties. The pre-conquest relics are all but entirely lacking in stratigraphical and other Canary dating evidence, relative and absolute; thus a mummy, a skull or a bone may be from 500 to 2000 years old (assuming always the immigration date proposed in the last chapter). Next, collection has been mainly unscientific, partially selective at least and without adequate record of provenance. The museums have muddled the specimens, so that most items can only be considered individually; thus, in the most recent major study (Schwidetsky 1963), the cranea (1334 male, 668 female) could not be associated with the long bones (1288 male, 772 female). There are notable collections in Madrid and

Paris as well as the three island museums. Lastly, and less beyond repair, a handicapping nomenclature is still in use. As in many other zones of prehistory, the material has been classified and named with distant types and migration theories in mind, these selected sub-jectively and themselves liable to change. Even where general agreement exists on the remote origin of an archipelago type, there is no question of exact identity. Had Canary archaeology not been long the province of Europeans, the types of physiques would have had local names, perhaps those of each type's main site — for example, 'Gáldar' man rather than 'Semitic', 'Berber', 'Eurafricanoid' and 'Mediterranean', all used of this type though not identical with it.

The second group of reservations concerns two non-physiological aspects of the recent anthropological studies on which these chapters are based: the effects of the topography and of historical events upon human settlement and movement appear inadequately studied, casting doubt on aspects both of the collected data and of the hypotheses. A detailed study of habitation distribution and of the communication networks should have preceded the collection of material on physical type; it will be suggested that on Gran Canaria, scene of the most detailed work, the socio-geographical divisions used simply do not correspond with reality. Similarly, careful examination should have been made of the results of the century of conquests: the French and Spaniards emptied or decimated whole islands and island regions, these being deliberately or casually re-stocked from other islands and regions. The century from 1476 brought massive man-hunts on the adjacent Sahara coast, so that the eastern islands in particular became overwhelmingly populated by captured Africans and their progeny: this element has been utterly ignored, probably since it is unmentionable in official histories of the Canaries and so is unknown to the anthropologists. The detailed grounds for these criticism will become clear as the book proceeds. The basic problem is of course that Schwidetsky in particular needed a team and major resources for the vast study she has so heroically been carrying out.

The third form of problem is inherent in the study of the modern islanders. The surveys have not of course attempted to single out 'pure' descendants of the pre-conquest people but have sought to establish the broad extent to which their characteristics have been transmitted to the present islanders. However, there was a wide area of overlap between the fifteenth-century Canary Islanders, the Iberian *conquistadores* and settlers and the captured N.W. Africans — the 'Mediterranean' type is common and perhaps predominant in each population. Thus, neither clear evidence nor definite conclusions are to be expected. This problem interlocks with the criticisms made in the last paragraph.

It should be underlined that the anthropologists' techniques are not in question, only some of their assumptions and conclusions. Further, these conclusions have been used to set up far-reaching theories of immigration and social hierarchy which, in turn, must be examined. Since they draw upon the equally-complex subject of pre-conquest burial practice, together with aspects of society in the pre-conquest period, these hypotheses will best be treated at the end of Chapter 7.

PREHISTORIC SKELETAL DATA: CRANIAL TYPES

Schwidetsky (1963) concluded that the pre-conquest islanders ranged between two poles: a 'Cromagnoid', particularly distinguished by a broad robust face (Fig. 7a), and a 'Mediterranean', the face comparatively high and delicate (Fig. 7b).

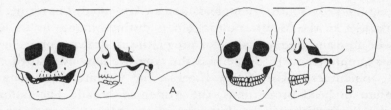

Figure 7   *Cromagnoid (a) and Mediterranean (b) skulls, Gran Canaria*

	Crania		Long bones		Main sites and number of crania
Sex	M	F	M	F	
L	0	0	0	0	
F	16	3	50	26	
GC	790	441	944	565	Guayadeque 845, Sta. Lucia 65, Tejeda 48
T	388	163	275	166	Candelaria-Igueste 121, Orotava 104, Chorrillo 57
G	62	34	5	3	Valle Gran Rey 14, Teriguete 13, Hermigua 10
P	18	7	14	12	
H	60	40	0	0	Tablón 56, Bco. Guerra 13, Cuevas de las Tablas 6

Table 8: *Crania and long bones by island (Schwidetsky 1963)*

In detail, the extreme Cromagnoid's face was wide, low, with strong bones, robust supra-orbital ridges, marked forehead slope, intense curvature of the root of the nose, laterally-prominent zygomatic arches, broad robust nose tending to convexity, low eye-sockets with horizontal upper edges, strong lower jaw with laterally-projecting angles and, lastly, great width of cranial vault. Conversely the extreme

Mediterranean face was narrow, high, with delicate bones, delicate glabella, little forehead-slope and curve of nose-root, zygomatic arches flattened laterally, narrow small straight nose, high eye-sockets with edge sloping downwards and outwards, delicate lower jaw with unaccented angles, together with a narrow cranial vault. The cranial indices were close: 75.6 and 74.1, respectively, indicating heads of medium proportions (breadth to length). Schwidetsky's analysis does not produce a division into quantities; about 6% of the crania were 'ideal' specimens of one or other of the two types. The evidence for other type-groups, such as the 'Armenoid', 'Alpine' and 'Negroid' was felt to be statistically insignficant, though isolated characteristics and individuals did occur.

A rather different, more traditional description is given by Fusté (1966a), working only on the material from Gran Canaria. Finding the two main types just described, he added two minor groups: an 'Orientaloid' (or 'South Orientaloid') and an Armenoid. The former has similarities to the Mediterranean but is distinguishable by its long convex nose and frequent alveolar prognathism; drawing on its living Canary representatives, Fusté said the type has almond-shaped eyes and, sometimes, rather fleshy cheeks. The Orientaloid is long to medium in head proportions, the Armenoid broad. The latter is further distinguished by a flattening of the occipital region and a highly-convex nose; amongst the living islanders this nose is the largest and most fleshy, the tip pointing downwards. Fusté found no Negroid type amongst the prehistoric population and suggested that all those earlier workers who had done so (Verneau, Hooton, Falkenburger) had been either simply wrong or had perhaps been misled into including the skulls of slaves from post-conquest plantation cemeteries.

PREHISTORIC CRANIAL TYPES: DISTRIBUTION BY ISLAND

Schwidetsky's system placed the ancient islanders in relation to the Cromagnoid and Mediterranean poles. This can be represented as:

Crom.	G	T	P	F	H	GC	Med
O	6.7	46.3	48.8	54.6	66.7	73.9	100

Table 9: *Type polarity by island (available data)*

Schwidetsky felt these statistics indicated a central group, Gomera and Tenerife, and a periphery, the rest, but it seems rather, on this evidence, that Gomera had the peculiarity of a very strong Cromagnoid element and the rest were well mixed, tending in Hierro and Gran Canaria towards the Mediterranean type. The cranial indices are generally typical of the indicated polarity, those of Gomera proportionately the longest and those of Gran Canaria just the broadest (Table 10).

	All islands	Gomera	Tenerife	Palma	Fuert.	Hierro	Gran. Can.
Crania & sex	1325m 690w	62m 34w	382m 164w	18m 7w	16m 3w	60m 40w	787m 442w
Cranial index	75.4 76.8	77.8 78.6	76.5 77.9	74.4 76.8	75.8 78.7	75.3 76.6	74.8 76.3

Table 10: *Cranial indices (Schwidetsky 1963)*

PREHISTORIC SKELETAL DATA: LONG BONES, BY ISLAND
As noted, since a long bone is not usually associated with any particular skull, this material cannot be used to give data on the different types. Table 11 summarizes the height calculations, based on the bone measurements, by island (in the order of the two previous tables, for comparison).

Pearson formula	Gomera	Tenerife	Palma	Fuert.	Gran Canaria
Bones & sex	5m 3w	275m 166w	14m 12w	50m 26w	944m 565w
Height (cm)	162.4 153	164.2 151.9	166.7 151.7	171.7 159	166.8 153.2

Table 11: *Height, by island*

There are too few bones from Gomera to do more than note that the men seem again to be at an extreme, the only islanders just on the 'small' side on a world scale (below 164cm). The women were clearly small (below 153cm) or close to this on four islands. Fuerteventura is this time quite distinct, both men and women being in the 'tall' group (above 166.9cm, 155.9cm, respectively). Taken overall, the eastern islanders were taller than the western people.

Schwidetsky also compared the robustness of the long bones to their size and, thus, to the height data. She found that the more robust the bone the shorter the accompanying stature.

PREHISTORIC SKELETAL DATA: DISTRIBUTION WITHIN THE ISLANDS
Most work has been done on Gran Canaria. Schwidetsky (1963) divides the island into mountain and coastal people but, as noted, the

settlement-cum-social-relationship pattern would have been far more complicated:

a) there were two separate populous coastal plains, on the east and in the north-west

b) the central mountains would have received their population by spread up the vast radial gorges

c) the N.W. to S.W. quarter was comparatively cut off from the rest of the island, limited communication being until recently by boat—a means of transport all but lacking in pre-conquest times.

Thus, future study could consider four radial segments as a basis, these running from the coast to the centre: north (Agaete to Tamaraceite, the extent of the ancient Gáldar chieftanship), east (Tamaraceite to Juan Grande, including the gorges of Guayadeque and Tirajana), south (the Fataga and Arguineguín gorges and their coastal zone), west (the Mogán and San Nicolás gorges and coast).

Gran Canaria		Gran Canaria		Tenerife	
Cromagnoid pole	0	Island average	73.9	Cromagnoid pole	0
Angostura (NE)	27.9	Acusa (C)	75.5	La Orotava (N)	20.2
Temisas (Centre)	38.6	Isleta tumuli (NE)	77.4	El Masapé (N)	24.5
San Lorenzo (NE)	44.7	Gáldar caves (NW)	77.6	Candelaria (E)	41.2
				Island average	46.3
Sta. Lucia (C)	55.9	Guayadeque (E)	78.3	Adeje (SW)	46.3
Tejeda (C)	59.4	Arguineguín tumuli (S)	82.1	Chorrillo (E)	52.5
San Nicolás (W)	62.5			El Becerril (NE)	55.7
Tirajana (C)	64.9	Mogán tumuli (SW)	82.2	San Miguel (S)	66.7
Agaete (NW)	72.0				
(cont. in next column)		Gáldar tumuli (NW)	89.4	San Andrés (NE)	67.0
		Mediterranean pole	100.0	Mediterranean pole	100.0

Table 12: *Crania type-polarity, by settlements*

This said, Schwidetsky's conclusions will be given. On Gran Canaria, the ancient mountain people had faces and a shorter stature a little nearer the Cromagnoid pole than the rest of the island; the Mediterranean was particularly well represented on the desirable north coast. However, on Tenerife it was just the fertile north rather than the arid south which had the Cromagnoid preponderance. Schwidetsky links these two Cromagnoid regions to the generally Cromagnoid people of Gomera. However, the same monograph's tabulation of 'settlements' in order of type-pole orientation of their cranial (male) characteristics underlines that there are exceptions to these generalizations. The indications in brackets are simply to enable the reader to locate the sites, rather than indicating groupings. The table shows that, in fact, the north-east of Gran Canaria falls in part nearest of all to the Cromagnoid pole. Very local differences occur: Angostura is only a few kilometres from La Isleta whilst Temisas, Sta Lucia and Tirajana lie along 7 km of mountain track. These local variations are explained away as due to factors such as endogamy and genetic drift.

PREHISTORIC SKELETAL DATA: TYPE ACCORDING TO BURIAL VAULT

The archipelago's death rituals divide basically into cave and tumuli burial, the former subdivided between 'mummification' and non-mummification of the corpse, the latter into large multiple tombs and individual graves (Pls. 3, 4bc, 8a, Figs. 12be, 13). The resting places and their rituals will be fully described in Chapter 7.

Fusté (1961) has thoroughly analysed the material from the large multiple tombs of Gáldar (N.W. Gran Canaria), excavated by the Museo Canario in 1935 (no report). He worked on 32 skeletons and nine other crania (26m, 15f).

	Cephalic index		Facial index		Height (different formulae), cm		
						Dupertuis-Hadden	Trotter-Glaser
	Range	Mean	Range	Mean	Pearson		
Men	70.37–79.89	74.65	85.95–99.22	90.73	172.15	175.77	176.38
Women	70.74–82.14	77.50	82.81–100.0	93.43	159.10	163.40	164.00

Table 13: *Skeletal data from the Gáldar tombs*

In other terms, most crania, large and robust, with long high vaults, were technically groupable as dolicho-mesocephalic; the faces were of middle value on average but many were high and orthognathous in profile, except in the alveolar region; there was a tendency towards high eye-sockets. The body, with large stout long-bones, was on the tall side of humanity. Fusté typed these men and women as 'Robust Mediterraneans'; significantly far less present were the Cromagnoids and Orientaloids. The main tomb, La Guancha, has a single C14 date of about the eleventh century AD; the second in importance, El Agujero, held a pot (Fig. 16g), part of the painted-ware group most likely to have been first made in the fourteenth century; it is probable that the large common tombs were in use over at least 300 years.

Fusté then drew attention, first, to the tallness (no measurements given) of pre-conquest skeletons from 'similar' tumuli elsewhere in Gran Canaria, such as at Arguineguín on the south coast; these have now disappeared but Verneau's nineteenth-century description of the southern tumuli, given in Chapter 7, does not suggest diagnostic similarity. Secondly he remarked the comparative unimportance of the Mediterraneans in the notable collection of cave-burial skeletons from Guayadeque, the eastern gorge; these have C14 dates of sixth and eighth centuries AD.

Schwidetsky (1963) assessed the material (88 crania) from all the Gran Canaria tombs—both collective and individual—dividing them into two groups, those from Gáldar and the rest:

Sex	Gáldar	Rest	North			South		
			Isleta	Agaete	Arguineguín	Mogán	Arteara	Fataga
M	22	37	10	5	10	9	1	2
F	14	15	4	2	6	2	1	0

Table 14: *Tumuli burials (crania), Gran Canaria*

She compared this material to that from 1142 cave burials (729m, 413f) spread throughout the island, including the Gáldar area. She concluded that the tumuli burials were nearer the Mediterranean pole than those of the caves and than the island average, with the Gáldar material the most extreme. However, there were many characteristics in which the tumuli crania differed amongst themselves. The Gáldar long-bones gave a male stature of 169.5 cm (compare Fusté, above, 172.15cm), the other tumuli came out at 169.3 cm average; these were each well above the overall island average, 166.8 cm—and did agree amongst themselves. Thus the cave burials must have been rather under the overall average height (no absolute measurements were given) and so differed in stature as well as in cranial type from the tumuli subjects.

Recently (1976) Schwidetsky has described the tumuli people as having 'Negroid tendencies': 'broad noses and relatively-strong prognathy'. She adds that these survive—with full lips and dark hair—in the present west-coast people of Gran Canaria.

The hypotheses based on the difference found between bodies buried under tumuli and those placed in caves must wait until Chapter 7, together with theories stemming from the difference proposed by Schwidetsky between the 'mummified' and the non-mummified, described in the next section. In the meantime, though, a qualification needs to be made. A period of 1500 years is under consideration: if settlements close together could evolve clearly distinguishable physical types (Table 12), then the whole island could equally evolve considerably . . . if tumuli burial were a late development, then the difference between its subjects and those found in caves could be due to evolution rather than, as Schwidetsky will be seen to propose, to physical (almost racial) and class distinction in the form of burial.

PREHISTORIC SKELETAL DATA: 'MUMMIFIED' AND NON-MUMMIFIED CAVE-BURIALS

There is material from four islands. Schwidetsky classed a skeleton as mummified if there was the least trace of visceral material. Yet is is known that sun-drying of bodies was common practice amongst the ordinary people; conversely, the mummies had little protection against rats, so that many would have lost all their soft parts. So, once again, extended theories of physical type and social position in relation to a burial practice have to be considered with caution.

Rite		All islands M	Non-M	Gran Can. M	Non-M	Tenerife M	Non-M	Gomera M	Non-M	Hierro M	Non-M
Crania	M	267	1028	156	628	79	283	10	52	13	46
(numbers)	F	164	514	122	310	24	128	7	26	7	32
Cranial index	M	75.2	75.5	74.6	74.8	76.4	76.9	75.6	78.2	74.0	75.5
(averages)	F	76.4	76.8	76.1	76.3	77.8	78.0	76.4	79.3	75.8	76.8
Long bones	M	266	935	156	770	110	165	0	0	0	0
(numbers)	F	112	617	71	492	41	125	0	0	0	0
Stature	M	166.9	165.9	167.9	166.4	164.7	163.7	—	—	—	—
(averages)	F	153	152.9	153.5	153.1	152.2	151.8	—	—	—	—

Table 15: *Physical data: 'mummified' against non-mummified*

The table, together with the facial and other indices, shows those 'mummified' to have been rather longer-headed, taller and more slender in body than those not mummified. Though the figures show 'the mummies had the higher faces, narrower noses and higher eye-sockets' (Schwidetsky 1963, p. 154), later the monograph states that 'the facial characteristics, so important in the Comagnoid-Mediterranean polarity, scarcely differ' (p. 170); the second quotation comes from a passage in which Schwidetsky is propounding her theory, discussed in Chapter 7, that a *limited* differentiation by class self-selection separates the 'mummified' from the non-mummified — rather than a *strong* racial distinction. Physical differences were also discerned between the 'mummified' men and women, the latter nearer the Mediterranean pole; discussion of Schwidetsky's explanation of this will also be deferred until Chapter 7.

MODERN PHYSICAL DATA: DISTRIBUTION BY ISLANDS

The reader is reminded that all modern statistics should have been collected and studied in the light of the vast population modifications resulting from the conquests and colonization of the Canaries by European and further African peoples. Fusté's published work (1958, a little altered by his later papers) covered only Gran Canaria (362 men, aged 18–50, mainly rural). His conclusions were that six types are now discernable on the island. Three large strong forms: the described Cromagnoid and Robust Mediterranean together with the well-known Nordic. Three types of medium size, these the Armenoid and Orientaloid together with a 'Slender Mediterranean'; the first is broad-headed, the other two long-to-middle in head proportion and difficult to distinguish one from the other. It is not certain that the two newly-described types (Nordic, Slender Mediterranean) were not present in the prehistoric period. Fusté said the first two types are still the most common, the Armenoids and Nordics the least so. Although in Agaete (N.W.) he encountered two men who had 'undoubtedly' a strong Negroid element and in spite of distinctively Negroid characteristics here and there in the island, Fusté discounted any 'established assimilated Negroid element' in the population.

Schwidetsky's study (1975) was again the wider. She collected data from 6800 schoolchildren, throughout the seven islands, converting this into adult equivalents; Table 16 gives the two most important aspects. Each subject's background was considered; the table is laid out in likely order of endogamy, Gomera the highest, then the other western islands, close together, then the eastern group, also close together.

Schwidetsky concluded from her many analyses that a majority of the islanders fall, as in the pre-conquest period, on a line between the two poles, Cromagnoid and Mediterranean. However, as the two types now have flesh as well as bone to be classified, with crania and long bones associated, a more complete picture can be given. The current Cromagnoid tends towards the proportionally longer head; lower

Male	All Islands	Gomera	Ten.	Hierro	Palma	Lanz.	G.C.	Fuert.
Cephalic index	78.1	77.2	77.9	77.4	78.1	78.0	78.7	78.8
Stature (cm)	169.1	167.3	168.1	167.9	169.9	168.6	170.6	169.2

Table 16: *Modern physical data*

stature; shorter broader face, more sunken eyes, more prominent cheekbones, concave rather than convex nose, straight rather than curved mouth, thinner lips, angular rather than rounded lower jaw. Though each island has its peculiar features too, there appears to be a broad progression from a more endogamous, Cromagnoid west to a more matrimonially-mobile, Mediterranean east.

MODERN PHYSICAL DATA: DISTRIBUTION WITHIN THE ISLANDS

The details of Fusté's study of the Gran Canaria men are given in Table 17; this is based on his concept of the settlement pattern. The San Nicolás figures are probably unreliable, the men thought to have been 'selected' by the local authority.

Region (individuals)	SW (50)	SE (79)	W (29)	N (114)	C (79)
Main settlements	Mogán Veneguera	Tirajana Agüimes	San Nicolás	Telde Gáldar Agaete	Artenara Tejeda
Cephalic index	79.35	77.92	77.79	78.73	76.55
Stature (cm)	167.06	170.52	176.52	171.66	169.34

Table 17: *Modern physical data, Gran Canaria, by region*

The north and south-east are each 'tall'; though all regions fall in the mesocephalic range, there is a significant difference, said Fusté, between the longer heads of the centre and the broader heads of the south-west. The table's diversity is also to be seen in the islanders' facial contours, nose shapes and so on.

Fusté also left notes on the type distribution. The Cromagnoids are mainly in the centre. Robust Mediterraneans occur primarily in the north and secondarily in the centre, in each region the most common type. The divergent south-west has the strongest numbers of Slender Mediterraneans, Orientaloids and Armenoids. The few Nordics are in the north.

Schwidetsky's 1975 monograph was again much broader. Her findings are both voluminous and complex—only simplified conclusions can be given. Within each island, as across the archipelago, there is a broad correlation between social isolation, inferred endogamy and the Cromagnoid pole. In Gomera, the remote villages of Chipude and Arure contrast with the outwards-looking banana-exporting settlements of Hermigua and Vallehermoso, for example. In Palma the isolated north-west corner was nearest the Cromagnoid pole. On Lanzarote, with a comparatively-uniform topography, the Cromagnoid extreme was found in Teguise (Pl. 14a), the long-stagnating, early post-conquest capital, and three villages close by to the west.

On Gran Canaria, this anthropologist's approach found the Cromagnoid-Mediterranean polarity to be most extreme between the mountains and the coast and, to a lesser degree, between the arid south and the fertile north. Dividing the mountains themselves into north and south, the first differed more from the densely-populated coast to their north than did the second from the well-peopled plain to the east.

The present people of the west of Gran Canaria have a marked incidence of high rounded faces, broad noses, thick lips and a colouring—a subject covered in the next chapter—darker than the rest of the island. The aspects recognizable in the skeleton have already been remarked in the tumuli subjects. Schwidetsky first called these features 'southern' or 'African' but not Negroid (1975, published in Spanish by the Tenerife Island Council) yet referred to them as 'Negroid tendencies' soon after (1976, published in English in Holland).

Tenerife gave much the same modern general pattern as Gran Canaria: Cromagnoids mainly in the mountains and the poor south, Mediterraneans around the coast, primarily on the north. As an example of a variation: the islanders in the broadly Mediterranean north are in fact shorter than those of the Cromagnoid south, though the coastal people are taller than those of the mountains.

The reader is again reminded that the early post-conquest immigrants from both S. Europe and N.W. Africa will have included a great many Mediterraneans but few Cromagnoids. Thus a strongly Cromagnoid area is probably in line of descent from the pre-conquest people—but a Mediterranean area may be the result of a post-conquest immigration of this type. There is no way in which an anthropologist could trace his sample's ancestries back to the fifteenth century; at the most, recent immigrants can be eliminated from the survey.

Finally, an interesting and rather different type of conclusion was reached by Schwidetsky in her very first paper on the Canaries (1956, published in German in Austria). In Tenerife's two towns, Sta. Cruz and La Laguna, Cromagnoids were commoner in the outskirts and poorer quarters than in the centre and the richer neigh-bourhoods . . . a socio-economic aspect which, unlike the differences between the forms of burial, she did not follow up — nor, in the Spain of 1956, would it have been possible to do so officially. This has of course direct relevance to the subjects of colonization, slavery and continuing widespread poverty in the archipelago, all discussed in the last part of this book.

CHAPTER FOUR
Flesh and Blood

Amongst the various physical data given in this chapter there are elements new to Canary anthropology. Not only is there thus no earlier material against which to assess these statistics but the techniques used in collection and elaboration are of an extreme complexity beyond all but other specialists in these fields. The conclusions, with the most vital statistics for those able to interpret them, are all that will be given here. The author's reservations over population settlement and movement apply again; indeed this and the last chapter could be usefully read again after those of Parts Five and Six.

PREHISTORIC AND MODERN EYE-COLOUR

The only pre-conquest material comes from five mummies from Tenerife and from one from Gran Canaria. Rohen's examination showed they all had dark eyes.

Half a century ago Fischer gave statistics for 870 Canary soldiers. Their eyes were 5% black, 87% brown, 8% blue, grey, green.

Fusté (1958) also recorded the eye-colours of his sample of Canary men:

Group	Colour	All	SW	SE	W	N	Centre
Dark	Brown	46	63	55	52	42	31
Medium	Green (hazel to pure)	42	25	34	41	41	61
Light	Blue, grey	12	12	11	7	17	8

Table 18: *Eye colour (%), Gran Canaria regions*

The 'green' of the first four regions is in fact an eye with a green iris and a light brown aureole around the pupil. There is a clear difference between the central mountains and the other regions selected by Fusté. The maximum of blue and grey eyes came mainly from the Agaete-Gáldar region. Fusté did not indicate the eye-colour of the Cromagnoids and Robust Mediterraneans but, of his other four living types, three have brown eyes and the fourth, the Nordics, light blue eyes.

Schwidetsky's first statistics (1958) are unusable due to suspected variations in sampling criteria. Her 1960–3 survey (1975) found no correlation between eye-colour and her two type-poles. Nor were there significant differences between the islands. The table lists these from darkest to lightest:

G: Darkest: Chipude, Valle Gran Rey (together in west)
F: Betancuria (first European capital, Pl. 14b) outstandingly light in island and Canaries
P: Darkest in remote north-west
L: Rather lighter in Teguise (first European capital, Pl. 14a) and area
GC: Light tendency in mountains, darkest on west and south coasts
T: Light in mountains, dark on north coast
H: Mocanal (N.E.) very light

Table 19: *Eye colour, by and within islands*

Schwidetsky and Fusté appear to disagree over the mountain people of Gran Canaria, unless the former simply means that they have lighter eyes than the rest. Her own statistics (Table 4) in fact suggest no marked distribution pattern within Gran Canaria. The point is noteworthy in view of the supposed division of the island between the main physical types.

PREHISTORIC AND MODERN HAIR COLOUR AND TYPE
Schwidetsky's 1963 study considered the 88 hair samples, 'mostly' from Gran Canaria, then held by the Museo Canario and the Museé de l'Homme, Paris. There were 26 loose specimens and 62 on mummies (6 children and 56 adults; latter were 31m, 25f, mainly over 40 years old). There were difficulties. Hair undergoes colour changes after death. Mummification — the use of astringent plants, long exposure to the sun — also causes alteration, in particular towards a reddish hue. For example, a Guayadeque (Gran Canaria, east) mummy had hair varying from a lightish blond to a dark chestnut. The study found the proportions of fair hair to be 15% for men, 11% women, 14% all adults. Children were 29% fair, reaching 71% if light brown were included, against which there has to be blanced the frequent darkening of the hair by adulthood; the fair children were all from Gran Canaria. Schwidetsky found no correlation between hair colour and physical type of mummy. Of course, if the mummies were not an average group of islanders — in accordance with Schwidetsky's theory — then their hair would not perhaps be typical either.

Three workers' studies will give an idea of the hair colour of the modern islanders. Fischer's soldiers were 11% black, 78% brown, 11% blond. Fusté (1958) produced statistics (Table 20) for his regions of Gran Canaria, showing a predominance of dark hair; in accordance with his eye data, the north appeared the lightest in hair colour.

Group	Colour	GC	SW	SE	W	N	C
Dark	Black, dark brown.	90	88	93	92	89	91
Medium	Light chestnut, dark blond	7	10	6	8	4	9
Light	Light blond	3	2	1	0	7	0

Table 20: *Hair colour (%), Gran Canaria*

Fusté did not indicate the hair colour of the living Cromagnoids and Robust Mediterraneans. The hair of his three other types was black, that of the fourth, the Nordic, being blond, occasionally ashy; he added that the skins of these were, respectively, dark, with sometimes an olive tint, and very white, often with freckles. The Nordic element could stem from Europeans shipwrecked on the island in pre-conquest times and from the many Flemish settlers (the much-visited Caldera de Bandama is called after a Van Dam); the Cape Verds, uninhabited until their discovery by the Portuguese in the fifteenth century, now also have a proportion of blue-eyed, fair-haired inhabitants.

Schwidetsky affirms (1963) that the present children are also very fair: in two Gomera villages, 45% of those 5–6 years old, 19% of those 11–12 years old (confirming their hair also darkens with age). Her wide study of 1975 listed the islands from darkest to lightest in hair colour — Gran Canaria, Lanzarote, Palma, Gomera, Fuerteventura, Hierro, Tenerife — with the differences considered pronounced. In Palma the remote N.W. quarter had the lightest hair, in Gran Canaria the darkest was in the N.W.–W. sector (Agaete-San Nicolás), in Tenerife it turned out to be the south. In 1975 (p. 49) this worker noted that the Cromagnoid usually has the lighter hair but in 1976 (p. 23) she said there was no correlation between hair colour and the type-poles.

Type of hair has been less considered. The 43 mummies (Schwidetsky 1963) had 78% straight, 19% wavy, 5% curly, with adults having 88% straight hair. The Canary soldiers of 1930 (Fischer) had 85% straight hair.

PREHISTORIC AND MODERN BLOOD CHARACTERISTICS
Data has been collected by the Spanish (Guasch *et al* 1952, Bravo 1958, Parejo 1966), the Germans (Schwarzfischer 1963, Rösing 1967)

and the English (Roberts *et al* 1966). The reader is reminded that, as with all physical remains, the mummies' ages are unknown—the samples may be from 500 to 2000 years old.

Subjects	Worker	No. of Samples	0%	A%	B%	AB%	p	q	r
T. mummies	Schwarzfischer	81	83.95	9.88	4.96	1.23	—	—	—
G.C. ,,	,,	191	94.76	2.62	2.09	0.53	—	—	—
T. living	Parejo	?	41.10	44.77	10.20	3.91	25.6	5.8	56.9
T. ,,	Rösing	376	43.35	42.82	8.51	5.32	—	—	—
G.C. ,,	Guasch	404	41.50	41.50	12.75	4.95	—	—	—
G.C. ,,	Parejo	?	43.84	40.65	11.31	4.20	23.3	6.5	60.7
G.C. ,,	Roberts	1001	48.70	38.00	10.20	3.20	—	—	—
G.C. ,,	,,	182	47.80	35.16	11.54	5.50	22.2	8.9	68.3
Palma ,,	Bravo	1255	49.72	39.28	8.93	2.07	—	—	—
Palma ,,	Parejo	?	45.67	43.47	7.68	3.18	24.9	4.4	63.3
Gomera ,,	,,	?	52.13	35.79	8.47	3.61	20.5	4.8	72.2
T. province ,,	,,	?	46.30	41.34	8.78	3.56	23.7	5.0	62.6
G.C. ,,	,,	?	43.77	40.50	11.56	4.16	23.1	6.6	60.6
Canaries ,,	,,	20,089	42.51	43.22	10.29	3.95	24.8	5.9	57.7

Table 21: *Blood and gene groups, ABO system*

The table shows a very high O reading, positively determined, amongst the prehistoric population, greater in Gran Canaria than in Tenerife. It is still higher in the eastern island though it looks as though the greatest proportions now occur in the lesser western islands; unluckily Parejo had not enough samples from Hierro or the extreme eastern islands. It would be interesting to have the ancient and modern blood groups also by physical type.

Table 21 showed that the O blood group has been about halved since the conquests, at least in the two main islands. Two obvious factors are the deaths and deportations amongst the islanders, before, during and after the conquests, and, secondly, the immigration of the Europeans and Africans. A third factor is that the O group is an index of isolation and recedes the more a people intermarries with the outside world. However, Rösing and Schwidetsky (1970) feel further, accelerating factors to be necessary, invoking contagious diseases, notably smallpox, this probably brought in by the immigrants and common until the end of the last century: it is thought to swing the blood-group proportions in favour of the carriers, comparatively immune. The two German workers construct a model for Tenerife, for example, based on a 2% Spanish immigration rate in each generation of 27 years (accepting Wölfel's estimate of the Spanish contribution to the island as a third by the mid-twentieth century) and a selection co-efficient of 10% (the rate at which the diseases acted against the ancient O group), thus explaining the changes in the blood groups between 1492 and 1966. Such a model seems grossly over-simplified in many ways — as an example, the mummies could as well be 2000 years old as date from 1492.

Regional statistics were produced by Roberts *et al* for Gran Canaria, using Fusté's geographical divisions:

Group	GC(1001)	SW(70)	SE(95)	W(56)	N(90)	C(90)
O	49	49	48	37	48	60
A	38	34	38	49	39	26
B	10	14	11	9	10	9
AB	3	3	3	5	3	5

Table 22: *Blood groups (%), Gran Canaria*

Again, it seems that the central mountains (Artenara, Tejeda) and, to a lesser degree, the west (San Nicolás) are different from the rest of the island. However, the north (69% of the whole sample on Gran Canaria) has in fact a wide range; for example, Las Palmas had 60% O group (only 45 samples, though) and San Mateo 51% A group. For Tenerife, Parejo's calculations gave 39.50% O group in the north against 43.29% in the south.

To throw light on the regional ABO data, the English workers made an assessment of Gran Canaria endogamy. Information was collected on marriages spread throughout the island:

GEO-GRAPHICAL MOBILITY	*Present generation:*	Number of marriages 299	Both local 58%	One incomer 27%	Both incomers 15%
COUSIN MARRIAGE	*Past generation:*	Number of marriages 998	Between cousins 8.2%	*Present generation:*	Number of marriages 399	Between cousins 12.5%

Table 23: *Indices of endogamy, Gran Canaria*

Though the mobility was considered 'quite high', cousin marriage was 'strikingly frequent'. In fact, in the present generation, cousin marriage in Mogán (SW) has reached 26% and Artenara-Tejeda (C) 24%, with San Nicolás (W) about 24% in each generation. Clearly, cousin marriage seems linked to isolation and may even be increasing. This degree of endogamy would permit genetic drift—in other words, the regional differences in the blood groups (Table 22) could as well be due to differentiation since immigration as to the arrival of people in different groups. Fusté (1958) in fact quoted an unpublished study by Gavilanes showing areas where up to 90% of marriages are between such close relatives as to need canonic dispensation.

The English broke new ground by grouping a further 182 Gran Canaria individuals not only on the ABO system but also under the MNS, Rhesus, P, Kell and Duffy methods:

MS	Ms	cde	cDe	cDe^s	P$_1$	K	Fy^a
28.24	27.53	32.66	7.58	3.5	41.63	4.21	29.29

Table 24: *Gene frequencies (Roberts et al)*

The cDe and cDe^s figures, totalling over 11%, suggest a negro element in the islands. The authors' extraordinary conclusions over the origins of the majority of the Canary Islanders will be discussed in Chapter 4.

Fusté (1965ab) studied the haptoglobin types in 139 Gran Canaria individuals:

Phenotypes	Hp^1/Hp^1 30	Hp^2/Hp^1 64	Hp^2/Hp^2 45
Gene frequencies	Hp^1 0.46	Hp^2 0.54	

Table 25: *Haptoglobin types (Fusté)*

Compared to 24 Caucasoid and 22 Negroid groups, this result is 'close to the top of the Caucasoid range but . . . still well below any . . . recorded for Negroid groups'. The islanders are 'especially close to the Spanish in particular'.

MODERN PALM PATTERNS

Fusté and Pons (eg Fusté 1965) collected the palm-prints of 367 Gran Canaria subjects, classifying the terminations of the main line 'D' (according to the Cummins and Midco typology):

Percentages	Right hand	Left hand	Both
Type 7	11.58	23.88	17.75
,, 9	34.18	48.60	41.41
,, 11	54.24	27.53	40.85

Table 26: *Palm patterns, main line 'D', Gran Canaria*

Four other groups of palm-pattern statistics were also produced. The data was claimed to solve 'one of the major problems', the presence or otherwise of the Negroid element: taken overall, the analyses placed the islanders amongst the European populations, towards the end nearer the Negroid indices.

Since the aim of Fusté's blood and palm-pattern work seems to have been to disprove Negroid influence, other relevant evidence should be recalled for summary here. Several competent anthropologists have discerned a Negroid type in the ancient skeletal material; Falkenberger suggested 11%; Schwidetsky noted the characteristics in the Gáldar tumuli skeletons. It is well-known that negroes were brought in to work as slaves in the early post-conquest sugar plantations; until at least the end of the last century (Stone, Verneau) there was a colony of negroes in the Tirajana area of Gran Canaria. Both Schwidetsky and Fusté himself noted Negroid traits in the west of the island, the former also in the Gomera mountains. And since Fusté states in his paper on palm-patterns that the data will only show up 'group differences, rather than those of individuals', a minor Negroid element would not be evidenced by this study. Finally, Fusté did not say where in Gran Canaria his sampling was done: it would be interesting to compare Tirajana and San Nicolás to the island average.

MODERN FINGERPRINTS

Schwidetsky (1975) gave an index of fingerprint complexity, tabulated now by island, from most ('advanced') to least ('primitive') complicated. The archipelago results are not self-explanatory, beyond the closeness of the eastern islands. As usual, some remote regions produced extreme statistics.

L: highest in northern half
F: no interior pattern discerned
P: lowest in N.W.
H: no interior pattern discerned
T: highest in mountains; south exceeded north
GC: highest in N. mountains; S. coast exceeded N. coast
G: highest in 'banana villages'

Table 27: *Fingerprint complexity*

PALAEOPATHOLOGY

The most informative of Bosch Millares' studies (1969) is concerned with three forms of skull surgery. Scarification was much the most common: vertical incisions, through the skin, into the right and left sides of the frontal bone, or forehead. Espinosa (1558) referred to pre-conquest scarification of 'the arms, head and forehead', using the common cutting stones, described in Chapter 11; Abreu added that this was for acute pains, the place then being anointed with goat butter. A few crania show cauterization on the bregma or occipital. Others have undergone trepanning, usually a round hole cut out of the left parietal. Some operations had been carried out after death.

Bosch Millares (1961) found no traces of rickets, TB, leprosy or, in spite of Verneau's affirmation, of syphilis; there were indices of rheumatism. Amongst the 32 skeletons he saw from the Gáldar tombs, Fusté found one case of rickets and thirteen of arthritis.

In his Gáldar monograph, Fusté also gave details of the condition of the teeth of his subjects, comparing this data to that from the burials in caves in the central mountains (mainly Tejeda, Acusa, Tirajana):

Burial type	Gáldar tumuli	Mountain caves
Subjects: adult	28	99
mature	7	29
senile	7	8
Caries (% of remaining teeth)	4–7%	13–22%
Teeth missing at death (% of sockets seen)	17%	21%
Teeth carious or missing (% of sockets seen)	19%	28%

Table 28: *Dental pathology, Gran Canaria*

Clearly, the mountain-dwellers had the worst teeth, especially since they were rather the younger group. Amongst the ancient peoples of Europe and N. Africa they seem to come low down in dental health. The Gáldar population would perhaps be average. As with many early groups, the caries in both regions, increasing to the back of the mouth, was concentrated on the first molar amongst the remaining teeth; correspondingly, the commonest missing teeth were the third and then the second molars. Powers noted that seven out of 47 'Guanche' skulls in UK collections have unerupted canines.

Fusté discussed four possible reasons for the poor dentition in the interior and for the difference between this and that of the coastal people. First, a lack of vitamins such as the shore and sea provide; but without an examination of the mountain people's diet, this is to assume that the world's inland groups in general tend or tended to go short of vitamins, by no means certain — indeed, in N. Africa the teeth of the people of the interior have been shown to be the better. Second, the use of rotary querns of volcanic stone adds abrasive material to the grain ground upon them; this supposes that the coast-dwellers ate significantly less grain than the mountain dwellers, not yet proved. Thirdly, dentition state may be linked to the difference in physical type between the two regions. Finally, since the Gáldar tombs may have belonged to a socio-economic elite, this may have been particularly well-fed and healthy; but then it must be remembered that the 'mummified' amongst the cave burials have been put forward as an elite too (Schwidetsky), though Fusté does not say how many mummy-crania are amongst his sample of 136 individuals.

AGE AT DEATH OF PRE-CONQUEST ISLANDERS

Group	GC			Tenerife				
Sex etc	M	F	M	F	Non-mum.	Mum.	North	South
Adult	26	35	39	37	32	20	31	42
Mature	58	46	44	42	52	58	37	46
Senile	16	19	17	22	15	23	32	11

Table 29: *Age at death (%), Gran Canaria and Tenerife*

These statistics (Schwidetsky 1957, 1958) show the islanders reached a good age, with every fifth or sixth beyond sixty. Women lived longer than men. People in the fertile north lasted longer than those in the arid south. The 'mummified' (?elite) longer than the unmummified. No distinction could be found between those buried in tumuli (?elite) and those found in caves.

However, Fusté (1963) again produced separate data for the 42 Gáldar individuals (26m, 15f recognizable), comparing this to data from 136 burials in the interior caves.

Group	Gáldar tumuli	Central caves
Adult	66	73
Mature	17	21
Senile	17	6

Table 30: *Age at death (%), Gáldar tumuli against central caves*

The tomb burials appear to have lived the longer. A comparison with the previous table shows the two workers have produced markedly different groupings for age at death on Gran Canaria, not explicable. Torriani (1590) had a further group: on Gran Canaria, he wrote, people had regularly lived to 140 years old . . .

It would be useful, for comparison, to have data on the ailments
and age at death of the present islanders. However, as with the
sociological implications of Schwidetsky's Cromagnoid-poverty
correlation, until 1975 this would have been politically unacceptable
unless it had shown the present islanders in the more favoured state.

SUMMARY OF PHYSICAL TYPES, ANCIENT AND MODERN
Throughout the archipelago's occupation, the islanders have been in
the majority on a line between the Cromagnoid and the
Mediterranean type-poles, most simply distinguished by their faces,
the former's broad and robust, the latter's high and delicate. Probably
the more Comagnoid were usually the shorter and sturdier in stature
but in some regions this type may have been taller than the
Mediterranean. Heads have changed from a middling proportion of
width to length towards a broader shape, the width increasing and the
length decreasing. On a world scale the ancient islanders were mostly
medium in height, with those of Gomera small and those of Fuerteventura tall; they are now all on the tall side, even those of Gomera.

The evidence suggests that the greater part of the islanders —
including the two main types — have always had dark-to-medium eye
and hair colouring. The arrival-date of the Nordic-type colouring is
uncertain but is to a degree certainly post-conquest.

In prehistoric times the Cromagnoid to Mediterranean range,
accounting for most of the islanders, would have been almost entirely
in the O blood group. Now, due to immigration and perhaps its
associated diseases, the archipelago's O group count is reduced to a
less distinctive level, in world terms.

In distribution the Cromagnoids have always been the more
common in Gomera and Gran Canaria; Tenerife's north coast was
also predominantly Cromagnoid in prehistoric times. The
Mediterraneans have always been at their most common in the eastern
islands, preponderating on the north coast of Gran Canaria and, now,
on that of Tenerife. Inter-island differences have decreased. The
anthropologists note a marked correlation between social isolation,
endogamy and the regions with extreme characteristics, in particular
those where the Cromagnoids are conspicuous and in others, less
clearly typed, such as N.W. Palma and the original capitals, now
stagnating, of the two eastern islands. Genetic drift is considered likely
to have also been a factor in the marked local variations.

The major differences between islands and between regions, in the
pre-conquest period, are usually explained in traditional terms:
Schwidetsky, for example, proposes two separate immigrant waves,
Cromagnoid and then Mediterranean. Since these formed distinct

groups in the Mesolithic and perhaps early Neolithic of N.W. Africa (Chapter 5), say until 5000 years ago, she sees the two types arriving separately; as in Africa the 'primitive' Cromagnoids would have come first, being later driven into the mountains on Gran Canaria, though not on Tenerife, by the 'advanced' Mediterraneans. Drawing on the low opinion archaeology once had of the Cromagnoids' culture in N.W. Africa (Chapter 5) and assuming the evolved cultural material of Gran Canaria was actually initiated by the Mediterraneans (the evidence of the later chapters leaves this issue open), she suggests that the Cromagnoids were an inferior race doomed to stagnation and extinction.

The author's alternative view is that the major immigration, almost 2000 years ago, held each physical type. Total numbers would have been small—Tenerife's oral tradition, that there were 60 original settlers, is recalled. The shiploads may have been mixed or, if drawn from particular tribes, tending towards one or other physical pole. Once set down upon an island, a founder effect could take its people preponderantly in one direction—and away from a neighbouring island, contact being at once lost due to the lack of vessels. Or the island might always remain physically well mixed. It will be equally important to bear in mind right throughout Part Four that this founder effect is also likely to have played a vital part in the evolution of speech, belief, structures and everyday life, with these further diversified in response to the new range of habitats. It is probably due to the founder effect that all sorts of physical and cultural similarities and divergencies can be found between islands, no matter whether close together or far apart. Fashion and individual psychology amongst archaeologists are to the fore in the diffusion-evolution debate—in the Canaries the long search for an acceptable pedigree has always predisposed workers towards diffusionist theories. The existence of several cultures in isolation yet geographically close to each other may allow at least one rule to be formulated: the more a physical or cultural feature is repeated across the archipelago the more likely it is to have come in from outside. *Within* each island the founder effect could also occur; once moving in a certain physical or cultural direction, a group might keep apart from the other groups, due to topography and the Berber custom of endogamy (as already discussed in relation to Table 12 in particular).

The Gáldar tumuli held individuals physically Gran Canaria's nearest group to the Mediterranean pole. The archipelago's 'mummies' are said to form a group nearer the Mediterranean pole than those apparently buried without mummification. Tumuli and mummified burials were each an elite—their inter-relationship seems unexplained—with the tumuli subjects more so than the mummified people. The ancient Canary Islanders were healthy enough on average and lived to a good age.

Most of the foregoing summary is based upon and only valid for the past and present two main types. The general opinion is that other types, much less common, always existed alongside them. Fusté, the most recent worker in this school, has proposed an Orientaloid and an Armenoid; amongst the present islanders he also distinguishes a slender form of the Mediterranean and a Nordic type. There is also evidence that the Negroid type was to a small degree included in the ancient people and, reinforced since the conquest, is also minimally present in the modern islanders.

In Chapter 2 it was proposed that the first islanders were Berbers deported from N.W. Africa during the Roman occupation. The next chapter will consider how the described physical aspects match those of the late prehistoric and proto-historic inhabitants of the Maghreb.

CHAPTER FIVE
Physical Origins in N. W. Africa

A whole book could be written on this aspect alone. It is necessary to be clear as to the meaningful scope of comparisons between the Canaries and N.W. Africa. If one places the main immigration during the Roman period, then one can seek physical parallels amongst the recalcitrant Berber fringe of the colonized Maghreb; here the problems are that there is little skeletal material firmly dated to this time on either the Canaries or the African side and, less important, the exact southerly limits of the Romans' interaction with the Berbers is none too accurately known; Fig. 5 gives the zone under their control by the middle of the third century AD, but they had outposts beyond this and also made expeditions yet further afield. Nor, of course, are the Berber tribes likely to be now in the same territories as two millennia ago.

Beyond this, comparisons become even hazier. For example, consideration of the current islanders against the present people of the Maghreb. The surviving prehistoric islanders have become mixed with French, Spanish, Portuguese and Flemish, with the W. Saharan people caught between Cape Nun and Cape Blanc, with negroes from Senegal and Guinea. The Berbers of the Maghreb have received massive immigrations of Arabs and also the people expelled by the Portuguese and the Spanish, by then a mixture of pre-Islamic Iberians, Berbers and Arabs; this amalgam is said to be anthropometrically indistinguishable from the present Spaniards.

Studies of the present Maghreb peoples range from data on individual tribes to broad regional and racial-type statistics; only a few comparisons can be made here. Berber groups believed to have remained relatively unmixed do provide evidence on which to widen the prehistoric comparisons. Such Berbers occupy isolated zones — and for this reason may once have been akin to those *insoumis* deported by the Romans . . . as in the twentieth century they proved the hardest for the Romans' colonial successors to 'pacify'.

The two previous chapters described the ancient islanders by their skeleton, by this in relation to the burial forms, by blood, by eye and hair colour, palm patterns, fingerprints, by palaeopathology and by age at death. This chapter has to limit itself to N.W. African skeletal and blood data, the most widely-collected material: the skeleton will be summarized from the later Stone Age down to the present, adding then the data on the modern blood; the paucity of well-preserved bodies in N.W. African prehistory means there is no data on the prehistoric blood groups. It is not pretended that this chapter is a definitive comparison of the two regions' human types.

SKELETON: THE MAGHREB MESOLITHIC

About 22,000 years ago (Posnansky), the Algerian littoral was developing into the centre of the Ibero-Maurusian or Oranian culture, this lasting until the seventh millennium BC; in Morocco its known range was fourteenth-ninth millennium BC, in Libya eleventh-ninth millennium BC. These nomadic hunter-gatherers have usually been credited with an unenterprising culture. The physical type, notably found at Mechta-el-Arbi and Afalou-bou-Rhummel, both Algeria, and at Dar-es-Soltan, Morocco, is a Cromagnoid ('Mechta-Afalou' type) similar to that of the ancient islanders but for its still more robust features, greater height and larger neurocranium measurements (Schwidetsky 1963). This is in line with the normal trend from 'primitive' to modern man.

Work still in progress (Charon) has just produced a valuable extension of knowledge on these people. The sites of Izriten (Tarfaya) on the Moroccan coast right opposite Fuerteventura have yielded human remains of Mechta-Afalou type. The C14 dates are 8480±180BC (GIF-2910) and 7500±160BC (GIF-2908), at the end of the culture's known span in Algeria. At first glance this raises visions of an immigration by W. Saharan Cromagnoids but neither the details of their culture (the stone-tool types and the lack of pottery) nor the primitive state of their physiques (above) in the least support such an arrival at this early date. Their descendants will however be considered shortly. The prehistory of the coastal Sahara, excluding this new work, has already been summarized by the author (1976).

The Oranian gave way to the Capsian culture. Its timespan was late-eighth to fifth millennium BC, with isolated dates now appearing of the fourth millennium. The Capsian approached the Oranian centre from the south-east and became itself established over the Algerian littoral and in Tunisia. The physical type, best evidenced at Ain Dokkara and Aioum Beriche, both Algeria, and at Ain Meterchem, Tunisia, is a Robust Mediterranean which again only differs in its greater 'primitiveness' from the mean Mediterranean type amongst the prehistoric Canary people. This Capsian type had Negroid characteristics, presumably acquired by contact with the north-going negro migrations during the last wet stage of the usually-impassable Sahara desert: 'Amongst the N. African mesolithic people, as in the primitive Canary Islanders, there are negroid characteristics' (Schwidetsky 1963).

SKELETON: THE MAGHREB NEOLITHIC

In the sixth millennium (Posnansky), Neolithic cultural features from the E. Mediterranean reached the Maghreb and, adding themselves to the existing Capsian culture, produced the Neolithic of Capsian Tradition. Almagro (1968) summarizes a further much-debated element: a stream of immigrants and influences from Iberia. These, writes this Spanish worker, included the fair Slender (Gracile) Mediterraneans who now inhabit the Rif and Tell zones of the Maghreb littoral; also the conical-base pot. Fusté (1958) notes that both Mechta-Afalous and Robust Mediterraneans were present in prehistoric Iberia. Almagro felt (in 1968) that Iberian immigration lasted throughout the Maghreb Neolithic into the first millennium BC.

The Sahara soon developed its own Neolithic, a blend of the ancient local cultures, of northern and eastern influences and of responses to the changing habitat. It can be assumed that the arrival and duration of each cultural feature were latest and most long-lived on the western littoral: here many C14 dates fall in the last two millennia BC, down to fourth century BC in the area of the present Mauritania (Fig. 2). Nearest the Canaries are the Tarfaya sites again (Charon), with a dozen dates running from late-fourth to early-first millennium BC.

In the Maghreb, Neolithic culture is usually associated with Mediterranean physical type. Various workers have also found Mechta-Afalou characteristics in the human remains. Balout (1955) proposed that these original inhabitants of the Algerian *tell* survived in isolated zones such as the present Oran and Constantine hills, saying they are clearly distinguishable in the early Neolithic. Elements such as pottery and the domestication of animals would have been acquired by contact.

Skeletal material is extremely rare from the last few millennia before the Arab invasion. The Maghreb littoral was gradually absorbing new cultural traits during this time — stone tombs, metals — from the more advanced Mediterranean peoples. These percolated slowly into the hinterland and the Sahara. The stone tumuli themselves will be summarized in Chapter 7, since there is some resemblance to those of the Canaries. The skeletal finds are usually made in these tumuli — but dating of these, both on typology and by C14, is still inadequate. Bertholon and Chantre (in Alimen) suggested the megalithic burials showed the Mechta-Afalou continuing distinguishably right up to the Arab invasion. Alimen, on the other hand, says that the N. African tumuli (pre-Islamic) do not hold this type. Islamic tumuli are rarely opened, of course. The limited study of the Canary tombs does suggest that at least the larger, multiple-burial tumuli were the resting places of Mediterraneans rather than Cromagnoids, as has been seen.

The Sahara tumuli — also with limited similarity to those of the Canaries — contain only Mediterraneans. Almagro (1968) goes on to derive these tombs from those of the Maghreb *tell* of the last millennium BC. The Tarfaya evidence (Charon) shows that evolved Mechta-Afalous could however have also been present in the W. Sahara at this time. Thus the Canaries' two main physical types could have stemmed directly from the adjacent mainland. Nevertheless, historical reasons (Chapter 2) and many aspects of the pre-conquest culture of the Canaries (Chapters 6–11) combine to make the Maghreb hinterland the more likely source of the main immigration.

CONFLICT IN ROMAN AFRICA

The region dominated by Rome (Fig. 5) increased gradually from the mid-second century BC until the mid-third century AD, then contracting again until the close of the empire in the fifth century AD. Major conflicts were the wars with Carthage (265–146BC) and then the struggle against Jugurtha, king of Numidia, roughly the present Algeria. From about 29BC to c.AD20 the Roman protectorate of Mauretania was under a puppet king, Juba II; his territory ran from the Atlantic coast to about Constantine. Juba's expedition, with its report that the Canaries were uninhabited, has already been discussed.

The Romans had set up cities and had colonized the land, leaving the indigenous people the usual choices of slavery and serfdom or flight into inaccessible refuge zones. The littoral Berbers could only move southwards. However, dessication was then making the Sahara unattractive to its existing inhabitants. So it is likely that the Maghreb's Highlands became increasingly populated from all directions — inevitably a reservoir of *insoumis*. It is known that the Berbers in the hinterlands not only resisted demands such as taxes but also frequently attacked the colonized territories, including those under Juba. In addition to those mentioned in chapter 2, punitive expeditions are recorded, in 32, 30, 28, 21, 6, 5 and 3BC, against the 'Getulians' and the 'Garamantes'. These were major forays, victory sometimes meriting a triumphal entry into Rome. Deportation was a common Roman punishment — and exemplary transportation to the recently-explored and seemingly empty Canaries would be an obvious solution. With the evolved Robust Mediterraneans, the most common type, could have been rounded up Slender Mediterraneans (the *rif*) and evolved Mechta-Afalous (the Algerian hills). This would explain why the prehistoric Canary skeletons were so far ahead, in development, of their N. African Mesolithic ancestors — they were very late in arrival in the archipelago. Logically, their average age is only 750AD, assuming they span 0–1500AD. The Maghreb continuing under Roman rule until the fifth century, deportations may have gone on until this period.

It is recalled that Schwidetsky and others have said that, because the two main physical types were associated with different cultures in the Mesolithic and early Neolithic of N.W. Africa, they would have arrived in the Canaries in two separate waves. Obviously the Roman-deportation theory, with its late date, does not imply distinct immigrations of people or cultures. The only island to have two distinguishable cultural phases, Gran Canaria, probably received the second in the fourteenth century by contact with Iberians, as will be discussed.

Finally, a useful dating aid is the custom of removing the front teeth in the prehistoric Maghreb. Thus the Oranian-associated skulls, of both sexes, had lost their upper incisors, those of the women found with Capsian culture their lower incisors. The front teeth continued to be taken out, ritually, during the region's Neolithic, the practice dying out in the Roman period. None of the 2000 Canary crania show this deliberate removal of the incisors.

THE PRESENT BERBERS

Cromagnoids are still to be seen amongst the modern Berbers of N.W. Africa. The Mediterranean is the common type, Coon (1966) for example describing him as 165–172 cm tall, long or medium in head proportions, straight or convex nasal profile, faces and jaws narrow. Fusté (1966) remarked that the early, Robust form was not only still present but even dominant in some tribes, including amongst the Tuareg ruling class.

The present inhabitants of the Rif and of the Kabylie (E. Algerian *tell*), says Coon, have a marked incidence of broad faces, heavy jaws and snub noses, often associated with red hair, greenish eyes and freckles. These zones are amongst the most likely to have provided the original Canary Islanders. Coon gave data for the well-known light colouring of the Rif Berbers. Pinkish-white skin averaged 65%, reaching 86% in the fairest tribe. Light head-hair was seen on 10%, light beards, including red, on 45%; the fairest tribe held 24% blond in hair and beard, with 57% with light beards. The Beni Amart have eyes 18% dark, 73% green-blue mixed, 9% light. These mountain

Berbers are thus fairer than the S. European peoples. Hair-type in the Riffians is over 50% curly, in ringlets; there is no frizzy or woolly hair.

Comparing now these features with those of the ancient and modern Canary Islanders shows the Riffians to be much the fairer and to have a quite different hair-type. A shared incidence of Cromagnoid features is not enough to link the Rif directly to the Canaries — and, in the archipelago, there is anyway no evidence to associate the Cromagnoid pole with such light pigmentation as has been found.

BLOOD GROUPS IN THE MODERN MAGHREB

Against the groupings of the ancient islanders, known from their mummies, N. Africa can only provide the data from the modern isolated tribes; there is also general data on the modern inhabitants of the archipelago and of the northern sector of Africa. It should be said at once that a similar blood distribution does not prove a direct relationship, it only makes it possible; however, a dissimilar typing does rule out a close connection. The Mediterranean and Africa down to the Sahara are generally considered to form an 'old European' blood-group zone; the statistics of the ancient islanders (Table 21) fall within this zone too.

Subjects	O	A	B	AB	p	q	r
Tenerife mummies	84	10	5	1			
Gran Canaria mummies	95	3	2	1			
Ait Moghrad Berbers (High Atlas)	82	11	6	2			
Ait Haddidu Berbers (High Atlas)	79	12	8	1			
All mountain Berbers	75	20	5	1			
All Berbers	68	21	11	1			
Tunisian Berbers	58	32	8	1	19	5	76
Moroccan Berbers	39	39	17	5	25	12	63
Maghreb Arabs	38	37	19	5	24	13	62
Sahara: Tuareg nobles	56	34	8	1	20	5	75
W. Sahara: Izarguien	53	24	18	4	15	12	73
W. Sahara: Reguibat	39	21	31	8	16	22	63
Egyptians	55	24	21	1			
Spanish	46	44	7	2			
Canaries living	43	43	10	4	25	6	58
Tenerife ,,	41	45	10	4	26	6	57
Gomera ,,	52	36	8	4	21	5	72

Table 31: *Blood group comparisons (various sources)*

The mountain Berbers, in particular those of the High Atlas (Morocco) are the nearest now to the Canary mummies in blood groups. Unfortunately no figures have been found for the other ranges of N.W. Africa, such as the Rif, Tell, Aures and Tibesti, nor for the Algerian Berbers in general. The all-Berber data, seen against that from Morocco and Tunisia, implies that those in Algeria would be the nearest to the ancient islanders as a broad regional grouping. The Moroccan Berbers have the same blood divisions as the Arabs, due presumably to inter-mixing. In the desert, the Tuareg nobility and the Izarguien, each endogamous, have retained more primitive groupings than the Reguibat, well-known to have built up their size and power by their openness to new blood, including Arab (high AB).

The Spanish zone's data shows the Canaries are now much like the Peninsula in blood groups — except that the B and AB counts are now higher in the archipelago. The table suggests these high figures must ultimately stem from Arab blood in Morocco and W. Sahara, obviously then brought in by the slaves resulting from the large-scale raids on the adjacent coast between 1476 and 1593. These two groups may in fact get lower as one goes westwards across the Canaries (Table 21) — it would be interesting to compare Fuerteventura to Palma in this respect. The N.W. African slaves constituted the bulk of the population in the east, were a common element in the middle islands and, probably, were less often to be met in the west.

A glance at other regions to have received the *conquistadores* is informative. Spain now has O counts ranging between 41% (south) and 47% (north). Venezuela O reading is now 41%, Mexico 44%, Cuba 46% — but the indigenous Americans, where they can still be found in pure form, have 89–100% in the O group.

N.W. EUROPEAN ORIGINS . . .

Before summing up the whole of the N.W. African physical evidence, some comments must be made on the conclusions drawn by Roberts and his English colleagues from their blood-group fieldwork on the modern islanders: 'Taken together, the results suggest a population essentially European in frequencies of the blood group genes and gene complexes, though with some African influence. Within Europe affinities with the north-west are on the whole most suggestive'. Statistically, the paper said, 75.1% was drawn from N.W. Europe, .3% from Iberia, 18.3% from N. Africa, 6.3% from W. Africa. Since there has been no major immigration from N.W. Europe since the conquest, this team reasons that 'This component must have been present in the pre-Spanish gene pool'. And, it concludes, the ancient islanders must therefore have come from N.W. Europe. Amongst other work drawn upon is Hooton's physical comparison (one of many) with the Londoners of the seventeenth century and the lesser similarity with the Romano-British, the Gauls and other ancient N.W. Europeans. It was noted that the palm-prints are in the European rather than the negro group.

These conclusions, based no doubt on sound fieldwork within these workers' speciality, are the result of a very limited understanding of Canary and N. African prehistory. First, it is not mentioned that the 'N.W. European' contribution is not in fact to be seen in the blood groupings of the mummies themselves. The mummies' high O simply shows they could have been drawn from any of the world's isolated peoples; the Berbers were the nearest geographically. The modern islanders' gene statistics were compared only with those of Europeans and of negroes, in the absence of data for the Berbers. Over Hooton's skeletal comparisons, it is simply naïve to abstract those made with N.W. Europeans and not consider the people of the adjacent continent. The 'European' palm-print group, doubtless thus named by Europeans rather than by Africans, in fact reaches down to the Sahara, as does the blood region of the same name. Schwidetsky (1970) demolished the conclusions on further technical grounds. The English paper of course completely ignored the cultural evidence linking the Canaries to N.W. Africa.

SUMMARY

The general physical comparisons indicate that the Canaries' main immigration was of Berbers from the mountains of N.W. Africa. The limited detailed evidence points to the Algerian Tell and the Moroccan Rif and High Atlas. As will be shown next, the cultural comparisons support these impressions—and reduce the focus to the first of these regions in particular. However, it may just be that, as the Algerian Tell was the centre of the prehistoric cultures of the Maghreb, a search for the origins of the Canaries' physical types and culture would inevitably find all the archipelago's characteristics in that region.

PART FOUR

PREHISTORIC CULTURE

CHAPTER SIX
Speech and Symbols

This chapter will describe the relics of the most intangible aspects of the ancient islanders' culture, their two main forms of communication. The second, alternatively called their 'art', shades into their 'beliefs', discussed in the next chapter. The early chronicles and travellers' notes will now be used, both to help interpret the archaeological evidence and to fill gaps caused by the lack of material relics from various aspects of pre-conquest life.

PREHISTORIC ALPHABETIC INSCRIPTIONS
The evidence for speech consists of inscriptions; the notes of past observers; surviving words and place-names. Not relatable now to these is the whistled speech of Gomera, unique in form.

The rock-incised alphabetic inscriptions (Fig. 8) have been discussed by Alvarez (1964). They are cut on lava-flows and the walls of ravines, outcrops and caves in Hierro (Caleta, Candia, Julan, Tejeleita), Palma (Tajodeque) and Gran Canaria (Balos, Bandama). A painted inscription recorded (CAMC) for Gran Canaria, in a cave up on Roque Bentayga (just off Pl. 1b), could not be made out by the author. The most extensive sites have been known for a century and, subjected to a corresponding period of vandalism, are now greatly beyond study.

Occasionally the engravings are on the shore (Caleta); most are well inland (Balos, 7 km from the sea, Pl. 5); one has been located in the heights (Tajodeque, 2000m, on the N.W. rim of the Taburiente Caldera). Some were probably related to burials (Candia). Those in the Julan are close to a meeting place or *tagoror* (Pl. 10b), with a shell midden beside it. Some share surfaces with other forms of engraving (Julan, Balos).

Percussion with a stone tool appears the usual technique, the line being formed by a series of overlapping pockmarks; Alvarez suggests some may have been made with a metal point and that those of Balos may have been gone over with a 'polisher', a Sahara technique. Superimposition (Julan) has suggested to Alvarez that these characters are the youngest of the Canaries' several forms of rock engravings.

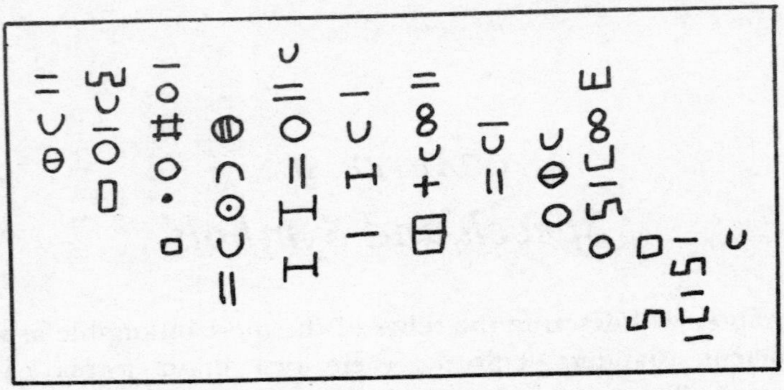

Figure 8 *Inscription in ancient Saharan alphabet, Hierro*

There is general agreement that the inscriptions (Fig. 8) are in a version of the ancient Berber alphabet, first recorded during its rapid expansion in the reign of Massinissa over Numidia, third–second century BC. During the following period of Berber-Roman conflict, its use in the Maghreb was curtailed by the Europeans; the Arabs ended its use there altogether. In the Sahara, however, it has continued to the present, as Tifinagh, used by the Tuareg. The writing is normally downwards. In the Canaries, translation has suggested proper names and invocations.

Archipelago dating evidence is sparse. Alvarez proposed that the inscriptions were the work of the many W. Saharans brought in as slaves from 1476. However, a major new discovery (Diego and Galand 1975) has shown that the writing was used in the islands in the first millennium AD. On Hierro (Guarazoca), the Hoya de los Muertos burial cave has yielded an inscription on a pine bier-plank, the associated human bones giving a C14 date of ninth–tenth century AD; a second date for wood from a lower 'funeral level' came out at eighth century AD. Those who made the bier probably had a metal tool, said the report. Partially missing, the inscription could not be read, but Galand did say that the characters are nearest the western versions of the Berber alphabet, in particular that of the Tuareg, past and present.

Finally, the Canary Islanders had no writing at the time of the fifteenth-century European invasions. Inscriptions in the old Berber alphabet have also been reported from the Cape Verd Islands, uninhabited when the Portuguese arrived there early in the fifteenth century. If the Saharan writing was an accomplishment of members of the main Canary immigration, it is odd that it should have fallen out of use; probably limited to an elite, the knowledge would have been vulnerable.

SPEECH AT THE TIME OF THE CONQUEST

The prehistoric tongue is known from a few sorrowful songs, of which one of the shorter examples is given in Chapter 22; two dozen phrases, such as *zahanat guayohec* or 'I am your vassal'; a couple of hundred common words; four thousand place-names. Many of the early records are untrustworthy. The Genoese slave-catcher, Recco, in the islands early in the fourteenth century, records the numbers from one to ten with an Italian flavour: *nait, smetti, amelotti, acodetti, simusetti, sesetti, satti, tamatti, aldamorana, marava*. Other words sound suspiciously Castillian.

The French conquerors, 1402–5, noted that the islands were of *divers loys et de divers lengages*. The many inter-island similarities suggest divergence from a common tongue. *Guanigo* was the name of a common pot everywhere but Palma. *Tamarco* was a body-covering, of skin or vegetable fibre, in the three easterly islands. *Aho*, milk, in Fuerteventura, Lanzarote and Tenerife. *Banot*, the fighting staff of Hierro, Gomera and Tenerife. Important common words still in use include *gofio*, everywhere a flour made of toasted grain; *Guanche*, correctly only the ancient people of Tenerife but now often used for all pre-conquest islanders; *jaira*, goat, *baifo*, kid, *guanil*, a free-roaming animal, *gambuesa* (Pl. 16), a common round-up of the *guanil* animals. The best-known Canary playwright, Pérez Galdós, spent part of his time as a nineteenth-century student noting the pre-conquest element in the speech of his own circle, even there collecting a total of 436 words (Nuez Caballero). The words which survive have done so because they describe island customs, foods and natural objects for which there is no Castillian equivalent; and, as these disappear, so the old words will too. Examples will be met throughout the book.

Ancient place-names abound. Alvarez (1956) summarized them, finding 21% began with A- (Gran Canaria: Arteara, Artedara, Artenara); 5% Be — (Gomera: Benchijigua); 12% with G- (over half of these with Gua-, as in Guarazoca, Hierro); 12% T-, 4% Ch-, often the same value (Teide on Tenerife, Chipude on Gomera). Several philologists have worked on special aspects; as an example, Río Ayala recently suggested that a radical F is found significantly often in the names of high, commanding places, such as the rock of Idafe (Pl. 6a).

The origin of the ancient speech is not hard to find. Several dozen of the known words occur in much the same form in the present Berber dialects of N. Africa (Glas, 1764, was perhaps the first to point this out). For example, *tamocen*, barley (Fuerteventura), against *tumzzen* by the Shluh Berbers of the Moroccan Atlas. There are informative place-names too. Gomera against the present Ghomera tribe of the W. Rif, a part of the Masmouda Berber confederation. The ancient Palma people called themselves the Beni Hoare, the name of a tribe now divided between the Sahara, the Middle Atlas and the Moroccan Sus (Marcy). Both African tribes are now Arabic-speaking. The Hierro people, recorded as *bimbachos* by the Spanish, were probably the Beni Bachir. Similarly, the probably garbled personal names, frequently mentioned in the conquest descriptions, included many with 'ben' prefixes, meaning 'son of': Ben Como, Ben Taguayre, Ze ben Sui.

According to the French conquerors, the Fuerteventura people called their island 'Erbanne', Marcy saying this was really 'Arbaniy', meaning 'the place of the wall'. He compared this to the Djebel Bani, the cordillera which divides the Draa region of S. Morocco—and, as will be seen, the two kingdoms of Fuerteventura were separated, in the words of the conquerors, by 'a great stone wall which crosses from one coast to another' and is still there today (Mercer 1973, plate on p.36).

In summary, philologists have found parallels right across N. Africa, from Morocco to the Siwa Oasis on the Libya-Egypt frontier. A relationship to Berber is certain. However, many of the pre-conquest words have not been located in any other tongue and it may be that the islanders spoke a language with an older, more individual status than a mere version of Berber. Like Berber and Egyptian, it would be of Hamitic origin and have long ago have travelled westwards from beyond the eastern end of the Mediterranean.

It is possible that the unidentified element was a remnant of the speech of the Oranian culture, this having survived with the Mechta-Afalou physique in the refuge zones. The Capsian Mediterraneans' tongue, presumably the most common speech of the indigenous people of Roman Mauretania, would have provided the now easily recognized element of the prehistoric Canary tongue. Thus, the islanders' speech may be derived from that of the Oranian and Capsian cultures.

THE WHISTLED LANGUAGE OF GOMERA

In 1402, as noted, the French wrote of the Gomerans that 'they say there that a great prince for no crime had them put into exile there, and had their tongues cut out'. The powerful whistled language is unique in its finger-aided purely articulated nature (Classe). It is now used as a means of exchanging messages—transposed from Castillian—across the island's vast radial gorges. Could it have begun as a response to mutilation of some individuals but have been found, by later generations, to so extend the normal person's communication range that it became established?

Interest has centered on Gomera to the exclusion of the other islands. 'When an enemy approached, they alarmed the country by making a smoke, or by whistling, which was repeated from one to another. This latter method,' wrote Abreu (1600) of Tenerife, 'is still in use amongst them, and may be heard at almost incredible distances'. During the conquest of this island, the Spaniards noted how the Guanches whistled when attacking, concluding it was a war-cry — when it may have been a form of signalling, even approaching the whistled speech of the Gomerans. It was also recorded that the Guanches would whistle as a sign of approval, for example at a decision of a meeting. They once caused their flocks to break away from the Spanish — who were driving them off — by whistling to them. There is also a nineteenth-century example of whistling as a public summons, on Hierro (Chapter 23).

INCISED AND PAINTED 'ART'

As is usual at least in prehistoric times, 'art' is inseparable from 'belief'; the 85 sites (21 'others') in Tables 32–3 look likely, in the main, to combine the two aspects. There is no evidence of this kind from Tenerife or Gomera. Structures and as much as is known of the associated rituals will be summarized in the next chapter.

| | Island & site | Caves | | Outdoors, Ground | References. Key: Table 33 |
		Floors	Walls		
L	Zonzamas			C	A
L	Jameos del Agua			C	NFS
GC	Painted Cave	H	H		B74
GC	King's Caves	HC			CAMC
GC	Bentayga			HC	,,
GC	Cuatro Puertas	H	HC	HC	,,
GC	Pilas . . . Canarios	HC			,,
GC	Candiles Cave		H		,,
GC	Others	HC	HC	HC	,,

Table 32: *Holes (H) & channels (C) at major sites on Lanzarote & Gran Canaria*

Descriptions of the main sites, with additional data, will be given in the order of the tables. The Saharan-type alphabetic inscriptions were dealt with in the last section.

Zonzamas was the stronghold of the pre-conquest leaders of Lanzarote (Chapter 13); the carved boulder (Fig. 10a) has parallels amongst the three-dimensional work (Fig. 10b, c, d, f). Jameos del Agua: a smoothish surface in a lava-field has at least five parallel grooves, these up to almost 2m long and 30 cm in width. Julan: 200m of brown glossy lava (Pl. 10b) covered with engravings, including

Island site	Cave walls		Outdoor cliffs, rocks etc (incised)							Refs.
	Humans	Abstract	Humans	Spirals, circles	Meanders	Comp. work	Grids	Others	Alphabetic	
F Unknown									X	A
L Zonzamas				X						A
H Julan				X	X		X		X	A
H Misc. (3)					X		X	X	X	A
P Zarza (2)				X			X			H
P Caldera de Agua				X	X	X	X	X		H
P Misc. (44)				X	X		X	X	X	H,A
GC Painted Cave		P								B74
GC King's Caves		P								CAMC
GC Majada Alta	P									J66
GC Moro Cave	P									J66
GC Bentayga		P								CAMC
GC Cuatro Puertas		I							Cave	CAMC
GC Balos			X	One	Few	X	X	X	X	B71
GC Péndulo Cave		P, I		Cave		Cave	Cave	Cave		J70
GC Candiles Cave		I								CAMC
GC Others		P,I								CAMC

Key   A: Alvarez 1964; NFS: no full study; H: Hernández 1977; B74: Beltrán 1974; CAMC: Comisión Arq. Museo Canario; J66: Jiménez 1966; B71: Beltrán 1971; J70: Jiménez 1970. P: painted; I: incised.

Table 33: *Main and representative 'art' sites, by island*

perhaps a hand. La Zarza and, close by, La Zarcita: the engravings are on basalt walls formed by abrupt steps in small ravines (Pl. 6b). Caldera de Agua: a rock-face on the side of a vast gorge.

Gran Canaria has the widest range. The Painted Cave is thought to have belonged to Andamana, an important pre-conquest islander (Chapter 16). Discovered in 1873 and restored a century later, the cave is now in the middle of the town of Gáldar and thus 2 km inland from the coastal tumuli supposed to have held the region's elite (Chapters 3, 7). The site consists of seven caves, artificial, each with traces of painting and with pits in its floor. The largest is about 5m wide and 3m high but its original length is unclear (Beltrán 1974). At the top of the wall at the end further from the entrance, this cave has a frieze, about a metre high, running right across and on to the side walls (Fig. 16a). The geometric design is composed of triangles, chevrons, squares and concentric circles. The colours are black, red and white. No analysis has been published of the colouring matter but Torriani reported that the women painted their caves with the juices of flowers and plants; Beltrán says red ochre was used in the Painted Cave and that animal fat (5%) was mixed in to hold the colouring matter together. The work has been done with thought and skill, the highlighting techniques bringing to mind the low-relief engravings of triangles elsewhere in the island, for example in Los Candiles Cave. Both these caves were sooner or later used for burials.

The King's Cave (Pl. 2) is in the westwards extension of the Bentayga massif (Pl. 1, Fig. 23). Also artificial, it is about 11m by 7m by 2m 50cm high. It too has been a dwelling, like many of the caves in this section. Verneau described an upper frieze of red circles right around the cave, above lines of red and black squares and other painted work, but little is visible now. However, the two small side-chambers do have entrances faced with white (Pl. 2b), this once highlighted in red. Some of the holes (44) in the floor can also be seen in the illustration. The similarity of the painting in important caves in the central mountains and on the Gáldar coast—together with a structural feature (Chapter 8)—adds to the doubt over the anthropologists' division of the island.

The painting of the caves, together with that of the idols (described shortly) and metal-style pottery (Chapter 10) are amongst the evidence, mentioned early in the book, used to construct a secondary immigration theory. There is a simple alternative. Some invading Mallorcans and Catalans, captured in the mid-fourteenth century, lived on Gran Canaria for many years. According to Abreu, 'they built houses, and painted them elegantly with the colours . . . from certain herbs and flowers . . . and fitted up neat apartments in caves, which remained entire long after the conquest'. It thus seems likely that the advanced cultural phase attributed to the Gáldar Mediterranean physical type and used to propose a secondary immigration was introduced to an existing coastal people by these Europeans; as will be seen, there were yet more stranded in Gran Canaria in the century before the conquests. Parallels for the general designs and for the pottery could be sought in fourteenth-century Iberia and, particularly, in Cataluña.

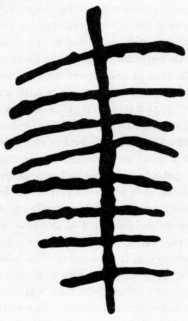

Figure 9 *Grid engraving on rock (31cm), Balos, Gran Canaria*

The Balos outcrop (in the south-east, near Agüimes) is marked out by its myriad engravings of humans; in turn, many of the men are distinguished by the portrayal of their sexual organs, often exaggeratedly large and thus indicating the virility-wish as the aim of the engravings (Pl. 5b). Many hands are also accentuated, with spread fingers. The grid of parallel lines crossed by one or more further straight lines, the design sometimes rake-shaped as a result, occurs here too (Fig. 9) as does compartmented work (Fig. 14c). An unusual form is a 'star', many fine lines radiating from a point. There is also the occasional horse and rider, but the best group of these, recently located, occurs higher up the ravine (Pl. 5b).

Two caves hold the only other human representations, painted however. Majada Alta, in the central mountains, has figures like those of Balos. Moro Cave, near Agaete, has a Balos-style human together with the representation, perhaps, of a fat woman, possibly related to the 'fertility idols', described shortly, and to the bride-fattening custom. Péndulo Cave, in the S.W. mountains, is reached by swinging into it on a rope; its painted and incised designs, 6m off the floor, appear to include circles, a grid and also compartemented work, with its walls, like those of many caves, plastered with 'ochre-coloured' mud.

Cuatro Puertas Cave (east, near Gando airport) is the principal chamber, 17m by 7m by 2m high, with four entrances, of an extensive complex of caves and rock platforms. Apart from a few triangles, the site is notable for its holes and channels of various shapes and sizes. As Table 32 shows, these are a feature of many 'art' sites. However, one cave appears to have only holes and channels, these collecting the dripping water; its name, Pilas de los Canarios, refers to 'basins' or 'fonts' of the ancient islanders. The recent CAMC inventory interestingly suggests that the astonishingly perfect shaping of these pits — with one at least oval — and odd lay-out of the channels points not just to water-collection but to a water-cult. However, the cave could equally well have been the scene of an early *post*-conquest water-cult, such as the author noted (1973) to be then still active on Fuerteventura (Virgen del Tanquito); the spring had once supplied the ancient islanders' fortress on the top of Monte Cardón.

For the interior floor-holes there is again a simple solution: they probably took posts which held up partitions, the 'neat apartments in caves' of the captured Iberians coming to mind. One of Gáldar's painted caves has six large holes laid out symmetrically in its floor (Fig. 14b). Berthelot noted of mid-nineteenth century Tenerife: 'Part of the population still lives in the caves, the compartments being formed by partitions of reeds', together probably with palm and split-bamboo work. There are also records of important caves being 'lined' with wooden panelling. Perhaps the modern cave-dwellers (Chapter 23) should be consulted.

There are still the distinctive pits cut in the ground-rock of two open-air *almogarens* or 'temples', Bentayga (central mountains) and Jerez (Bco. de Silva, coast near Gando). Plate 1b shows the former, looking east at the Roque Nublo. Bentayga's ridged eastern end, rising away slightly, has been quarried out, presumably with stone tools, to form a small windswept platform about 3m each way. Its low side-walls rise eastwards, the back wall, some 1m 25cm high, holds a broad seat or shelf, a small pit in its N.E. corner. Channels up to 10cm deep run around the walled sides of the main area and, probably using natural fissures, to the pits at the nearer, open end. The large pit, 75cm diameter, is grooved right around; the small pit, 30cm by 15cm, is the deeper. There are more pits elsewhere on the ridge, one in a natural platform. The cave said to hold a painted alphabetic inscription is on the north side of the ridge. The Jerez *almogaren* has three linked pits, clearly for the same purpose. Gómez Escudero (c. 1485), writing of the pre-conquest vestal virgins (Chapter 7), thought to have lived in the Cuatro Puertas caves, said 'the *maguadas* took vessels of milk to pour in these ritual places'. Others have said the famous caves' occupants were brides in retreat before marriage . . . in which case the libations remind one that bride-fattening on milk and *gofio* was customary, as will be seen.

As in the photograph, the smaller pit on Bentayga collects up rainwater. The massif was one of the pre-conquest people's last strongholds against the Spanish; its fortifications, much like those on Monte Cardón on Fuerteventura (Mercer 1973, plate on p. 36), are still visible. The quarried area, with some further embanking, could have been used as a rainwater catchment during siege. However, that such rocks were the scenes of worship is certain, so that their pits may well have been originally made to receive libations.

There is a little dating evidence for the archipelago's incised art. The engravings are either in outline or worked all over, in each case usually by pocking by percussion; occasionally they are incised, perhaps with a metal tool. Palma's spirals, concentric circles and meanders are the best work; some Palma pottery (Figs. 10j, 18n), not yet firmly dated, bore comparable decoration, incised; so too did a rotary quern (Fig. 10i), discussed shortly. Upon such designs at the Caldera de Agua site (N. Palma) there are incised—rather than pocked—two grids of fine lines. At Balos (Gran Canaria) where the spiral and its associated forms are extremely rare, the grids and rakes are battered by percussion, in the same way as the human figures— here too the straight-line designs are informative, since a grid cuts across a Saharan alphabet inscription (Crawford). At Balos the 'stars' are made of fine incised lines. The significance of the grid and rake forms (stylised and distorted humans or human hands?) is unknown— they are potentially the most instructive. The Balos horses, post-conquest since there were none in the Canaries until the Europeans came, were battered out at the main site and faintly scraped out at the new site up the ravine, in each case the whole body being gone over. Patination at Balos supports the suspicion that some ancient-style engravings have been done recently.

To summarize the engravings, they appear to fall into three groups, characterized by spirals, by combinations of straight lines and by human figures, together with alphabetic work. Superimpositions suggest the spiral group may be the oldest; the other three groups cannot be placed in relative order of age. The engraving of concentric circles, the outer starting to spiral, on a rotary quern seen by the author in Palma's museum, shows this group's period of currency falls

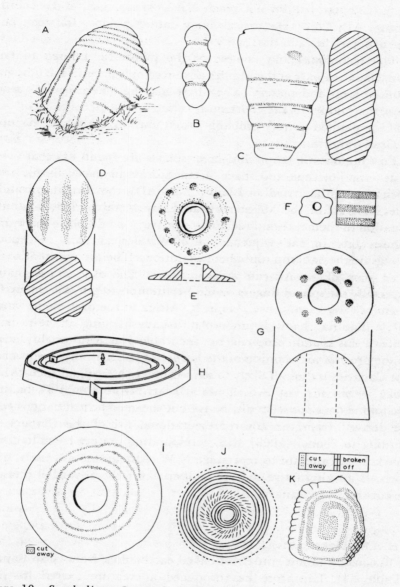

Figure 10   *Symbolism. Grooved: boulder, Lanzarote (a), pebble, Fuerte-*
ventura (b, about 6cm), stone 'animal', Lanzarote (c, 13cm), pebble, Palma
(d, about 7cm), beryl crystal, Gran Canaria (f, 6 x 5mm). Pitted: quern,
Palma (e, 27cm), clay disc, Gran Canaria (g, 28mm). Spiral: temple,
Fuerteventura (h, after Torriani), quern, Palma (i, about 35cm), pot bottom,
Palma (j, about 30cm), flattish stone, Tenerife (k, about 8cm)

at least partially after the time of Christ, since this form of grinding stone (Chapter 10) did not reach N.W. Africa until about the first century AD. This is the first absolute dating evidence for this type of engraving in the Canaries.

The techniques and designs of the paintings, limited to Gran Canaria, are a part of the island's advanced culture, this including the painted idols and pottery. The phase may be no earlier in opening than the middle of the fourteenth century. The decoration of caves and the painted pottery probably lasted until long after the conquest of Gran Canaria.

Looking outside the archipelago, spirals are found to occur over a wide range of time and space, from Europe in the Neolithic to N. Africa up to the arrival of Islam (c. 700 AD); the African spirals are late survivals of the Mediterranean Early Metal period. The combination of theme, technique and low artistry would place the human figures late in the sequence of N.W. African 'art', acceptably alongside the Saharan-alphabet inscriptions. The pit and libation has been part of N. African animist ritual. The exaggerated hands, especially the spread fingers, could be attempts to put the 'evil eye' on enemies ('five in your eye'), as in N. Africa to the present; to ward it off, a 'Fatima's hand' is now worn, usually hanging at the neck. In spite of this Islamic prophylactic, the whole practice probably existed in the pre-Islamic animism of the Berber tribes. The engraved work of the Canaries is thus all likely to stem from N. Africa and to have been done within the last two thousand years. Gran Canaria's painting technique does not seem distinctive but the geometrical designs could be derived from the non-representational art of the Berbers; according to Zeuner (1966), the corresponding pottery bears hammer-marks in an attempt to reproduce N.W. African metal vessels. This, then, is an alternative source, to Iberia, for the advanced phase of culture on Gran Canaria.

THREE-DIMENSIONAL 'ART'

This consists almost entirely of baked-earth 'idols' from Gran Canaria (Table 34). Lanzarote has produced a creature carved in shelly limestone (Fig. 10c, Tejía; Dug Godoy 1974). Tenerife: a flat stone, the sides notched in places, bearing an incised spiral presumably associated with such engravings on other islands (Fig. 10k, Bco. de la Arena). Fuerteventura has yielded grooved and polished cylindrical pebbles (Fig. 10b, Tuineje). From Palma there are fluted and polished ovoids, the grooving flattening out and dying away towards the ends (Fig. 10d). Gran Canaria has also produced grooved stones.

Distortion or selection	Trunk	Head and limbs	Head, frags. only	Sexual organs	Misc.	References (see key)
Gáldar (Painted Cave)		1		2	2	Z, MC
Gáldar (Agujero)			1D			Z
Valerón (granary)		1(?)	1D			RH, Z
Moya Montañeta	1					Z
Arucas (Hoyo San Juan)			1D		1	J, Z
Jinámar (Los Barros)		1				
Telde (Tara)	1	1	XH			H, Z
Telde (?)		1			3	H
Agüimes	1					Z
Juan Grande (Bco. Hondo)				1		MC
Arguineguín					1	J
Mogán			1P		1	J, N
San Nicolás (Caserones)					X	J, MC
Tirma					4	
Acusa					1	MC
Sta. Lucia (Fortaleza)			1D		1	RH, J
Temisas (Risco Pintado)				1		
Sites unknown	3	1	X	1	X	Various

Key Z: Zeuner 1960; MC: in Museo Canario; RH: *Revista de Historia* 30; J: Jiménez 1958; H: Hernández 1952; N: Naranjo; D: draped; H: hollow; P: plain; X: more than one.

Table 34: *Idols, Gran Canaria*

The table is presented clockwise from Gáldar to San Nicolás, followed by the central mountains, crossing them eastwards. The N.W.–E. sector is distinguished by two forms of idol. First, the poorly-made violin-shaped plaques, stylizations of the trunk of the human body (Fig. 11e, site unknown). Second, a more imaginative figure with minute head and bulging upper arms and legs (Fig. 11a, Sta. Lucia; 11d, Tara). Its head was perhaps of three types: plain, draped with hair or a head-dress (Fig. 11b, Arucas) or, perhaps to hold a bundle of real hair, hollow on top. The bulging shoulders may have been, in

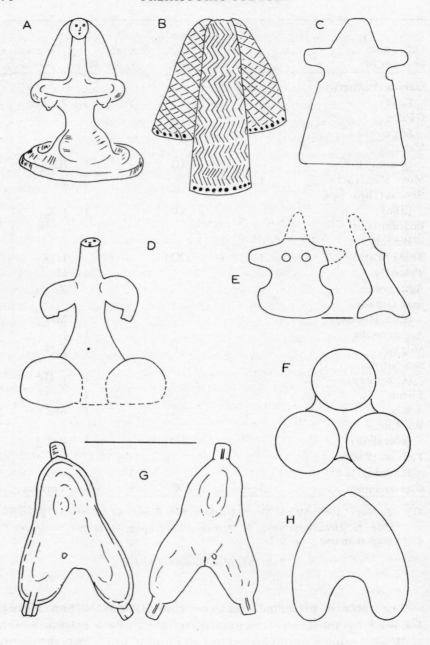

Figure 11   *Symbolism, Gran Canaria: clay 'idol' (a, Sta. Lucia), back of head, 'idol' of previous type, clay (b, Arucas), stone 'idol' (c, about 60cm, San Nicolás), clay 'idol' (d, 26cm, Tara), 'violin-shaped idol', clay (e, site unknown), carving (f, about 4cm, site unknown), milking tray, wood (g, 75cm, Juan Grande), carving (h, about 8cm, site unknown)*

fact, the representation of a cape (Zeuner 1960). A second Tara figure (fragment) which led to this suggestion is painted with red and yellow geometric patterns similar to the cave and pottery decoration: a strip of chevrons across the shoulders, a separate pattern on the torso, with the forearm left plain. Zeuner's reconstruction suggests a cape exposing a flat, decorated chest. Torriani described a dyed cape worn by the islanders, this probably however a post-conquest importation (Chapter 22). The people of Gran Canaria painted their bodies as well as their coverings, probably one of the uses of the baked-earth stamps, *pintaderas* (also granary seals, as will be seen); these print geometric patterns (Fig. 16b) and are all but limited to this island. However, most workers see the upper bulges as huge breasts, the lower as massive thighs—obviously with the Venuses of the European Stone Age in mind. To be logical, Zeuner's cape idea would have to postulate bloomers below (Fig. 11d, undecorated). However, the Sta. Lucia specimen (Fig. 11a) perhaps supports the cape proposal since it has both breasts and rather bulgy shoulders. The Painted Cave example has the lower bulges extended in a closed ring around the back, so that this figure stood up by itself, being similar in this way to the cross-legged Jinámar example (one violin-shaped figure, Fig. 11e, was also made to stand up). The fragmentary heads in Table 34 are all likely to belong to this general type, so that at least a dozen are preserved. Marín (1687) wrote that 'The fat and bellied woman had many suitors and was much lusted after and courted, the thin women not being popular'; bride-fattening was the custom—it will be shown to have lasted into the nineteenth century (Chapter 22).

These bulging female figures were not, however, made with indicated genital organs. Two distinct 'idols', both from the Painted Cave, each have *both* a penis and breasts. No figures are notably similar to the virility-wish engravings at Balos, although the Museo Canario does have many broken-off sexual organs from clay figures, male and female. So these suggest female figures with accentuated sexual organs did occur; Alcina (1962) mapped this general type's distribution as the Mediterranean and the centre and north of S. America. Unique is the famous legged milking tray carved with a female sexual organ (Fig. 11g). Two other three-dimensional though flattish carvings (Fig. 11f, h) may be highly-stylized associated forms.

Images are known to have been part of the pre-conquest worship. Recco's 1341 expedition entered a Gran Canaria temple and—setting the precedent for the European looting of African 'art' treasures—took away a carving of a man holding a globe in his hand. The 1375 planisphere of the Catalan Abraham Cresques depicts such a figure; possibly Recco invented the Canary figure in order to give status to his expedition by claiming to have reached a legendary kingdom. The two eastern islands had idols in human form, according to Torriani. Bernáldez (1479) said the Gran Canaria people had 'a prayer house called Tirma and in it a wooden idol the length of half a lance, in the form of a naked woman, with two goats about to couple in front of her. There they poured their milk and butter, as offering or tithe or first-fruits'. This historian added the reassuringly first-hand comment that the place stan. of rancid milk and butter.

There are further uncommon types. At Telde, three small stone obelisks, cigar-shaped, up to about 70cm tall; Hernández (1952a) saw human features on one, Crawford later disagreeing. The Acusa figure is distinguished by a necklace indicated by impressed dots. The west-coast mountain of Tirma and the Fortaleza de Sta. Lucia, the islanders' very last fortress, have between them yielded five further idols, type and present ownership unknown; it can be noted that through 'Tirma' was the name of a temple to Bernáldez and has since become the name of a mountain believed sacred, it was used as an invocation by the ancient people (Chapter 16) and was thus perhaps one of the names of their deity (Chapter 7). Many more three-dimensional figures have been found but are inadequately known (Jiménez 1958).

Finally, a numerous group on Gran Canaria were fired-earth figures of animal-human hybrids; Jiménez (1966) describes woolly dogs, pigs and birds, noting Hoya de San Juan, Los Caserones and Arguineguín amongst the finding places. Abreu said the Gran Canaria devil took the form of a dog, Tibicena. On Palma the devil was a shaggy dog, Irvene according to Abreu, Haguanran to Torriani; the latter added that he lived in the sky, *tigotan*, and in the peaks of the mountains in the Tedote territory (Fig. 23). As will be seen in the next chapter, on Hierro a sacred pig acted as intercessor with the people's deity; this at least was of non-Islamic origin.

Searching for parallels outside the Canaries, it is seen that the two most distinct forms of 'idol', the violin plaques and the women with small heads and bulging 'limbs', each have reasonably similar counterparts in the E. Mediterranean of the Neolithic and early metal ages (Zeuner 1960). It is not known how long they continued to be made but the former at least also occur in the W. Sahara (Mercer 1976, Fig. 7, Nos. 14, 17). However, both types were made in the same way as the red-burnished pottery, part of the advanced culture, its inception just dated to the middle of the fourteenth century. The preference for fat women, together with bride-fattening, is an ancient custom amongst the Berbers of N. Africa.

CHAPTER SEVEN

Worship and Burial

The varied forms of 'art' just examined were, in the main, symbols in the pre-conquest people's beliefs. Many related ruins also survive, throwing further light on this side of their lives; as will be seen, there is a need for their scientific excavation. However, the 'art' does not appear directly linked to the burial practices. Places of interment abound and have been widely dug or opened up.

WORSHIP

The history by Abreu, a priest, notes the existence of the concept of a supreme being on five islands; he probably had no information on Gomera and Hierro. This deity was called Acoran (Gran Canaria), Achoran (Tenerife) and Acora (Palma), with other titles meaning 'Maker of the world' and so on. The people of Gran Canaria and Tenerife believed in a heaven and, as will be seen, those of Fuerteventura and Lanzarote raised their arms skywards when at prayer. The image Recco said he found on Gran Canaria could have represented Acoran; this would break the Islamic prohibition on representational 'art', if one is to accept the obvious linkage with the Koran (Chapter 2) as a sign of minor, late contact with Moslem N.W. Africa. Abreu expressly stated there were no images on Tenerife.

A religious establishment existed at least on Gran Canaria. The leader was the *faicagh* or *faycan*, the high priest. Then there were *magadas* (*harimaguadas*), nuns; these were virgins and wore a white ground-length dress (? of unpainted white skin). Hernández (1952a), another priest, said these vestals were 'a reaction against prostitution, such a common depravity in the Palaeolithic'. Abreu recorded that the nuns lived in 'houses of god', *tamogonteen Acoran*; these were daily sprinkled with milk from goats allowed to keep their kids. Criminals could find sanctuary in these houses. During local conflicts the sacred places of the enemy were respected. The nuns were probably the virgins whose work it was to wash new-born children all over with water. Torriani, writing of Tenerife, referred to 'baptism' by 'venerable' women (? midwives as well) who became the children's relatives as a result; perhaps this was a compensation for being 'never allowed to marry' (Abreu, on Gran Canaria).

Tenerife had its genesis myth, designed to support the class structure along the rich-man-in-his-castle, poor-man-at-his-gate lines: God created the first men and women in equal numbers, gave them flocks and all they needed . . . but then he decided to make some more people and when these asked for animals and other necessary possessions he told them to go and serve the others, they would be looked after in exchange. Tenerife society was composed of the *achimenceys*, being those of the family of the chief (*mencey*), the *cilhiciquico* or gentry, the *archicarnay* or common people (Abreu).

There were also prophets. All helped the European invaders, either making catastrophically optimistic forecasts — Yore of Hierro was introduced in Chapter 2 — or simply foretelling disaster if the islanders resisted the incursions. The prophets included a chief (Palma), a mother and daughter (Fuerteventura) and a head nun (Gran Canaria). Some will be encountered in the narratives of the conquests.

There appear to have been lesser cults on some of the five islands which believed in a supreme being. On Gran Canaria they adored fire, the moon, the dog star and, especially, the sun, Magec, saying the human soul was its daughter (Marín). Sun and moon worship was also noted on Tenerife (Ca da Mosto) and Palma (Abreu). The Gran Canaria harvest festival, the *beñesmen*, began on midsummer day according to Marín; on Tenerife it was at least a month later, probably in fact in August, *beñesmen* there in fact the name of this month. The three main islands kept a calendar in lunar months; that they could count is shown by their often-remarked proficiency in knowing the exact size of their flocks.

The information on pre-conquest religion comes, then, almost entirely from Christian priests. To them the ancient islanders were almost all idolaters; to the humanist there would seem to be a great area of overlap between the beliefs of the observed and of the observers. Hernández (1952a): 'They were clearly idolaters, in accordance with their cultural level, for the concept of a single God can only be reached by peoples of highly-evolved culture, or through Revelation'.

Examination of the remaining religious structures carries two general cautions. First, the islands hold a good many stone-built enclosures of types considered religious by earlier workers; the structures range from small to large and from a mere outline to a wall a metre high or more. There is usually no way of deciding either their construction date — before or after the conquests — or their purpose. They will be discussed amongst the secular structures. Secondly, most of the Canaries' sites published as 'devotional' in the last 30 years have been the work of Jiménez, a man whose varied papers have been much criticized. A glance at those now under consideration (eg 1966b, a

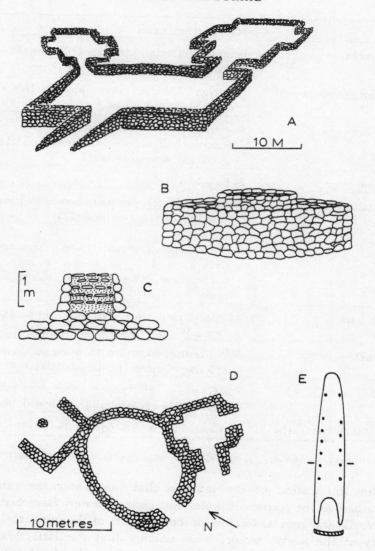

Figure 12   *Structures. Gran Canaria goros: San Nicolás (a, after Verneau), Tauro (d, after García Marquéz). Tumulus, Agaete, Gran Canaria (b, after Verneau). Altar, Julan, Hierro (c, after Cuscoy). Bier, Tenerife (e, about 2m 50cm)*

summary) show their author to have a strong religious bent himself. Table 35, due greatly to his work, summarizes the most acceptable remains. It can be mentioned that Jiménez saw representations of the sun, moon and stars amongst the Balos engravings, in the crescentic (? U-shaped) wall-channels at Cuatro Puertas and the arcs (some horse-shoe shaped) of walling at Tauro Alto, in the pottery ornamentation and so on.

Type	Main sites and notes
Main rocks	Bentayga, Tirma, Umiaya, (?)Nublo; Palmés, Narices (J)
Platforms (*almogarens*)	Bentayga, Umiaya, Jerez; Jiménez lists eight more, some with altars
Stone-built *goros*	Arguineguín, Tauro, San Nicolás (Los Caserones, disappeared this century; idol from site-area), Mogán, Arteara
Bleating place	El Baladero (Telde)
Divination cave	La Montañeta (Moya); pit in floor with 7 smaller roundabout, these with ashes (J)
Altars	S.W.: Veneguera, Mogán (4 sites), Arguineguín. Groups of 1–3; 1m 20–1m 60 high, well made, some with stone circle around; no cist below
Walls (arcs)	Mogán (Tauro Alto), crescentic and horse-shoe, face S.W., associated with tumuli (J)
Obelisks	S.W., centre, 90cm–1m 40, often within or part of a ring of stones (J). Burials, in fact?
Wailing benches	La Guancha, El Agujero (built into tumuli); Temisas, Veneguera (all J). Only with burials?
Ritual shell-fish feasts	La Guancha tumulus, *Cyprea* species (J)

Table 35: *Belief, structural remains, Gran Canaria (J: Jiménez 1966)*

One implication of the table is that the *almogaren*, already described in the section on holes and channels, may have been the N.W.-E. and central mountains' counterpart of the *goro*, the sanctuary of the S.-W. sector. This assumes that the latter was not secular—the related word *tagoro(r)*, correctly used only of Tenerife, was the name of the place of public assembly. A supposed *goro* (Fig. 12d) near the highest point of Montaña de Tauro is described by García Márquez. Still standing to 1m 90cm, it has an open-sided artificial platform to the north, with an artificial 'pinnacle' (? tumulus) at the centre of this, and a cruciform-plan chamber to the east. This agrees well enough with Verneau's section on *goros*. They occurred, he said, at Mogán and Arteara, in each case near cemeteries—the second is described shortly—and also at San Nicolás and Arguineguín. Verneau wrote also of small *goros*, considering them dwellings, perhaps due to a second-hand report of the finding of roof beams. He described one of two large *goros* at San Nicolás, this time with two cruciform enclosures (Fig. 12a); there were seats, let into the wall, around the main enclosure.

An *almogaren* was described by Marín several centuries ago. Umiaya (Humiaga, Amagro) has been since identified by some as the Cuatro Puertas complex but Alvarez (1956) places it between Gáldar and Agaete, on the mountain now mapped as 'Almagro'. Marín's muddled notes suggest a flat perhaps paved area high up and on a precipice edge: there were three 'braziers' in which all kinds of produce were burned, except meat; the embers were then transferred to an altar like a huge wall and, according to whether the smoke went straight up or to the side, the future was then divined. The *almogaren* of the Fortaleza de Sta. Lucia consisted, by Verneau's time, of an esplanade with an altar of stones. It can be noted that odd-shaped pieces of 'walling' occur at many Canary sites, especially perhaps in the east — possibly devotional (? Islamic), they are unstudied.

In the Telde region of Gran Canaria there was a bleating place, now called a *baladero*. It consists of a platform and many artificial caves, with holes, channels and two rock-cut cists, these once holding burials. Abreu: 'When it didn't rain and the flocks had no grazing, they got the sheep together in certain special places . . . and thrusting a staff or lance into the ground, separated the lambs from the ewes, and put the bleating mothers round the lance, and with this ceremony the natives thought God would be appeased and would hear the bleating and send rain'. Abreu added that the people sat in a circle and lamented, neither they nor the flocks eating. The Gáldar region had a related reaction to drought. A procession, carrying palm fronds and led by the nuns, went up to a sacred rock, such as Tirma; libations of milk were poured out, the people danced and sang laments. Then they all went down to the sea and, in unison, beat it with the branches; at each blow they gave out a great cry, doubtless to their deity. By the noise it gave off, the water too was being made to take part, in much the same way as the sheep were made to bleat their appeal. Siemens (1969) made a comparison with a custom in the Tchad: the women on the Ubangui River go into the water and beat it with their cupped hands, producing a rhythmic drumming.

The only Tenerife vestige of any pre-conquest religious structures appear to be the 'abundant' *baladeros*, such as that in a commanding place in the Anaga mountains (Diego 1968a). The practice was at its most developed on Hierro. First, the bleating was tried for three days and nights, at a rock called Bentaica. If this failed, a holy man went to the Asteheita Cave (? Tejeleita, near Valverde, or Teseneita, near Mocanal) to ask the gods to send their representative, the pig Aranjaibo. This was then brought to Bentaica. The people and the pig, wailing and squealing respectively, walked round and round the

Island & type	Main sites and notes
F Temples (*efeguens*)	Llano del Sombrero (?), place names
F Wailing benches	Llano del Sombrero, Lesque de la Pila, Casas Atlas (J). Only with burials?
F Altars	Jiménez 1966 (abbrev. to 'J')
F Walls (arcs)	Face east (?associated with tumuli), J. Islamic prayer walls?
F Obelisks	Listed by J. (adds the Zonzamas boulder, on Lanzarote — Fig. 10a)
T Bleating places	El Baladero (Anaga); 'abundant' (Diego 1968a)
T Hell	Teide volcano (Pl. 7a, 8a)
P Rock	Idafe (Pl. 6a)
P Tumuli (not burial)	Garafía, recently disappeared; associated with engravings (Hernández 1977), presumably spiral type
P Sacrificial altar	Said to have existed in Los Sauces area (N.E.)
G Altars	Fortaleza (Chipude), beside 3m *enceinte* (Verneau)
G Rocks	Above Agulo (north), according to Verneau
H Rocks	Bentaica (Los Lomos), including bleating rite
H Altar	Julan (Diego 1966, Fig. 12c)
H Ritual shell-fish feasts	Julan (beside *tagoror*, Pl. 10b)

Table 36: *Belief: structural remains other than Gran Canaria*

shrine. Abreu avers that it then rained at once; the pig, released, scampered back to its cave. Darias, on the other hand, describes how a sacred pig was shut up in the holy cave, there presumably interceding with the gods on behalf of the people.

Fuerteventura's place of worship was called the *efeguen* (Fig. 10h, redrawn from Torriani). The map holds suggestive place-names, such as Esque, Esquen, Lesque and Lesquen, the variation probably due to the slurred, lisp-avoiding and truncating speech of the Canary peasantry. Montaña de Escanfraga may be the mountain of the brambly or overgrown *efeguen*. About halfway down the eastern cordillera, at El Esquen (E. of Mña. del Sombrero), the author located a great circle of foundation stones, near a spring. Abreu described the *efeguen* as 'round, composed of two walls, one within the other, with a space between . . . strong, and having a narrow entry. In these temples they offered to their god (for they worshipped only one) milk and butter'. The 1402 MS of the French conquerors said 'the people are very firm in their faith and sacrifice in their church'. The spiral *efiguen* depicted by Torriani, 'like a labyrinth', is to be linked to the spiral engravings, underlining that these were cult symbols. Torriani probably saw the *efequen* on Lanzarote too; spiral engravings occurred at least at Zonzamas. Glas compared the *efeguen* to the Shluh (Berbers of S. Morocco) word for priest, *fquir*, but the origin of this appears to lie in Arabic. The Catholic priests probably had the old sanctuaries demolished — or where they were not so easily dismantled, annexed them instead (Pl. 6a).

There is evidence that high rocks were places of worship in all seven islands; in addition to the known sites of Tables 35–6, there is the record of Abreu that the eastern islanders took goats' milk up into the mountains, there pouring out libations and lifting their hands to heaven. This was probably the general practice. On Gran Canaria the procession was usually led by the chief priest.

On Palma it was the Idafe rock itself (Pl. 6a) which was worshipped. It was accurately described by Abreu, who also compared it to the pillars of Hercules: 'each pillar supporting a brazen image with its hand lifted up and pointing backwards'. The people were afraid the rock would fall down, bringing disaster. Whenever they killed an animal, a piece, roasted, was taken by two of them to Idafe. One, who carried the offering, sang:

> *Y Iguida, y Iguan, Idafe*
> It will fall, Idafe

to which the other replied:

> *Guegerte, y guantaro*
> Give to it. and it will not fall.

Then the meat was thrown down and they went away. The custom must have been limited to those who lived near this most inaccessible rock (Fig. 23). Each of the other several districts of Palma had 'a great pillar or pyramid of loose stones piled up as high as possible, and so as not to fall down'; these may have been images of Idafe, in fact.

The Hierro people had a man's god, Eraoranhan, and a woman's, Moreiba. These came to Bentaica, two rocks according to Abreu, to be adored by the islanders. Darias identifies the place with Bentegis, on the Lomos heights west of Valverde. Hernández (1952a) said the rocks are now known as the Santillos de los Canarios, the old islanders' saints. Related may be the name of Palma's sacred rock, Idafe (radical 'f' suggests 'high place' to Río Ayala) and 'Nisdafe', a place at the eastern end of Hierro's highlands. It is worth noting that the Idafe rock was in Palma's canton of Eccero (the near-impregnable Caldera, the only zone to resist the *conquistadores*, as will be seen) and that the very name of Hierro perhaps stems from *eccero* or 'fastness' (Alvarez 1956).

The devil was also present in the Canaries. On Tenerife, Teide (Pl. 7a, 8a) draws its name from *echeyde*, hell; out of its often-smoking crater, especially at night, came Guayota, a devil or evil spirits. Devils in animal form have already been encountered, as baked-earth figures. Palma's dog-devil, Haguanran, was taken butter and milk in the mountains where he lived (Torriani). One or both of the two small western islands had a closely-similar demon, a hairy man called Hirguan.

Finally, the two tables suggest that five islands had small tumuli, not covering burials — and Diego's Hierro excavation (1966) has demonstrated clearly that these were sacrificial altars. The zone of the investigated tumulus, the Julan (Pl. 10b), holds also a common burial cave (El Tablón), a meeting place or *tagoror* with a spread of limpet-shells alongside, and a number of hollow cairns, *taro*, all to be described shortly, in addition to the lava-flow engravings already discussed. Diego chose one of 15–20 ruined tumuli. The section (Fig. 12c) shows the stepped exterior; inside there were five levels of sand, ash and burned goat bones, including many horn-cores. Two slivers of basalt, the most common Canary cutting tool, were also found inside; roundabout were more pieces and a chip of poor local pottery, pale brown, of sand over-mixed with the scarce clay. Unfortunately no C14 dates were obtained for this site. Diego said he had seen similar structures on Palma.

In fact there is no dating evidence for any of these religious sites, beyond the chroniclers' notes suggesting many were in current use at the time of the conquests. Numerous aspects of the prehistoric worship are comparable to surviving vestiges of pre-Islamic N.W. African animism; the stepped altars, like the stepped tombs described next, probably derive from ancient Berber structures.

BURIAL

Popular interest in Canary prehistory has always centered on this aspect, due to the frequency with which burials come to light and the ease with which the local skull and pot collectors have, in the past, been able to find them. Respect for the dead is clearly recorded for the post-conquest descendants of the islanders and the burial-hunters have usually been Europeans — travellers, scholars, settlers. However, the opening of the thousands of Gran Canaria tumuli to get at the planks of mature pine-wood, probably comparatively recently, has perhaps been the work of ordinary islanders. And, for at least the last hundred years, the rural people have been at once destroying any

| | Caves | | | Tumuli | |
	Burial	Cremation and burial	Mummification	Large, multi-burial	Small, single burial
F	16m, 3f				x
L	x				x
GC	575m, 291f		156m, 122f	22m, 13f	37m, 15f
T	308m, 139f		79m, 24f		
G	52m, 27f		10m, 7f		
P	18m, 7f	9 sites	?		?Garafía
H	47m, 33f		13m, 7w		

Table 37: *Burial forms, with recovered skeletal material, by island*

bodies they have found (Verneau; Diego 1976); the reason for this is not clear.

Table 37 gives the forms of burial with the numbers of crania held by the museums (Schwidetsky 1963). Burial in a cave was the most usual practice. Mummification was common except in the two eastern islands; here perhaps the good natural conditions for preservation made it seem unnecessary. On Palma, mummification may have been replaced by cremation—a practice only very recently recognized (Hernández 1977). Verneau heard of Lanzarote tumuli similar to those of Gran Canaria; Jiménez records many for the eastern islands (those of Fuerteventura are summarized in Mercer 1973).

A few hundred burial sites are known throughout the islands; Diego (1968a) lists 162 burial caves for Tenerife (the reader is reminded that La Laguna University is at present mapping all the islands' sites). A few caves have been excavated in the four western islands. Otherwise, the sites' most attractive material has simply been collected up, greatly destroying the now more essential evidence. The comments made in the Introduction are particularly relevant to the burial sites . . . as a result, little is known beyond the divisions given in Table 37, with their physical types (Chapters 3–4).

Of the cave-burials, plain interment was the usual practice everywhere. The floor might be levelled with slabs and volcanic ash. The burial might be enclosed in walling (El Morro, Gran Canaria; Fusté 1958a). In the western group at least, tree trunks, branches or shrubs were often spread over the floor, a wide range of species being recorded; in the two eastern islands, skins were placed below and upon the body (Abreu). A stone or wooden head-rest was commonly provided.

There is ample evidence from Tenerife of the use of a wooden bier, *chajasco*, of pine or juniper. One (Fig. 12e) from Teno was a single somewhat-hollowed plank; at one end there are two projections, these believed to have sat on a bearer's shoulders; along each side there were holes to take cords to tie on the corpse (*xasco*). The cords might be plaited vegetable fibre or strips of skin. Another *chajasco* (Risco de los Guanches, Tacoronte, Tenerife) consists of a grid formed of pieces of wood, the slender ones passing through holes in the thick ones, these last being oddly triangular in section. The *chajasco* from Hierro, engraved with the inscription in the old Saharan alphabet, has been described (Hoya de los Muertos, Guarazoca). Abreu says that in Hierro a dead man was buried in his everyday skins, a board (? inscribed, then) at his feet, his staff beside him; the cave was then sealed.

Body orientation, at least as reported, was haphazard. The corpses were left on their backs, arms down their sides. However, an E. Gomera site (Los Toscones Cave, Bco. de Avalo) produced two corpses on their backs, arms crossed on their stomachs, above five more which were crouched and lying on their right sides (Lorenzo *et al*); in Espigón Cave (Puntillana, Palma) a skin-wrapped corpse was crouched on its right side (Hernández 1977); in Chabaso Cave (Igueste de Candelaria, N.E. Tenerife) there were two bodies, crouched on their left sides (Lorenzo *et al*). The Gomera burials were also unusual in that each body had a slab of rock *upon* its head. But then Darias recorded that Tablón Cave (Julan, Hierro), discovered about a century ago, had held a score of bodies on their backs and covered with stone slabs; the present author noted human bones, still scattered around, during a recent visit. Often the Canary corpses were not buried but simply placed in the cave and the mouth of this then sealed with rocks and earth.

The small finds in the caves include a great many of the objects described in Chapters 9-11, in particular pottery and stone tools. Belief in life after death is well attested: Marín says the spirits of the dead were held to be simply invisible and, as they carried on another life of tasks and troubles, they were taken food. The tombs were visited on special days, the people making fires and offerings at them. The caves have yielded remains of most of the foods discussed in Chapter 9.

Diego (1951) contrasted the believed grave-goods of mountain and coast. Those from the former — with the burials of goat-herds — consisted of their staffs, good obsidian tools, often found by their hands, and throwing balls. The bodies lay on tree trunks, their dogs with them . . . perhaps as food offerings, for they did eat dogs. Down on the coast, clay beads were common, with bone punches and poorer stone tools; the bodies lay on branches or hewn planks. In the mountains, kids were offered, on the coast pig-meat was placed with the corpse.

Perhaps the most notable feature common to the five islands whose burials have been investigated is the presence of the shrub *Cneorum pulverulentum*, especially of its seeds; it does not anyway grow naturally in the two eastern islands. The shrub also occurs with mummy burials. Verneau reported it in tumulus burials too. The species has been seen inside the *goro* enclosures, suggesting these were used for the drying out and mummification of corpses. It is supposed that the plant sweetened the air and slowed down putrefaction — the body may have been laid on a bed of it — but its components do not seem to have been chemically analysed. A decoction is said to be still used as a substitute for quinine. Several of its names in the islands include the adjectives 'good' or 'holy'.

The Llano de Maja site (Pl. 8a) will illustrate the islands' burial caves. At 2200m on the east rim of Teide's crater, a huge bubble formed in the lava. The resulting cave is about 14m high and 10m across, the entrance hole in the middle of a wall, high up. At least 45 shepherds were buried there, together with grave-goods typical of the high pastures (Diego 1964b).

Interest has centred on the mummies but their geographical distribution on the two main islands does not seem to have been plotted. On Gran Canaria the best sources have been the central mountains (Acusa, Guayadeque) and the south (Juan Grande, Arguineguín). Tenerife appears to have had mummy caves right around the island.

First, the archaeological evidence. Men seem to have been more often mummified than women. Diego (1976) distinguishes two grades, good and bad, of mummification. Surprisingly, he found no sign of an incision on any Tenerife mummy, the intestines being still in place; though this raises the question of whether true mummification did occur — as opposed to mere sun-drying — it will be seen that the early descriptions of the process did include the removal of the intestines nevertheless. Necklaces might be worn by the corpse, whether male, female or of a child. The corpse was wrapped in reed mats or in skins, the latter sometimes dyed, yellow or chestnut; the skins were over-stitched together, with doubled animal tendons, except for the outer seam, this flat-stitched with a fine throng. As many as seven shrouds have been found on a single corpse. The shroud might be bunched and tied above the head, giving a sack-like result. Hooks have also been mentioned as fasteners. The body would then be carried on a *chajasco* to the cave and there laid on a trestle. The grave-goods have not been distinguished from those of the plain burials. Some Acusa (Gran

Canaria) mummies were in coffins of pine and dragon wood. Marín's history notes that, on Hierro, the 'enbalmed' bodies were laid out with their heads to the north. There is no archaeological evidence to back the several early accounts that mummies were also stood up against the cave walls.

The most thorough archaeological report is that on Roque Blanco, 1970m (above Orotava, Tenerife; Diego 1960a). Amongst the cave's six burials were three mummies, including that of a child. The wrappings were of sewn skins. There was a potsherd and a number of obsidian and basalt tools.

The early histories can now be examined for further details of mummification. The alchemist Frances Barrett referred to the mummies as monsters, the results of marriages between devils and men: 'Tude-squils, Stude-quills or Stew'd quills . . . so small that a boy might easily carry one . . . upon the palm of his hand . . . clear and transparent . . . their bones flexible like gristles; against the sun . . . their bowels and intestines were plainly to be scene . . . the destroyed race of pygmies'.

There are other less fanciful English descriptions. Thomas Nichols (Cioranescu 1963) said he had seen Tenerife caves with up to 300 corpses propped against the walls; he mentions vessels of milk and says that those in authority had each a staff at their sides. Herrera claims that in S. Gomera there are still inaccessible caves holding standing mummies. The best of the old descriptions was by one of a group of 'considerable Merchants and Men worthy of Credit' (in Sprat 1667). He was taken to a Güimar cave (Tenerife) as a reward for doctoring some of the islanders; this 'endeared him . . . otherwise it is death for any stranger to visit these Caves'. The mummification process was explained to him by the local elders, some over 110 years old. It had been the sacred secret of the priests, of an endogamous tribe. They always had ready a balsam made of goat butter, and perhaps pig fat, boiled up with four herbs: a lavender (on the rocks), the gummy *lara* (tops of mountains), a kind of cyclamen or sow-bread, and sage. A corpse was first disembowelled and, if a poor person, they 'took out the Brain behind'. The body was now many times washed in an astringent derived from pine bark, then dried in the sun or, in winter, 'in Stoves'. Next they rubbed in the preserving balsam, inside and out, until it had penetrated the skin right through and the muscles could be seen. The body was by then very light. It was next tightly sewn up in goat skins, with skin thongs, the seams of 'incomparable exactness'; the rich had soft hairless skins. This traveller saw 300–400 mummies in several caves: 'some of them standing, others lie on beds of wood', these perhaps artificially hardened so as never to putrefy. He was also told of 'twenty Caves of their Kings and great Persons, with their Families'. A final note was that, in Gran Canaria, the bodies are found 'in sacks, and quite consumed, not as these in Teneriffa'. In the eighteenth century a cave in the nearby Bco. de Herques (Arico) was found to hold over a thousand mummies, not only in rows but in layers too, still on their trestled biers.

Other variably-reliable reports from different islands give further details and also variations. The mummy preparers were social out-casts, a major contradiction to the old men's tale. Women were mummified by women, men by men. There was a wide dissecting table of stone. The viscera and brains were not always removed. Other stuffings used were sand, powdered pumice, pine resin, the ground bark and cones of the pine, decayed heath, the crushed fruits of *Visnea mocanera*. The body was smoked with a scented wood. Sun-drying took 14–20 days. The body might spend a period in burnt sand. Some, doubtless the poor, were buried in their everyday skin clothing, the rich had up to sixteen wrappers. The best animals were kept specially to provide mummy-wrapper skins; a corpse could afterwards be distinguished by the brand-marks. The men had their arms by their sides, those of the women were crossed over their stomachs. Important mummies were placed in coffins of juniper wood, these then stood on end against walls or in niches. Chiefs were buried in special caves, the corpses marked for later recognition. It is clear that, as one would expect, practice varied from island to island.

Hernández (1977) gives nine Palma sites where burnt human bones have been found. At Cuervo Cave, stratification and the pottery sequence suggested cremation was an earlier rite than plain burial. The pottery, unburnt, had been placed, after the cremation, with the ashes. However, Hernández's current excavation of Espigón Cave (Puntillana) itself underlines how unwise it may be to theorize yet on the sequence in the lesser Canaries. There were two burial areas, one with two skeletons 'retaining their skin in places' and 'partially covered by perfectly-cured skins stitched with vegetable cord'; one corpse lay on its back, the other was crouched on its side, upon bedrock covered with pine-needles and other leaves; some *Visnea* fruits were associated. The preliminary report does not refer to these as mummies. As noted (Diego 1976), many accepted Canary 'mummies' appear, externally, to be untreated. These factors, together with the sharing of caves and of the grave-goods of the 'plain' burials, suggests that Schwidetsky's recent sharp mummification and non-mummification division has been an over-simplification. A series of stages between the two ex-tremes seems more likely. Schwidetsky's deductions from the supposed division will be considered at the end of the chapter.

Death, in Palma, was met with fatalism and stoicism. Seen ap-proaching, its prey called together his relatives and friends to announce 'I want to die', recorded by the Castillians as *vacaguaré*. He was then taken to his chosen cave, laid on a bier covered with soft skins, a big pot of milk at his head, and the entrance sealed up.

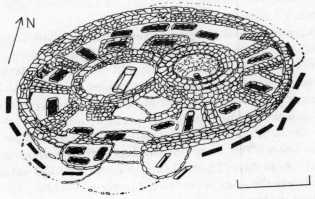

Figure 13   *Tumulus of La Guancha, Gran Canaria* (Scale: 4m)

Tumulus burial can only be discussed for Gran Canaria, for lack of reliable evidence from the two eastern islands. Large tumuli only occurred at Gáldar and Telde, the major settlements. In each case the structures were built on the shore. All that is known about La Guancha (Pl. 4b, Fig. 13) is that there were 42 unmummified burials, with two in one of the cists. The cists within the tumulus were stone-faced, those outside were simply trenches in the soil. The body in the eastern, main chamber lay in a coffin of pine planks, as did that in the lesser, western vault. Each burial included quantities of limpet shells. The whole tumulus was originally covered in earth. The radiocarbon assay, on a piece of wood, showed the tumulus to have included the eleventh century AD in its period of use.

The Agujero tumulus, nearby, was smaller, 14m diameter, and stepped (Pl. 4b, c), each level 60cm–1m wide, with its summit 6m 40cm across. Its undated burials, number not recorded, were in unlined trenches, 30cm deep. One grave held a fine red-ware pot, decorated, with triangles, in black and red (Fig. 16g); it was full of limpet-shells. If, as has been suggested, the painted ware was only introduced in the fourteenth century, this will show that the tumuli at Gáldar spanned at least three centuries. El Agujero was also originally covered with earth.

Close by, to the west, are a few smaller cairns. One example (Pl. 4b), still recognizably well-made, is clearly also tiered, though in only two levels, with steps up through the lower one (in the plate, a white box stands on one of these steps). This whole set of striking ruins is quite unprotected; at present they are used as rubbish dumps.

The Telde cairn, La Garita (Jiménez 1966b), sounds like the smallest Gáldar structures. Some 3 km from the town and 300m from Punta de Salinas, it was oval, 10m by 9m 50cm, 75cm high, with two slab-lined cists, 2m by 65cm by 40cm deep, these covered with pine planking.

A tumulus also perhaps more related to the common tombs than to the individual cairn-burials described shortly has been examined at Tauro Alto (S.W., Mogán; Jiménez 1964). Overall it is 5m 50cm across but, as far as the report can be understood, consists of a central mound separated by a 40cm gap from an outer ring of stones. The inner structure was built over four 'radial' cists (each 2m by 80cm) with slab covers. Each cist was marked by an obelisk (1m 10cm high).

Three further intermediate forms have been recognized. Verneau saw 40 tumuli at Agaete which were in shape two-tier versions of the Agujero tomb; the crowns were made up of yellow, black and red stones in sequence. Verneau also reported small and very well made domed tumuli at San Nicolás and Mogán, up to 1m 50cm high, each with surrounding wall and three red stones placed on top; they seem to have been built beside rather than upon the burial. Also in the Mogán region (Mña. Redonda, Tauro Alto), two structures closely similar to the Hierro altar (Diego 1966) in fact covered cists; like low-crowned, broad-brimmed hats, one was 2m 80cm across the base, its centre cone now only 70cm above the ground (Jiménez 1964). However, this last type is probably only the penultimate form, a century later, in more collapsed condition.

Schwidetsky, comparing the extreme Mediterranean types from the large Gáldar tomb to the physical remains from the disappeared Arguineguín tumuli (south coast), assumes the structures were also similar, this reinforcing her burial-elite-race hypothesis. Verneau in fact described Arguineguín's sepulchres at about the time when the bones were collected. In order of quantity, there was a common grave of about 20 corpses under a sand heap with a few stones for shaping; a stone tumulus holding two layers of cists, three in each layer, with slabs lying upon the bodies; there were individual burials covered either by stone tumuli or heaps of sand.

It can be seen that the multiple-burial tumuli varied in design and occurred all round the coast of the island. It is the present author's opinion that they held local leaders, such as the kings and dukes referred to by Azurara (1443, 40 years before the conquest of Gran Canaria). In assessing the differences and similarities of these tombs and their physical types, the founder effect, endogamy and topography must again be borne in mind.

In contrast to the few, large tumuli are the thousands of small cairns which humped the island's lava-fields. Little is known about them, yet much could be gleaned from the remaining cemeteries; these are still in existence, even if rifled, because of the undesirability of their terrain. The main sites seem to have been La Isleta, Jinámar (both N.E.); Arteara (Pl. 3), Mogán (both in the southern mountains); San Nicolás, Agaete (W.).

These single-corpse tumuli can be up to 7m 50cm across, thus overlapping in size—but not shape—with the multiple-burial tombs. The cist underneath may have any orientation. On La Isleta (long a military camp, access forbidden) the cists had been covered with pine planks before the tumuli had been built over them. Here Verneau saw stone covers kept off the bodies by forked sticks. At Arteara (Pl. 3, 1977), the cists were stone-lined. Verneau heard that similar tumuli existed on Lanzarote (Guatiza).

One Agaete tumulus (2m 75cm across, 1m 80cm high) covered a crudely-walled cist (2m 65cm by 80cm, 86cm deep), this planked with pine: inside was the unique coffin hollowed out of a pine trunk (2m 34cm by 50cm diameter, the walls 35–40cm thick) with a lid held to the trunk by wooden pegs. The coffin gave C14 dates of eighth century AD (conflicting dates have been published, also given in Appendix Two). Abreu: 'Some of their dead bodies were put in chests, and afterwards deposited in a kind of stone sepulchre'; Torriani suggested the fourteenth-century Mallorcans introduced pine coffins (interred with the head-end to the north, he added), perhaps mistakenly in view of the C14 date. Hollow trunks are in use today, in the islands, as drinking troughs (eg at La Zarza, Palma, by the engravings).

Grave goods were perhaps rare—but since the tumuli were all opened and looted long ago, none are likely to have reached the museums even they existed. Pots of fat have been found (Arucas), a link with the Fuerteventura custom of burying butter to increase its medicinal properties (Chapter 9). Near the head of a burial at La Gabia (Telde) there were pots, one holding a wooden spoon and limpet-shells, and also perforated shells.

If it is supposed that the chiefs were buried under the large tumuli, it follows logically that the individual cairns sheltered the remains of the far more numerous nobles—and there is some evidence, given shortly, that the common people were interred in trenches *without* tumuli above them. The connection of these last with their equals in the caves—mummified or not—will also be discussed soon. If this third type of tomb did occur, then, inconspicuous and certainly little sought by archaeology, there may still be undisturbed burials of this simplest kind to be found.

In summary, the five investigated islands each practised plain and mummified burial in caves, though Palma's inclusion needs confirmation; the C14 dates show that each form was current in the first millenium AD, with the Palma and Hierro dates so far rather later than those of the two main islands. Palma's cremation ritual is placed near the beginning of the island's occupation, by Hernández (1977), with C14 dates for the associated pottery of ninth century AD (the two earliest Belmaco datings, Appendix Two); but the same pottery at El Humo has a date of fourteenth century AD (Pellicer 1976). The reader is reminded that the Canary archaeologists, though quietly shortening their overall chronology, have not yet publicly accepted any C14 dates.

There seem to be only two tumuli dates: large, La Guancha, eleventh century AD, and small, Agaete, eighth century AD. Another Agaete date, of about 1000 AD, may also relate to a small tumulus. There is thus at least partial contemporaneity with the cave burials.

Looking across to N.W. Africa, it is seen that cave burial, undistinctive of course, was common enough up to the Islamic period. True mummification, as known from Egypt, did not occur. However, as Pellicer (1971a) well summarizes, a Tangier necropolis of the sixth-seventh century BC, showing Punic influence, has yielded dried bodies in skins; in the Tibesti (Fig. 2) and Ennedi (E. Sahara), there were burials in skin sacks, current practice at least during the first half of the second millenium AD; Pellicer also noted that the Tangier form was practised in black Africa until recently, for example amongst the Hausas, these linked to the Tchad culture (S. Sahara). The Canaries' most advanced treatment of bodies falls between these types and full mummification—could it have been an archipelago development of N.W. African practice? Cremation, obviously the least easy form of burial to recognize, has been found as rarely in N.W. Africa as in the Canaries.

The early Neolithic graves of N.W. Africa were simply trenches in the open or in caves, just like those in the lava-fields and caves of the archeipelago. The Mediterranean megalithic zone diffused its tumulus-building element to N.W. Africa. The only diagnostic feature of Gran Canaria's large round tumuli is the stepping, allowing safe comparison with the Berber *bazina*; 5-150m across, the latter may hold one or several elongated burials, either just laid on the ground or placed in trenches covered with flat slabs. The *bazina* lasted until the arrival of the Arabs; Pellicer actually limits them to the first three or four centuries AD. The small individual tumuli are similar to the *chouchets* of N.W. Africa; these are 3-5m across, 2-3m high, with two or three burials at the most, these crouched and on the old land surface. Made of an outer cylinder of large stones then filled with smaller ones, this aspect of the *chouchet* recalls Cuscoy's Hierro altar-tumulus. Alimen particularly notes that *bazina* and *chouchet* occur together in the Constantine region of Algeria. In the adjacent W. Sahara there is a wide range of tumuli: round, oval, keyhole, horned and others, little understood. The *bazina* form does not seem to occur but *chouchet* types were opened by Almagro and Mateu, during the Spanish occupation, and found to have appropriate burials.

Two comparisons in particular are significant. First, the N.W. Africans spread red ochre on their corpses up to Roman times; available amongst the volcanic products of the Canaries, red ochre has never been recognized in the archipelago burials. Second, the N.W. African bodies were placed in the crouched position, usually on their left sides, until the arrival of the Romans: almost without exception, the Canary dead were laid out on their backs. The W. Sahara *chouchet*-type corpses, like those in the large tombs, were in the crouched position; their date is unknown, but then the Romans probably did not influence the region. On each score, then, the Canaries' immigrants are unlikely to have left N.W. Africa before Roman times.

BURIAL, CLASS AND IMMIGRATION

The anthropologists' deductions from the relationships they have proposed between physical type and burial form can now be considered. In doing so, much information on Canary prehistoric society will be introduced.

First, Schwidetsky (1966) said that the mummified, seen against the non-mummified, had 'the characteristics of the upper class everywhere': in each island they were larger, more slender in facial details and long bones, longer lived. They were thus nearer the Mediterranean pole, the women in particular, than the non-mummified. Second, the burials under tumuli in Gran Canaria, both big and small structures, were again tall, slender and Mediterranean when compared to that island's cave burials, these including the mummies. Of the all-Canary mummies and the Gran Canaria tumuli burials, the latter had the higher skulls, nearer to the Mediterranean pole, and also a comparatively simple median suture. The burials in the big Gáldar tumulus were very similar to the human remains from the supposedly-similar Arguineguín tumulus (long disappeared, as noted).

Schwidetsky next quotes Azurara (1443): 'Two kings and a duke, elected, reigned in Gran Canaria. But the real rulers were the nobles: they had established their own assembly, never to be below 190 or above 200, keeping up its numbers from amongst their own sons . . . The nobles kept themselves apart from the lower classes, their line being of the purest . . .'. She then concludes that these nobles—rather than the kings and dukes—were buried in the few large tumuli. Referring to Torriani, in a debatable interpretation, she next proposes a second group of nobles, not hereditary, whom she identifies with the mummy-elite of Gran Canaria.

Schwidetsky goes on to suggest that the all-Canary class distinction she sees between the mummified and the non-mummified is not due to separate immigrations but to local endeavour: the more Mediterranean type has lifted itself in the social scale, then perpetuating itself as the elite. On the other hand, the extreme Mediterraneans of the Gran Canaria tumuli burials may, she feels, have arrived in a secondary immigration.

The basic anthropological data cannot be assessed here but the conclusions can discussed. The early writers, such as Torriani, certainly implied that the mummies were an elite; however, as in Egypt, different grades of mummification were practised, with mere drying by sun and fire of commoners. Mummies and plain burials shared the same cave and ritual, suggesting that correlation with class was not extreme. Nor is it possible to accept two classes of nobles on Gran Canaria—the ceremony seen by Schwidetsky as ennobling commoners was in fact only open to the sons of nobles and should thus rather be seen as a coming-of-age rite for the sons of the single elite group. According, perhaps, to period and place, so the nobles were either mummified or buried under tumuli.

The correlation of the *large* tumuli with the nobles also needs reappraisal. Schwidetsky has the nobles buried in these few massive tombs. But the council of 190–200 men would, in the course of time, turn into thousands of bodies—the Guancha tumulus, for example, held only 42 burials, as described. Hence the author's suggestion that it was Azurara's few kings and dukes who were interred, probably over a long period, in the large tumuli. Torriani did say that, buried in the lava-fields, only the nobles had tumuli over their graves—these would be the thousands of conical cairns described earlier. One is thus left to find the resting places of the commoners . . . Abreu provides the clue: 'The lower classes . . . were buried in the Mal Paices, in holes *covered with dry stones*; and excepting those bodies which were placed upright in caves, all . . . were laid with their heads towards the north'. Unfortunately, it is arguable whether the italic words describe a tumulus or not—if not, then a third-class burial for commoners is confirmed. However, Verneau can be brought in to support this: at Las Huesas ('The Graves') he saw burials, with pre-conquest pottery, in trenches without tumuli. Such distinction is certainly to be expected. Archaeological fieldwork could yield proof or otherwise.

Next, the proposed burial-race correlation. It is surely surprising that such a clear pattern should be discernable, in view of the basic uncertainties in the raw material. A major query must be placed after Schwidetsky's criterion for a Canary mummy, 'the least trace of visceral material'; for example, it is known that the dead who fell against the Spaniards on Tenerife were sun-dried in quantity. Then one must question the assumed rigid distinction, made for Gran Canaria, between tumulus and cave burial. Abreu having described how the mummies stood up in caves, went on: 'But if no proper cave was at hand, they carried the body to one of those stony places they call Mal Paices, where, levelling the ground and fixing the loose stones, they made a coffin of very large ones, placed so as not to touch the body; then they took another large stone, two yards in length, wrought into a round form, and with this they closed the coffin, and afterwards filled up the nich between the top of the round stone and the outer part of the sides of the coffin with small stones.' Abreu seems to be referring to the burial of nobles (with no mention of tumuli!); mummies may thus have been buried in the lava-fields. Above all, the opening line makes one wonder whether the growing population on the coast, faced with a choice between the carriage of bodies to caves, often awkwardly placed, with shallow soil or entrances difficult to block, would not probably have soon come to prefer the easy disposal available in the lava-fields. In the mountains, with less people and more caves — and no flat lava-fields — burials may have always been in caves.

Schwidetsky's argument that the mummies were a self-selecting elite comes up against an obstacle. Her thesis begins by assuming that all elites vary in a certain direction from their associated commoners. The elite would chose as marriage partners those of its own type. In the Canaries the general movement was, according to Schwidetsky, towards the Mediterranean pole. The flaw in the argument is that it ignores the well-known fact that it was fat women who were most sought after in the islands (continuing the Berber preference) — and the Cromagnoid women would probably have been the fattest naturally and the most easily fattened for marriage.

Finally, the linking of immigration to burial, class and race by Schwidetsky. She proposed that though the Mediterraneanization of the mummy-elite was an archipelago development, the Gran Canaria tumuli-elite, also Mediterranean, stemmed from a secondary immigration. This brings up a range of possibilities beyond detailed coverage; some have been led to propose three immigrations, respectively bringing universal plain burial, mummification and tumulus interment. Mummification and tumuli overlap only on Gran Canaria (Table 37). If mummification came with the first wave, say, why did it not take root also in the two eastern islands, doubtless occupied at the same time? If this could occur, then tumulus burial

could also have come in at the beginning and not have reached the
four western islands. In fact, the varied practices and their
distribution could be the result of a mixture of founder effects—both
between islands and, on Gran Canaria, between regions—and of the
influences of climate, topography and, with time, population
pressure. More evidence is of course needed.

CHAPTER EIGHT

Secular Structures

This chapter covers the remaining constructions, those not used for worship or burial. A new problem arises: it is likely that most commonplace structures, not posing a threat to the settlers and the incoming church, continued in use after the conquest, many right to the present. One result is archaeological doubt over the existence and certainly over the type of pre-conquest stone huts in many islands. Table 38 gives only the distinctive ruins. Life usually revolved around simple caves, huts and corrals.

	Assembly & justice places	Fortified summits	Advanced cave dwellings	Sunken houses	Communal corrals	Hollow cairns	Various
F	x	x		x	x	x	Jandía wall
L	x			x	x		Zonzamas fortress
GC	x	x	x	x	x		Cross-plan houses, Valerón granary
T	x		?				
G		x					
P	?						
H	x					x	

Table 38: *Distinctive secular structures*

CAVES

There were cave-dwellings throughout the archipelago. To make a cave habitable, the mouth might be walled, stone slabs brought in as seats, stone beds built against the inner wall and surfaced with gravel; the beds were padded with dry grass or bracken, the bedding was of skins. The floor might be levelled, with a layer of vegetable matter then spread upon it. Cooking was done near the cave-mouth. Eventually the cave might become its occupants' sepulchre, with the vegetable layer considered by the modern archaeologist as part of the burial ritual.

Artificial caves occur mainly in Gran Canaria but have not been systematically studied in the archipelago. Cave-cutting was with animal bones and stone tools (Chapter 11); Pellicer says the most famous complex, Cuatro Puertas, was quarried with metal tools, however. Cave-cutting was a specialist task in conquest-time Gran Canaria.

Torriani, having described this island's stone huts, said there were also 'older' dwellings 'under the ground', occupied by kings, nobles and old men. These might be made in the tuff or the *soils* of a *sloping* hillside. First the cutters quarried out a chamber with no front wall and, from this, 'in the middle of each wall they cut a door and then large and small rooms'. This produced a cross-shaped plan, showing these dwellings to be linked to the cruciform houses, to be described shortly. A good example of such an artificial cave is to be seen in the King's Cave complex (Bentayga); the main cave (Pl. 2b) has only the two depicted chambers off its eastern wall. Other features said to have been usually cut out were a window above each door, niches as seats and storage places, two cistern-like pits by the entrance. At their most evolved (eg Cueva Pintada) these caves were partitioned (Fig. 14b) and and painted (Fig. 16a), believed a fourteenth-century development as described; Torriani said the designs, in colours extracted from plants and flowers, were non-figurative.

Probably there were no evolved cave-dwellings on the other islands. Tenerife's best sound to have been the King's Cave of the Bco. de Chimisay (Güimar), artificial according to Verneau, and the Prince's Cave at Realejo. Berthelot visited the latter, saying it had belonged to Ben Como, the leader of the Taoro territory (Fig. 23) and chief opponent of the *conquistadores* of the last decade of the fifteenth century. Reaching it with difficulty, Berthelot found it had 12–15 rock-cut seats at the entrance with a higher one in the middle of the cave; improbably, there were still staffs on the seats, recalling those carried by dignitaries (Chapter 11) and with which, as has been seen, they were buried. This cave sounds to have been used as a meeting place.

The only Canary caves in which stratification has been recorded — to examine now the archaeological evidence — are Roque de la Campana (Mazo, Palma; Diego 1970), discussed in the section on pottery (Chapter 10), and Arena Cave (Bco. Hondo, Tenerife; Pellicer & Acosta 1971, 1976). There are also advance notes on three Palma caves with stratification: Belmaco (separate excavations by Diego and by Hernández), Humo and Los Guinchos (both by Pellicer and Acosta). Hernández (1977) works these, together with several more of his unpublished Palma excavations, into the Canaries' first 'clear cultural succession' but until the many sites are published in detail it is impossible to assess the sequence. Pellicer (1968) lists a dozen Hierro sites with untouched occupation deposits.

The Arena Cave excavation is worth summarising since it gave the earliest C14 datings in the Canaries. The site, at 670m, is 7km N.N.E. of Candelaria, in the upper part of Bco. Hondo. The cave is a volcanic tube 77m long; sealed almost 2000 years ago, according to its excavator, finds were made on the surface when it was first re-entered in 1970. The deposit, 2m thick, was divided into four main levels; the upper two yielded fragments of pots and rotary querns, with obsidian artefacts, whilst remains of the huge lizards, assumed eaten, occurred throughout. The datings (Appendix Two) ran from sixth century BC to second century AD. The absence of pottery in the two lowest levels may be due to a lack of human occupation — the lizards could have been brought in by birds of prey or have just lived and died there, the charcoal may have resulted from a fire caused by the island vulcanism. Alternatively, the lower remains may stem from human occupation but this could have been by individuals who had arrived before the proposed major immigration; Juba II's men reported traces of occupation.

STONE-BUILT DWELLINGS

The remote pastures, for example the Teide crater, contain innumerable shepherds' shelters, part walling part natural outcrop, thoroughly studied by Diego (1968a). Vestiges, usually the foundations, of simple round, oval and (? post-conquest) angular huts, some compartmented, have been described for most islands (Palma, Hernández 1977; Tenerife, Cruz et al; Gran Canaria, Jiménez, various; Fuerteventura, Mercer 1973). A few distinctive types will be described.

In the extreme west, the early writers refer to Hierro structures holding about twenty families; the constructions must have been subdivided and it is tempting to see the compartmented rock-engravings, commonest on this island (Fig. 14c) as plans, perhaps dedications, of these dwellings. They were said to have consisted of large circular enclosures, with narrow entrances; inside there were 'poles against the wall', covered with branches, bracken and dried grass. Since Marín said the result was domed, it sounds as if the poles were used somewhat like the cruicks of the Scottish Highlanders' huts — placed at 45°, braced against the foot of the walling and joined together at a central apex. Dry bracken was also spread on the floors and the beds — as will be seen, bracken roots were the staple food of Hierro, so the dead fronds would be plentifully available.

Tenerife's huts were comparatively ordinary. Cruz did note that at

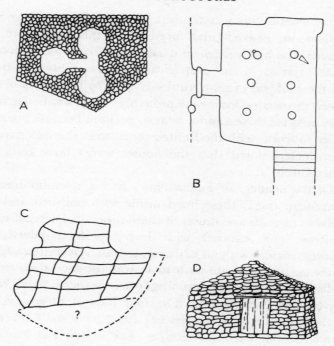

Figure 14 *Dwellings: pit-type, Tahiche, Lanzarote (a, after Verneau), cave with symmetrical holes in floor, Cueva Pintada complex, Gran Canaria (b, after Beltrán 1974), compartmented rock-engraving, Julan, Hierro (c), hut, Tunte, Gran Canaria (d, after Verneau)*

Guargacho (Las Galletas; unpublished) there may have been a hexagonal-sided dwelling, the walling of skins or branches held to posts set in stones; there was a hearth in the middle. This is the nearest structure to a tent ever recorded in the Canaries. The average Tenerife hut would have been round or oval, the stone walling up to 1m 80cm, flat-roofed with vegetable matter. Espinosa said that where there were no caves the people 'made houses of dry stone with straw on their walls'; Viera wrote of 'huts covered with dry stone and bracken'.

For Gran Canaria there are descriptions of huts perhaps little altered since the conquest, seen a century ago in or near San Bartolomé de Tirajana. Verneau pictured one at Tunte (Fig. 14d). They might be round, oval or, less often, square or rectangular; the oval plan may be limited to the north-west corner of the island. On the tree-trunk roof-timbers was laid a lighter layer of vegetable matter 'sometimes covered by earth and flat stones'. The largest took 20 people. At Agaete the huts reached 10m in diameter (Bco. de Guguy). Verneau went on to describe the dwellings as grouped in villages and aligned so as to have narrow streets between them — there had been hundreds of these at Arguineguín, for example. Stone (1887) saw a round hut. The walling was almost a metre thick at the base and rose to 2m 50cm, the peaked earth-faced roof a metre above this at the apex; inside, the hut was 5m in diameter, with an earth floor; there were built-in seats in the deep entrance and recesses in the inner walling; the roof was of pine trunks covered by two layers of strips of wood, then the earth. Doors were probably always small. Torriani says palm was used for these and for beams, perhaps because it was lighter and easier to work, with the limited tools, than the other trees. The early chroniclers noted that the houses were clean and, in fact, beautiful (Abreu).

The Gáldar leader, or *guanarteme*, had a splendid house, with walls 2m 50cm thick, these lined inside with polished and painted pine-wood: 'the walls are almost of three *varas* thickness, of such well-fitting stone and covered with huge, perfectly-joined, planed (*acepillados*) planks, without nails, mud, plaster or whitewash' (Viera). Carpentry, again done with stone tools, was also specialist work.

The distinctive cruciform buildings occur in the N.W.–S.W. sector: Gáldar, Mogán, San Nicolás. The four huts at Mogán (Lomo del Corral Canario, Tauro Alto; Jiménez 1964) have walls 1m–1m 80cm thick and are 5m each way inside. The design has already been described in relation to the *goro* (Figs. 12a, d). Its origin may lie, as proposed, in the natural architecture of the artificial caves. In turn, since these belonged to the elite (Torriani), so too may have the cruciform houses. The cruciform houses on the shore at Gáldar, a few hundred metres from the large tumuli, may thus have been the winter residence of the regional leader, the Bentayga complex (The King's Cave), with a cruciform cave, his summer retreat. Such migration of the court certainly occurred in Tenerife, as will be seen. The caves were superior dwellings, in terms of climate response, to the houses, since they were cool in summer and warm in winter.

The two eastern islands had not only ordinary huts but a range of others variably sunk in the ground. The author (1973, plate on p. 54) has described settlements in both solid and shattered lava-fields on Fuerteventura. At El Saladillo (Pozo Negro), for example, the dwellings consisted of single or grouped cells, sometimes with a common courtyard, all below the surface of the broken-up lava: roughly-circular spaces having been cleared by lifting out the loose blocks, the best of these had then been put back as roofing, corbelling over minute chambers, no more than 1m 50cm in height, with tiny entrances. It is hard not to feel these were in fact animal pens. Structures similar in size and shape occur all over the island. On the Risco del Carnicero (Río Palmas), they were again built into the ground, this time into a chaos of boulders on a high, easily-defended ridge.

However, the most interesting of the eastern dwellings were those of Lanzarote, an island with comparatively-few caves. Verneau described one at Tahiche (Fig. 14a): 'A great heap of stones . . . in the form of a cube . . . three little round rooms, one open to the sky, laid out in a triangle and linked by galleries . . . entered by climbing the heap and going down into the roofless room'. Further, it was half-embedded in the ground, construction having begun by sinking a pit and lining it with rocks to avoid collapse. Verneau felt the design was derived from the lava-field dwellings. Another type—which Verneau said also occurred on Fuerteventura—went to the extreme of being entirely sunken, the entrance a stone-faced ramp; the vaulted roof was of flat slabs. This form occurred, for example, at La Jenía (Yaiza), with a pottery kiln and cisterns, and at Masdache. Recently it has been said that the Yaiza casas hondas, as they are called by the Spanish, have been located, without further details.

In 1977 the author noted semi-sunken round houses, up to 5m interior diameter, at La Fortaleza de Sta. Lucia—on Gran Canaria, that is. The underlined words in Torriani's description of the artificial caves would fit these sunken houses. The Italian also mentioned the important settlements of Tara and Sendro, both near Telde, giving them the unlikely total of 14,000 dwellings: not far from Sta. Lucia, at these places the commoners' huts were above ground but those of the nobles were sunken, he said. The latter do not sound like artificial caves. Abreu made a brief but useful comment on the subject: the walls of the Gran Canaria houses were low, the floors below ground. It thus seems likely that the semi-sunken type of house occurred in Gran Canaria too—perhaps in the eastern Telde-focussed region, against the cruciform caves and houses of the west, perhaps diffused from Gáldar. In each case they were the dwellings of the elite, it seems.

COMMON CORRALS

The vast remote pastures required the shepherds to spend their nights away from home: in the evenings they came together, with their flocks, at the majadillas, large common pens with little rooms, like sentry-boxes, built into the walling.

The gambuesa pen (Pl. 16, Fuerteventura), is similar but for the absence of the rooms. It is used for a community round-up of the guaniles, the animals allowed to roam freely over immense desert-quality areas in search of their own pasture. Brought into the gambuesa, they are then sorted out for milking, marking, slaughter and so on, the survivors then released again. These communal structures may be limited to the eastern province.

ASSEMBLY PLACES

Public meeting grounds probably existed for each settlement, each territory and, if unified, each island. These places were used for important ceremonies, political debate, justice, duels, sport and feasting, each described later. Espinosa said there was a general Tenerife *tagoror* held at the Orotava (Taoro) dragon tree; perhaps this was before the island became broken up into principalities. The word *tagoror*, obviously related to Gran Canaria's *goro*, this seemingly of a religious function, is only correctly used for Tenerife's assembly places. Many, all over the Canaries, will have gone over to use as animal corrals.

Though there are suggestive place names, few certain ruins are known. Abreu said the places of justice, on Tenerife, were level stretches of ground with a large high square stone in the middle, for the chief to sit upon, with smaller ones, for the elders, on each side; these last were seated in order of seniority. This recalls the just-described Prince's Cave (Realejo). Diego says the *tagoror* was enclosed by a round or oval wall and was no bigger than a threshing pan (a further source of confusion).

The well-known Hierro *tagoror* (Julan) is upon a commanding hillock above the coast (Pl. 10a). The focal point is now a column of stone slabs, at the end over the sea, on the circumference both of a small circle of stone seats and of the ruined main wall which follows the outer edge of the hillock; at the inland end there are sunken enclosures. If this *tagoror* was also a place of ritual, then an altar and the sties of sacred animals are to be seen in the structures at the two ends. There is a white spread of limpet shells immediately to the east, thought to be remnants of ritual feasts. However, Hernández (1977) says this *tagoror*, used by many to define the structure in the islands, has been rebuilt since the conquest.

The other islands do not clarify the matter. At Gáldar (Los Mugaretes) the *guanarteme* dispensed justice in an oval recinct, said to be 2000 sq m in area, divided in two parts along the major axis: the 'back', sounding now particularly in need of clearance, has no discernible lay-out, the 'front' was a walled enclosure with concentric stepping in the centre. Verneau noted a *tagoror* at Corralejo, N. Fuerteventura, but it sounds more like a *majadilla*, just described. Jiménez recorded dozens of *tagorors* all over the eastern province but those seen by the author in Fuerteventura (1973) could equally have been corrals.

For Tenerife itself, Diego (1968) and Cruz have three sites: Tagoror del Rey (Granadilla de Abona), Taganana (N.E.) and La Victoria (N. centre). On Palma, ruins in the ravines of Los Cantos and Briesta have been proposed as *tagorors* but rejected by Hernández (1977).

Diego (1968a) also records the still-continuing use of the word *tagora* for a type of shepherd's temporary shelter on Tenerife. The structure consists of a semi-circular wall which rises towards the middle. This may be linked to the arcs of walling on Gran Canaria, considered to have had a ritual significance—and perhaps even a relationship to the Islamic prayer-wall.

There is information on some aspects of the events which took place in the public meeting grounds. Justice was usually meted out by the local leader or, at least in Gran Canaria, also by the high priest or *faycagh* (Abreu). There were prisons and trials. In the sentences one can again suspect a founder effect in action, by the similarities and differences between islands. Murder brought the death penalty in the three eastern islands and in Hierro—but in Tenerife it was felt that only their god could take life. In the two easternmost islands, execution took place on the shore: the convict's head was placed on a flat rock, his brains were dashed out with a round stone. His children were afterwards abhorred. On Gran Canaria, execution was carried out in the meeting place by the same means. However, if the murderer had sons, one of these, selected by lot, was despatched in his place; if he killed a man with a son and had himself a father, then his own father would be executed . . . far-reaching deterrents. Perhaps as a result, there was a definite attempt to educate children in social behaviour; this included the custom of choosing one youth as Vice and another as Virtue. Torriani said the Gran Canaria men, crossing in their small craft, as described, took their forms of the death penalty to the more easterly islands. Gran Canaria had its own way of locating a murderer: all suspects were given pieces of burning resinous wood to hold, the first to go out bringing execution . . . if they all went out together then all were executed. On Hierro the death penalty was carried out, by a special executioner, in the same way as the victim had died.

Clearly all these penalties are applications of the *lex talionis*, an eye for an eye. Theft on Gran Canaria and Hierro brought the loss of an eye the first time, of the other eye on second conviction. On Palma, conversely, efficient theft was socially honoured; if caught, the only obligation was to return the stolen object—on this island there was no justice, robbery being a form of livelihood.

On Tenerife, to return there, the murderer only lost his cattle and chattels, these given to the dead man's family, and was banished. Subsequent vendettas were forbidden, the murderer being henceforth under the chief's protection. Elsewhere, feuds were common—on Palma, of course, and probably on Lanzarote and Fuerteventura, since in the latter pair it was not punishable to kill a man if you entered his house through the door . . . only killing by surprise brought the death penalty. On Tenerife, corporal punishment was administered; the victim, lying flat on the ground, was beaten with the chief's staff by an appropriate official.

The coming-of-age ceremonies on Gran Canaria have already been mentioned in connection with Schwidetsky's second-class nobility hypothesis. Abreu is clear that although the initiation was essential to becoming a noble, it was only open to those born of noble parentage. The priest, in front of the assembled people, made the youth swear by Acoran to tell the truth, then interrogated him: had he ever prepared food, looked after, milked, slaughtered or stolen animals, acted wrongly towards women? If the youth passed, then his hair, grown long for the occasion, was ceremonially cut around the level of the ears; he was given a staff, *magada*. Otherwise, in disgrace, he had his head shaved — also the post-conquest commoner's normal tonsure in at least Lanzarote (Chapter 22). In this way the single-class nobility perpetuated itself. In battle the commoner was only to beat a noble with his stick, then let him go — it was death to kill him. This emphasis on class distinction rather than on defeating the enemy reinforces the theory of hierarchy in the tumuli zone, to which — as usual — the early narratives are to be limited.

HOLLOW CAIRNS

Diego (1966) discussed the Hierro *taros*, use unknown: these are oval structures of stone, for example 3m 30cm by 2m, entrance only 75cm high, facing north-east, with four big stone slabs inside, placed horizontally against the collapsed walling. The *taro*, Diego noted, is always positioned on a high open site. On Fuerteventura, the word survives as a place name, Rosa del Taro, the highest point of the eastern cordillera, but was meaningless to the islanders questioned upon it. In fact there is an early record of the use on Fuerteventura (Mercer 1973) of a hollow cairn for drying meat — presumably the reason for the entrance on Hierro facing into the prevailing trade wind, unlikely in a dwelling.

FORTIFIED SUMMITS

It is not known whether any of the Canary peaks were fortified before the European invasions. The place-name 'Fortaleza' now marks many of these summits. Fuerteventura had at least Monte Cardón (Mercer 1973). Ca da Mosto wrote of this island's resistance, renewed about the time of his passage (1455): 'the people are able to fortify themselves in the mountains in such a way that a serious siege is necessary to make them surrender'. On Gomera, there is the *fortaleza* of Chipude, seemingly without record of fortification or battle. However, Abreu refers to 'a strong natural fortress named Garagonohe', the name now preserved in the Alto de Garajonai, the island's summit; this was held by rebellious islanders 1488. Probably the rebels had in fact retreated to the Chipude fortress, not far away to the west.

The people of Gran Canaria stubbornly resisted the invasions of 1478–83 by entrenching themselves on numerous peaks, these events narrated in Chapter 17. The defensive walling on Bentayga (Pl. 1a) is still recognizable. The last confrontation occurred at 'Ansite': the site has recently been claimed by two adjacent rural councils in the Tirajana crater and official decision has identified it, perhaps correctly, with the Fortaleza de Sta. Lucia (Pl. 8b). This outstanding and clearly greatly-unexcavated site has thereupon been mostly destroyed by official action, to make a faked-up tourist attraction, in the best *folklórico* style, for the celebrations of the five-hundredth anniversary of the founding of Las Palmas (the site of the *conquistadores*' first fort in 1478).

Another peak probably fortified during the Gran Canaria invasion was Acayro (Fig. 23); also referred to as 'Aguayro' and 'Acuario', it was probably on the eminence called 'El Roque' on the 1:50,000 military map, its summit overlooking the eastern plain and the Balos engraving sites, one depicting the invaders' horses (Pl. 5b). Other *fortalezas* were Ajodar (unlocated), Artenara (W. of Tejeda) and Tirma (N.E. of San Nicolás).

MISCELLANEOUS

Fortified peaks were not recorded for Lanzarote. An island king, Zonzamas, on the threshold of history, as will be seen, had a stronghold about halfway between the two post-conquest capitals, Teguise and Arrecife (Fig. 23). The French, fighting his descendants in 1402–4, recorded: 'They have the strongest castles, built in their own style, that one could find anywhere'. Post-conquest occupation of Zonzamas' fort is implied by Viera's statement that the defeated king, Guadarfrá, was allowed to live on in his ancestral home.

Verneau described the site as an oval rampart, 22m by 12m by 2m high, on a rocky hillock; within it was the chief's cave, 20m maximum length, divided in two by walling; there were also unidentifiable structures. Berthelot, writing at much the same time, said the walls were 4–5m high. Pellicer has recently remarked that most of the ruins, squarish, lie upon ash from the massive 1730–6 eruptions and so are comparatively modern. The site, potentially informative, is in need of investigation; it is now under excavation (Dug Godoy 1972).

Fuerteventura was divided into kingdoms (Fig. 23) by a 5km wall.

Crossing the island from Matas Blancas to Playa de la Pared (Beach of the Wall), it was a metre thick and, now at least, is no more than waist high. All manner of stones have gone into it, unworked, simply collected off the surface along its trajectory.

The final structure is the common granary, known only on Gran Canaria. Moro Cave (Agaete), its paintings of human beings already described, had some twenty storage chambers. However, the best example of the common granary is just above the road on the Cuesta de Silva zone of the Gáldar coast. The Valerón site (Pl. 4a) consists of about 200 little chambers cut into a soft rock-face under a great overhang. The grain inside, the front of each small silo would have been plastered over with mud and this, whilst wet, impressed with the owner's distinctive personal seal; known now as *pintaderas* (Fig. 16b, Chapter Ten), one only was actually found at Valerón. The popular description of this granary as another dwelling of the *magadas* or nuns, together with its title, 'Cenobio de Valerón', is unfounded; not even the smallest of vestal virgins could have lived in the minute cells. Espinosa said Tenerife had granaries.

COMPARISONS WITH AFRICA

Canary prehistorians have long used the dignifying word 'megalithic' of the Canaries' structures. These, however, show neither the techniques nor distinctive designs of the Mediterranean megalithic zone. At the most, the Gran Canaria tumuli may be linked, through those of the Berbers, to the Mediterranean culture. None of the secular structures considered in this chapter appear to have any connection.

A number of these constructions can be seen to be local responses to special circumstances. The great wall of Fuerteventura, to the existence of two warring kingdoms and a conveniently-narrow isthmus. Communal corrals, to the need to allow the animals to roam freely over the poor but vast pastures, in turn made possible by the low population density and confining nature of an island.

N.W. African caves have been used as dwellings wherever they occur, being also quarried out, as in the Marrakesch area, where the rock is soft enough. Again, the Canaries have amply provided caves and thus encouraged troglodytism. The variably-sunken houses may have been local developments. In black Africa there are funnel-shaped pit dwellings entered through the narrow apex (Moal). The houses of the N.W. African highland zones could be studied in relation to the most distinctive Canary dwellings.

The common granary, if really called an *agadir* on Gran Canaria, of course suggests the port of the same name on Morocco's Atlantic

coast; its name means 'granary'. Marcy noted the common granary
and the *pintadera* seal in recent use amongst the Berbers of both the
Moroccan Atlas and the Algerian Aurès mountains. The meat-drying
tower, *taro*, has parallels from central Africa to St. Kilda (Scotland).

The original islanders would have had assembly places in their
home settlements. The *tagoror* is not distinctive. Any pastoral people
would meet naturally in a large common corral, adding seats as
gatherings became increasingly important in local life.

CHAPTER NINE

Daily Life: Dress and Adornment, Animals, Crops and Fishing, Food

The clothes, tools and other artefacts of the seven different island peoples, developing more or less independently over a long period, took a wide variety of forms, exhausting both to describe and to read about in detail. Worse, in important sections of life from which little concrete evidence survives, the description must draw on the early chronicles and reports — but these often differ amongst themselves, further extending the discussion.

DRESS

Archaeological material is limited. The Guayadeque burials (Gran Canaria) have produced two sets of clothing. One consists of a pig-skin upper garment with a palm-fibre skirt now reduced by fraying to only 50cm in length; the other set, entirely of palm, is a cape, of which only the upper 12cm remain, above a short skirt. Vestiges of rush clothing have also been found. Vegetable-fibre cloth is not known elsewhere in the Canaries.

The chronicles give more details for Gran Canaria. Recco (1341): the islanders went naked but for the married women, these wearing an apron, and the upper class, in skins painted in saffron and red; however, Recco's four captives, young men, wore aprons of palm or reed fibre coloured in the same way. The French, 1402–4, wrote of palm-leaf shorts, probably worn by the men, with the women covering 'their shameful parts' with skins; their hair was tied back in a plait; these islanders were a handsome people, recorded the chronicle. Tattooing appears to have been common: 'most of them had emblems cut (*entaillées*) on their flesh in different ways, each according to his fancy'. Tattooing has long been fashionable amongst the Berbers; this evidence may show that it was practised in N.W. Africa not only by 1402 but as long as 2000 years ago.

Abreu and Torriani are second-hand reports probably relating to a later period. The first said the Gran Canaria people wore a rush coat, tight and down to the knees, with a belt and hood; over the coat they put on a skin cloak, hairy side out in summer; their large hats were made of almost entire goat-skins, so arranged that 'they had a goat's beard hanging under each ear, which they sometimes tied under the chin'; all these garments were painted; others wore skin bonnets adorned with feathers; their shoes were of goatskin, hairy side outwards. Torriani also left pictures: a woman with long loose hair wears a single garment, a short-sleeved calf-length skin dress of almost Victorian modesty; the man, in a hat of Napoleonic magnificence (the trotters rather than the beard dangling on his shoulders), displays a thigh-length skin cloak, open to show a short-sleeved skin vest, which hangs over a skirt, also thigh-length, of palm and rush; the women plaited their hair with rush, the men had their hair long if a noble, shaved if a commoner.

Gran Canaria, the best evidenced on clothing, seems to show a progression from near-nakedness to almost an European degree of coverage. This can be put down less to a change in local temperature than to the clearly-recorded violations by the European soldiery and to the priests' ideas on morality—indeed, one Spanish archaeologist could even recently write on this that 'Decency is a result of habit, not of instinct'.

The more easterly islanders dressed much as those of Gran Canaria. Nude in the fourteenth century (Recco), they were clearly more covered by the time of the French invasion. On Lanzarote the men still had only a knee-length back-cloak 'and are not ashamed of their parts' but the women were now into ground-length skin tunics; the Fuerteventura men had only a skin tied around their shoulders but the women had also knee-length skins hanging from their waists. On Lanzarote, hair was worn long, though cut away across the forehead.

Abreu's wider description of the Lanzarote dress again links the Canaries to Africa. He wrote of a hooded skin-cloak, down to the knees, the *tamarco*; of the skin shoes, *maho*; of a goat-skin bonnet, *guapil*, with three large feathers stuck in it—as on Gran Canaria—to which the women added a red-dyed leather band. The oldest inscriptions in the Sahara, early first millenium AD, depict men wearing feathered head-gear; they also carry round shields and javelins which, as will be seen, were used in the Canaries. Abreu said the men of the eastern islands had long hair and plaited their beards—yet in post-conquest times those of Lanzarote apparently shaved their heads, wrote Torriani.

The skins shoes, also worn on Fuerteventura, may well have originated there, since the islanders were known as 'Mahohs'. Gaiters were also current. The pre-conquest men of Fuerteventura dressed in sheep-skin jackets, short-sleeved, above short breeches. Their caps sound like those of Gran Canaria.

There are even fewer relics from the four western islands. The gaiters, *guaycas* on Tenerife, have become the more acceptable since Diego (1961a) found a pair on a mummy in a burial cave on Mña.

Rajada (Las Cañadas); Berthelot (1835) has a picture of a Tenerife peasant in gaiters. Diego also recovered pieces of skin with finely-incised hatching and others dyed a bright clear yellow and a very dark red, almost chestnut. No clothing has been found in Gomera, Palma or Hierro. Neither Recco nor the French had much contact with the western people and so did not describe their dress.

So again one must rely on the late-sixteenth century writers. Abreu said that at least three of the western islands had used the skin cloak, *tamarco*. On Tenerife, the women's was longer than that of the men; both sexes rubbed sheep's oil on their bodies. The Gomera cloak was to the calf according to Abreu but Torriani depicts a woman in one reaching only to the waist, with a man in a short skirt and no cloak; the two authors concurred in the women being bare-bosomed and with a short petticoat. Abreu recorded a Gomera women's head-dress down to the shoulders, dyed and curiously painted; the men wrapped a band of softened rush, dyed red and blue, around their foreheads when going to war. In Torriani this became a dyed hair-band, red for both men and women, worn all the time. Abreu repeated his description for Hierro; with no head-dress, the women there made their hair into small plaits. Yet, for Hierro, Torriani pictures a man in a tight, short, sleeve-less skin tunic, his hair cut but with a long beard, beside a woman in a sleeve-less waistcoat which hangs over a loose skirt reaching to below the knees, with her hair long and flowing; in the winter, he added, they wore also the *tamarco* cloak. Neither author says much about dress on Palma — it sounds like that of Hierro. Shoes of pig-skin were current on Gomera and Palma, but they were more commonly made of sheep or goat skins on Hierro.

The general picture seems to be that, by the fifteenth century, the majority of the islanders were wearing one or two piece tunics; with little or no sleeve, these varied in length and tightness; the garments were made of skin and, on Gran Canaria, also of vegetable fibre. When it was cold the people added a skin cloak. Skin shoes were common. Clothing might be dyed, painted or have incised decoration. Head-dress and hair style varied.

The leather-working techniques have been studied by Mies (1960) and Diego (1961a) — they have already been summarised in relation to the mummy wrappings. It is known (Abreu, Torriani) that the red head-band of the Gomerans was dyed with the juice or roots of the *tajinaste* (*Echium* sp.); the historians mistook their blue-yielding plant for woad (*pastel* in Castillian). The clear yellow of the skins has not been identified but it is probable that the chestnut colour was obtained from lichens, in particular *Ramalina siliquosa*, used until recently in the Canaries (as *agicán*). Colouring matters abounded and, as will be seen, a valuable dye-lichen (*Roccella* spp., *orchilla* in Castillian) was one of the lures to the French conquerors. All aspects of dress-making, often described as of high quality, were in the hands of the women.

Important absences were the techniques of spinning and weaving, known in N. Africa by 4500 BC, at Fayum in Egypt for example. Some prehistoric Africans are known to have preferred leather to woven cloth, this hotter and less durable; after the conquest, skin cloaks went on into the sixteenth century at least. Moreover, the island goats were short-haired; goat-hair is anyway hard to work and perhaps, as at present in the islands, the original immigrants brought no tradition of spinning and weaving it. Some islands appear to have had sheep but these were not as common as goats; they too may have been kept for skins, meat and milk—it is now said that a mixture of goat and sheep milk gives the best cheese. Diego (1968a) avers that the early island sheep yielded no wool, without giving evidence. The present sheep, crosses, have short thick fleeces which give a little over a kilo of wool, after washing. Anyway, neither spindles nor looms have been found. Gran Canaria's vegetable fibres described as 'woven' (eg Diego 1961a) need examination.

ADORNMENTS

The ancient people took an interest in their appearance. It was never said that they were dirty; on Tenerife they washed often, including both before and after meals. It has been seen that they painted and tattoed their bodies, dyed their clothing. Though raw materials— stone, earth, wood, skin, bone, shell—were much the same across the islands, there is a good variety of three-dimensional ornament.

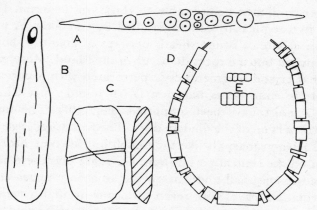

Figure 15   *Body ornaments: diadem of limpet-shells (about 40cm) on skin strip, Gran Canaria (a), wooden 'pendant', Palma (b, 13cm), stone plaque, Lanzarote (c, 6cm), bead necklace, clay, Tenerife (d), segmented beads, Tenerife (e)*

Nothing is known of Hierro's body ornaments. Gomera has yielded only some perforated seeds strung on a two-ply vegetable cord; the *tajinaste*-root red was used as a face or body paint by the women. Palma's peculiarity was a large 'pendant' of wood or stone (eg fibrolite), oval swelling below to pear-shaped (Fig. 15b); however, they look equally likely to have been fishing-net floats and weights. There were also circular beads of fibrolite. Hernández (1977) notes segmented clay beads, known otherwise only from Tenerife. In shell, there were pendants of limpet, necklaces of limpet-discs and of perforated *Trochus* and Columbella. Diego (1970) suggests a few 'polished' shell-discs were money, implausibly.

The segmented bead of fired clay had a wide distribution, in Africa being made up to the opening of the current colonial cycle; on Tenerife the bead has up to seven segments (Fig. 15e). Simpler and equally common clay beads were tubular and discoidal, also red-brown in colour; a necklace in which these alternated was popular (Fig. 15d). On Tenerife, both types were being made in the fifteenth century. Other Guanche beads were of polished stone, sliced tubular bone, holed fish vertebrae, small perforated *Conus*. There were also round plaques of shell. It was particularly the women, wrote Torriani, who wore the shells and other marine finds. Peculiar to Tenerife were angular strips of skin, again dyed yellow and chestnut, sewn to the clothing.

Gran Canaria, though usually presenting the more sophisticated culture, is poor in three-dimensional work — probably because of the popularity of tattooing, painting and printing; the granary seals, *pintaderas*, were used for this last too. Thus, the only good find is a 'diadem' (Fig. 15a), a strip of skin bearing ten large discs of shell, also found loose and then comparable to those on Tenerife. Otherwise there are five atypical ornaments studied by Garralda. A triangular pendant in calcite; a square bead, perhaps of goethite; both are of unknown origin but the rocks do occur in the island. More puzzling is a hexagonal crystal of green beryl, perforated with a perfect, cylindrical hole in spite of its hardness (7.5); found on a Guayadeque mummy, it must have been imported (Fig. 10f). The fourth is a baked-earth version of the diadem discs. The fifth (Fig. 10g), from the Cuesta de Silva granary, is like the fourth but for nine little pits in a circle around the central perforation; Garralda says these objects are also found in the shell-middens on the adjacent Sahara coast. The Moya 'divination' cave, with seven little pits around a central hole, comes to mind — it is close to the granary. More will be said about this when discussing the rotary quern.

Fuerteventura is notable for its distinctive shell plaques, attached to the people's clothing. Shapes were from square to rectangular, the longest having three holes. There were also necklaces of shell discs. The preferred raw material was a large *Conus* since parts of it are susceptible to being rubbed down to flat plaques. The 'diadem' found on Gran Canaria was recorded by Abreu for the two eastern islands — another close link if he is correct. A single Fuerteventura 'pendant' recalls those of Palma.

Lanzarote has produced unique grooved and polished flat stones, known in chalcedony, a coarse alabaster and basalt (Fig. 15c); it is not clear how, or even whether, they were worn. Dug Godoy (1972) refers, in a preliminary note, to shell adornments from her current Zonzamas excavations. This island has also yielded a barrel-shaped bead; possibly of fibrolite, it would then be a tenuous link with Palma.

As can be seen, there is little overlap even of the simplest forms. Further comparative work between the Canaries and N.W. Africa could be done on the more distinctive forms.

DOMESTICATED ANIMALS

Putting together the evidence of archaeology and of the chronicles, it seems likely that all islands had dogs and goats. It is usually very difficult to distinguish sheep bones from those of goats, other than by the horns and horn-cores, but Diego (1968a) claims to have excavated sheep remains in Tenerife. Abreu and Torriani record sheep on all islands except Gomera but Herrera (1965) says his island also had sheep. The pig has been present in excavations everywhere except the two eastern islands, though Abreu denied its existence in Tenerife — showing the caution needed in the interpretation of both archaeological material and the early reports. It should be recalled that dogs, pigs and goats all figured in pre-conquest beliefs, the first evil, the second an intermediary and the third good — but sheep apparently had no such role. The French of 1402 recorded 'wild dogs, like wolves, but smaller' on Gran Canaria; Abreu 'little dogs' on Tenerife. The French also distinguished wild from domesticated goats on Fuerteventura, the former doubtless the owned but free-roaming *guaniles*.

The only scientific study of the ancient animals has been by Zeuner (1958b), working on a mere seven Gran Canaria specimens (six from Guayadeque, one from the Cuesta de Silva). Two dog skulls suggested a primitive medium-sized animal like a small dingo; its modern representatives have reddish-yellow coats. A third skull was of a broader-faced dog, perhaps the ancestor of a current boxer-like animal, medium-sized, with drooping ears, dirty grey-brown in colour with a faint tiger-stripe. Zeuner described two other breeds now common in the Canaries, close to the Ibiza hound and the corgi.

Two goat skulls appeared to Zeuner to be of unevolved-mamber breed, still the most common in Gran Canaria and Palma; later (1963), he recorded a modified form on Tenerife (Las Cañadas). The breed is screw-horned, short-haired, brown with a wild stripe, this black, along the back, and its face and feet patterned in black and white. A horn core (Cuesta de Silva), yet more twisted, suggested a second type of primitive screw-horned goat. The Tenerife Museum holds horn-cores of one or other breed (Los Cabezazos, Tegueste).

A single pig-skull, with a long slender snout, belonged to a type similar to the small slender wild pig of the Mediterranean. This does not clash with Herrera's description of the Gomera 'wild' pig: between wild and domesticated species in shape, long in body with sharp-pointed snout, the adult male weighing 70 kilos.

Seven specimens from two sites on one island have thus suggested no less than five different breeds. Zeuner's conclusions cannot be extended beyond Gran Canaria.

Diego (1968a), making a thorough comparison of ancient and modern pastoralism in Tenerife, reached conclusions over the island's domesticated animals. The Llano de Maja shepherds' necropolis (Pl 8a) yielded the skull of a small fawn-coloured dog, mummified according to Diego. The goats, past and present, he divides into two breeds distinguished by their horns, straight-horizontal and curved-vertical. The first now keeps to the coast but the second is suited, by its horns, smaller udder and lighter build, for transhumance through the wooded level, lava fields and higher pastures; of course the practice of transhumance may be as responsible for the differentiation as the reverse. On the ancient sheep, attested only by Abreu—who supports himself with the Guanche word for the animal, *ana*—Diego supplies no acceptable evidence.

GRAIN CROPS

All that is known about land-tenure is that, on Tenerife, the holdings were given out by the leaders. Sowing, in the same island, was apparently in August (Abreu). Digging was generally done with wooden sticks, some tipped with goat-horns; sometimes the work was done communally. Irrigation was practised in places, on Gran Canaria by diverting streams into canals (Abreu). Harvesting probably varied widely with island, region and crop. On Gran Canaria only the ears of the grain were reaped. Threshing in the three eastern islands was with sticks and the feet, winnowing with the hands. It has been seen that there were granaries, common in at least the two main islands and on Gran Canaria sealed with personal stamps.

There is archeological evidence of barley on the two main islands and, in the chronicles, on the two eastern islands. Wheat has been

found in the stomach of an Acusa mummy, in a Guayadeque pot and
in other caves in Gran Canaria; the 1402 French recorded it here too,
and also, with 'other cereals', on Hierro, in need of confirmation.
Diego prefers Abreu's assertion that the Tenerife people had wheat
(*triguen*, suspiciously near the Castillian *trigo*) to Torriani and
Espinosa's denials of this—yet he has no archaeological support. Gran
Canaria grew beans, found in the caves; the chronicles recorded these
for Hierro and Tenerife too, with peas also on the last of these.

Grain distribution appears to place Tenerife with the eastern
islands, unusually. Barley, better suited to Canary conditions than
wheat, was the prime grain of the drier parts of N.W. Africa.

FRUIT TREES

Gran Canaria had figs, found at several ancient sites: Abreu gave two
names for them, *archormase* when green and *tehaunenen* when dried,
adding that the fig tree was probably introduced, by the captured
Mallorcans, not long before the conquest. The French found edible
dates on Gran Canaria and Fuerteventura, with olives, presumably
wild, on the latter.

Gomera is now renowned for its palm 'honey', an exudation from
cuts made in the top of the 'white'(?) palm (Herrera); this substance,
guarapo, is considered to have been a pre-conquest food. Maire (1690)
described the exact custom for the Senegal and it may be that, in fact,
the negro slaves of Gomera's sugar plantations brought in the idea;
but perhaps both the palm and the custom could be found in the
Maghreb.

WILD PLANTS

A consideration of the edible wild plants (eg Bramwell 1974a) suggests
that the early notes were scanty and haphazard. The general opinion
has been that the western islands grew no crops, providing their flour
needs from toasted and ground fern roots (*Pteridium aquilinum*,
Pteris arguta, *P. longifolia*). The Hierro people also ate the fruits of
the *mocan* (*Visnea mocanera*) and of the beech (*Myrica faya*), according to Darias. Abreu adds the sweet potato (*batata*) on Hierro,
perhaps meaning the yam, nowadays commonly cultivated in the wet
zones of the western islands. Food records for Palma also include the
seeds of the *amagante* (Hernández 1977: *Cistus symphytipholus*). It is
of course quite likely that these foods were widely eaten; Bramwell
records *Tamus edulis* (a yam) and the *Cistus* species as present now on
the five westernmost islands.

A similar range is recorded for the four easterly islands. Fern-root flour was eaten on Tenerife. One of this island's mummies had pine-seeds in its stomach. The *mocan* was also eaten in the two main islands, with the *bicacaro* berry (*Canarina canariensis*) on Gran Canaria (Abreu). Miscellaneous foods like salt (Lanzarote and Fuerteventura, according to the early French), honey (Tenerife, Abreu), lizards (Tenerife, Pellicer's excavation), and, doubtfully, rabbits (Verneau — but the animal had to be introduced to Madeira by the Europeans) may have been particularly wide in consumption.

FISHING

Shellfish were everywhere eaten. Fishing is evidenced by food remains in the caves and shell-heaps, with the rare piece of tackle. Chinama Cave (Taganana, N.E. Tenerife) has produced well-made 15cm hooks of wood and horn, a type found also on Gomera; according to Verneau, bone and shell hooks were also used. There are the possible net floats and sinkers from Palma.

In addition to angling with skin cords and hooks of goat bone and horn, the Gran Canaria people had several peculiar methods. Abreu: 'Their poor lived by the coast, chiefly on fish . . . caught in the night-time, by making a blaze on the water with torches of pitch-pine'. Traps were made of seaweeds, there were pens of stone (Marín). Thirdly, also Abreu: 'In the day-time, whenever they discovered a shoal . . . a great number of men, women and children waded into the sea, and swimming beyond the shoal, chased the fish towards the shore; then with a net . . . they enclosed and drew them to land, and there made an equal division'. Putting several accounts together, it is found that the key artefact, the net, was squarish, hung on a long pole and had stone weights on the bottom; it was made of a tough rush, dyed brown, or of palm; Torriani compared it to those in use on the Lombardy rivers.

Similar techniques have been summarized elsewhere (Mercer 1976) for the adjacent Sahara coast. In 1506 the Portuguese Valentim Fernandes recorded the use of nets of bark-fibre (*Leptadenia* sp) with floats of euphorbia wood and fired-clay weights. The nets were attached at each end to staffs and then 'the men go two and two to fish . . . they tie their two nets together, and, as soon as they see the fish . . . approach from either side, letting the net unroll gradually between them until they reach the shore. This takes place in shallow water . . .'. A mere ten years ago these people, the Imraguen — the W. Sahara's lowest caste, again a point of comparison with Abreu — were still fishing in this way. Anthonioz (1968) describes how the people watch for shoals, then attract the littoral's dolphins by beating the water with sticks — imitating the jumping of mullet, probably — and then wade or swim in a circle around the fish, these keeping inshore for fear of the dolphins. A good session could bring three or four tons of mullet and meagres, landed with the help of the women and children. But before linking the Canaries to the Sahara coast by their similar fishing techniques, it needs to be considered whether the method is not simply so basic as to have once been common to the whole coast of N.W. Africa; as a primitive version of the *madrague* it may have been practised on the Mediterranean shores two millennia ago.

Abreu said the people of the two eastern islands, good swimmers, used to kill fish with sticks; probably this means after they had been hemmed in, perhaps with delicate nets. A method believed ancient, described to the author on Fuerteventura, was to pour euphorbia juice into rock pools, this stupefying the fish, then collected up by hand. This island also had traps, perhaps pre-conquest.

The Fuerteventura country people had the custom, still current when the author was there, of regularly migrating—with animals, bedding and cooking-pots—to the shores, living there in lean-to shanties. Their time was spent fishing and collecting shellfish, a part being taken to the villages. Two points may be made. First, that this rich phase of the pre-conquest year's diet—assuming such migration to have been common throughout the Canaries—has not been taken into account by those who say the ancient people went short of vitamins. Second, it was the custom in the Sahara for the interior, dominant-class nomads—dependent otherwise on their goats and camels—to go to the coast about February, there to gorge themselves on the fish-hauls of the Imraguen and other tributary tribes. Another vestige of an ancient and perhaps remotely related practice, in the islands, was the seasonal migration of the pre-conquest Tenerife and, perhaps, Gran Canaria chiefs between coast and mountain. On the former, the elite went in procession, the chief with his staff of office, *añepa*, those he encountered abasing themselves and wiping the dust off his feet with their clothing.

There was of course no fishing from boats in the Canaries, no more than on the Sahara coast. Naturally, if the first islanders were Berbers from the Maghreb mountains, they would know little about fishing and have to develop their own techniques, limited to inshore work, as the midden species have shown (Serra 1957).

FOOD PREPARATION

Animal slaughter was carried out, at least on Gran Canaria, by an outcast group. It was seen earlier how, to become a noble, a youth had not to have tended or killed animals. The butchers were not to mix with other people or even touch their belongings—objects to be singled out involved pointing with a stick, always at a distance. As a recompense, the outcasts were publicly provided with all they needed. By law, all animals had to be killed in the public shambles (? ritually).

'Their method of obtaining fire, was by taking a stick of dry, hard, thorny wood, which they caused to turn rapidly round on the point, with a soft, dry, spongy thistle, and so set it on fire: this method has been used there to this day' (Abreu, on the two eastern islands). Verneau noted not only this rotation but also an up-down or lengthways movement of the hard stick. Lighting was done with sticks of resinous pine, frequently found stuck in the walls of caves; the method has lasted into this century. The pre-conquest people also used lamps of fired clay.

Food was eaten simply. Cooked meats; milk, butter and cheese; meal mixed with honey and fruit. The oven was a hole in the ground covered with stone slabs, the fire upon these. Butter and cheese were made by putting the milk in a bag and swinging it to and fro between two people; the cheese was probably shaped on a runnelled slab of stone.

Fermented drinks were made of the *mocan* berry on Hierro and Gran Canaria, of the palm exudation on Gomera. No other liquors or forms of drugs have been recorded—perhaps life on the Fortunate Isles required neither escape nor the artificial stimulus of consciousness.

The only distinctive food preparation was the universal grilling of the grains—barley, wheat, *amagante* and probably others—prior to grinding them into a meal. The fern roots were treated in the same way, grilled and pounded up. The result, *gofio*, was a pre-cooked flour which could thus be eaten cold. It could then be carried in a skin, *zurrón*, on a shepherd's back and, when he was hungry, all he needed to do was to splash in a little water, knead a ball with his hand and eat it. On Hierro, the newly-born were fed on the bracken-root flour mixed with butter (*aguamanes*). Today *gofio* is still a staple of the Canary working class. In times of famine a vast range of crop and wild plants are turned into *gofio*. Soon after the Civil War, Diego made a useful study of the harvesting of *Mesembryanthemum crystallinum*, then being eaten as *gofio de vidrio* in Tenerife. As *barilla*, the raw material of the soda-export trade, it was the centre of controversy between starving islanders and would-be exporters in the period 1750–1850. Bramwell treats the plant as introduced, however.

A few aspects are distinctive enough to merit comparison with Africa. Butchery has always been outcast work—in the *rif* it is even now done by negroes. Barley-meal is a Maghreb staple. In the W. Sahara, as *bulegoma*, it is prepared just as *gofio* (Mercer 1976); there too famine brings in the substitutes, including the *barilla*-like *Aizoon theurkauffi*.

MEDICINE

Archaeological evidence has been seen, on the skulls, of trepanning and scarifying. On Tenerife, bleeding was practised. The two main islands obtained an astringent, *chacherquen*, from *Visnea mocanera*, a tree valuable in many ways. Medicinal herbs are mentioned for the two eastern islands.

The most important single medicine on Hierro and the three eastern islands was goat or sheep butter. This was rubbed on the patient or used as a cautery, applied hot with a beaten rush, on an open wound. In the east it was believed that the butter gained in supernatural potency the longer it was stored. In Fuerteventura vast quantites of it were buried, in enormous jars, for this reason. Already by Abreu's time (1600) so much had come to light that he found it noteworthy. Zeuner had a study of this island's butter under way at his death. During the author's stay on Fuerteventura, a jar almost a metre high was said to have been found, in a round pit lined with stones, near Antigua. This distinctive custom may well have African parallels.

CHAPTER TEN

Women: Customs, Work and Tools

Much of the previous chapter consisted of a little archaeological evidence explained or enlarged upon by the early writers. This and the next chapter have a converse origin: the first Europeans said little about the islanders' artefacts but, luckily, these have been found in quantity.

SOCIAL STATUS OF WOMEN

With the early chronicles all written by men—and mostly priests at that—it is hardly possible to see life from the women's point of view. The material remains suggest their lives were comparatively full, for example against those of Arab women in recent centuries. Though the matriarchy proposal cannot be taken seriously on the limited evidence, the history of the conquests will show that much notice was paid to the women's opinions. As outstanding examples, there was a mother and daughter soothsaying partnership in Fuerteventura; the politically powerful Andamana, occupant of the Painted Cave, on Gran Canaria; the Palma woman who mediated between the *conquistadores* and the islanders and, seeing them enslaved as a result, went to law on their behalf on the Peninsula. The existence of nuns on Gran Canaria can be seen in various lights—but their leader, a noblewoman, was able to intervene to save the lives of 80 Spanish caught during the invasion. However, even if some Palma women were good fighters—the report on the conquest of the island does not give them a role in the battles, however—their normal function in the Canaries' conflicts was to back up their menfolk with food and medical attention.

Hernández (1952b) said marriages on Gran Canaria gave occasion to public feasts lasting fifteen days. For Lanzarote the limit of information is that polyandry was the custom, each woman having up to three husbands. At the opposite extremes, the Hierro men may have had several wives (Torriani) though it was also said they were monogamous (Abreu). A single spouse was the rule in the two main islands. Where blood restrictions were recorded, it was usually that a man was not to marry his mother or his sister—linking with the high incidence of cousin marriage at present; however, the elite males probably married their sisters if no one else of their class was available. On Hierro there was bride-price: the father was given some animals. The Tenerife man gave nothing for his bride. And on Gran Canaria the bride's family had to fatten her up to be socially correct, putting her apart for thirty days and stuffing her with milk and *gofio*, superficially not a sign of female freedom; it was in fact supposed to enlarge the womb and thus aid child-bearing. No justification has been noted for the Gran Canaria nobles' first night with virgins on the eve of marriage, though these women may have had the right to choose amongst the nobles (Bernáldez). This, incidentally, is a factor in the distribution of the Mediterranean-elite physique overlooked by Schwidetsky . . . nor, clearly, was class-distinction ultimately sacrosanct.

On Tenerife, a man could send his wife away at will, keeping the children himself; these were then, however, considered illegitimate, doubtless to allow those of his next wife to take precedence. On Gomera, belongings passed on death to a man's sisters' sons, since sexual relations were easy-going, to the extent of wives being loaned to strangers as a mark of hospitality. In spite of Tenerife's divorce custom, women were there treated with great respect in one way: if a man met a woman in a lonely place, he was to turn away, Torriani saying that even to speak to her against her will brought death.

The material evidence suggests that women had scope for creativity in their lives. Personal adornment was imaginative. As the preparers of skin clothing, as makers of mats and ropes, as the potters and, on Gran Canaria, the painters of the caves and houses, the women had ample possibilities for expression. Where they worked for their neighbours—as did the men who were cave-cutters and carpenters—they were paid in kind. Skin clothing and house decoration have already been described—the women's remaining work, with their personal tools, will take up the rest of this chapter.

GRINDING STONES

These fell into three types. A large flattish slab of stone with one lightly-concave surface; upon it was used a heavy roller-like stone. Second, a stone dish, normally elongated, occasionally round (Tenerife), used with a fitting rounded cobble; the museums have these from the two main islands and from Palma (Hernández, 1977, thinks these last may be from Gran Canaria, in fact). One or the other type would be needed to pound up grilled roots so that these tools ought to be found in all the western islands at least; however, since the roots are still eaten perhaps the dish-querns are still valued by the rural people. These tools are also suitable for preparing colourings

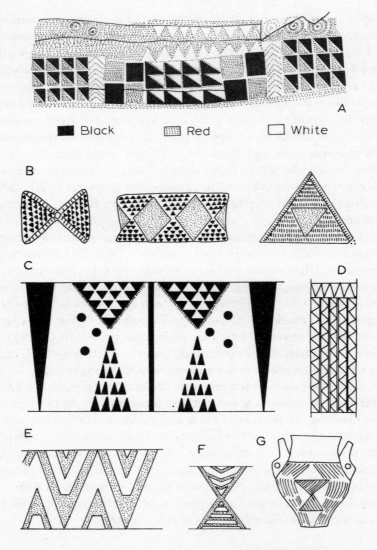

Figure 16   *Triangles, Gran Canaria: Wall decoration, Painted Cave (a, after Beltrán 1974), clay stamps (b, after Alcina 1956), pot decoration, El Agujero tumulus (c, after González 1973), club decoration, Guayadeque (d, also Fig. 19g), pot decoration (ef), pot, El Agujero tumulus (g, 23cm, after El Museo Canario guide, 1958)*

and pot-making materials. These three uses in turn imply that only querns from controlled excavations can be said to be of certain prehistoric age.

Sooner or later the rotary quern, the third type, came into use on all islands — those of the west may have originally made them for grinding up the wild seeds. This tool consists of two round stones; the lower, unmoving, is made or fitted with an upwards projection at its centre, the pivot, upon which fits the hole in the middle of the upper stone; pits on the surface of the latter take the turning sticks or the grinder's fingers. One stick, especially if crank-shaped and steadied overhead, allows a continuous forward motion; otherwise work is usually backwards and forwards with two sticks, one in each hand. The grain, dribbled in through the centre hole, drops down round the pivot and, ground, is ejected from between the two stones on to the skin upon which the quern is worked.

Diego (1968a) visited a quern-quarry in the Cañada de Pedro Méndez (Tenerife). A V-groove was used to separate the embryo quern from its parent lava-block; the central hole was biconical, being worked from each side. No real study of the rotary querns has been made but a glance at the collections shows there was a wide variety. Many from Las Cañadas are markedly domed. A main division would be between flat and collared querns, the latter perhaps with the more turning holes. Tiny querns, toy or votive perhaps, were made on the two main islands.

Other possible links with pre-conquest belief have been discerned. There is the Palma quern relatable to the spiral engravings (Fig. 10i). Another quern (Fig. 10e) had nine 'turning' pits, associable with the 'divination' cave and the baked-clay adornment (Fig. 10g), both of N.W. Gran Canaria and respectively with seven and nine pits around a central hole. That a number of other Canary querns have more holes than is essential — though none was seen with so many — does not clarify the matter. Since odd numbers are considered lucky in N.W. Africa — where at least the pitted ornament occurs — it might be worth considering how many Canary querns have an even number of 'turning' holes.

The dish-quern is undateable. The rotary quern was only invented just before the time of Christ, and then in the Middle East, so that it would have taken a while to reach the Canaries. Its arrival in the islands cannot thus be earlier than the first millenium. Pellicer (1976) reported its presence in Arena Cave (Tenerife) about the second century AD. This carries with it the partial dating for the spiral cult and, tentatively, for a divination-pit practice; as a result, study could be made of the lay-out of the hundreds of pits in the floors of the Gran Canaria caves and platforms (Table 32), together with an examination of the collections of artefacts in search of associated patterns in both functional and decorative work.

STAMPS OF BAKED EARTH

These occurred almost entirely on Gran Canaria; most were of fired clay, some were of wood. One has been found on Palma, carved out of volcanic tuff. Pellicer (1971a) mentions finds on Lanzarote (Malpaís de la Corona) and Fuerteventura (Cueva de los Idolos). The designs (Fig. 16b) consist mainly of triangles, chevrons and concentric circles; in outline, 37% are rectangular, 23% round, 20% square, 15% triangular, 5% varied (Alcina 1956). Most taper up into a handle, this often with a suspension hole.

These *pintaderas* are clearly to be placed with the geometrically-painted caves, idols and still-undescribed pottery. Traces of 'ochre' may show some at least to have been used for impressing coloured patterns though the French (1402–4) referred to the emblems 'cut' on the islanders' bodies and Ca da Mosto (1455) said that 'both men and women paint their skins green, red and yellow with plant juices'. Comparable stamps used for body printing have been cited, by various writers, for W. Africa and the Mediterranean. As granary seals, comparisons have been made with similar artefacts of Berber tribes in Morocco and Algeria (Crawford, Marcy). The Valerón granary (Cuesta de Silva), the finding-pace of a *pintadera*, is at the centre of the region of geometric decoration.

The *pintadera* also occurred in Mexico, the artefact thus amongst the links hazarded by archaeology between the Mediterranean and the pre-Columbus Americas. The winds and currents may also have taken across mummification and trepanation; Mourant (part of Roberts' team) has suggested the S. American blood groups may show a Canary contribution.

USE OF VEGETABLE FIBRES

The best available materials were palm (*Phoenix canariensis*), rush (*Luzula* spp, not now on Lanzarote and Fuerteventura) and sedge (*Carex* spp — Bramwell seems uncertain of their presence in the two eastern islands). Some uses have already been described: as a mummy shroud and as a cord to tie the corpse on the bier, as clothing, including the thread for stitching it together, as a fishing net.

Gran Canaria has provided almost all the evidence, with the craft probably at its most developed there. Abreu said the people had baskets (*carianas*) and mats of palm-leaves and rushes, 'made extremely neat, and very ingeniously wrought. There were . . . people whose sole occupation was to . . . manufacture mats'. To make the rush 'coats' they took the plant and beat it until it was quite soft like flax, and then divided the filaments and wove(?) them together. The cords were made by flat or spiral plaiting. The containers ranged from stiff baskets to flexible bags. One of the last basketmakers of Fuerteventura, visited at Sta. Inés by the author (1973, plate on p. 144), made all these goods, except the coats.

POTTERY

More has been written on this than upon any subject other than the islanders' physiques. The main studies are Diego (1971, highly detailed) and González (1971) for Tenerife; Jiménez (1958) and González (1973) for Gran Canaria; Hernández (1977) for Palma. The first four are simply subjective classifications of shapes, decoration and so on, unassociated with stratification or other excavated evidence. The fifth groups its subjects into a sequence based on stratification at four of the sites already discussed in Chapter 8 — and, as stated, until these are fully published, Hernández's sequence cannot be assessed.

Only the broadest sketch of the Canaries' pots can be given here. Knowledge of Hierro's pottery is limited to a few sherds, such as the coarse specimen from Diego's altar excavation in the Julan. Gomera has produced undistinctive pots, from near-ovoids to hemispheres and of an extreme simplicity; similar vessels occurred on Tenerife, alongside much more striking pottery. Diego (1971) links Hierro and Gomera to Tenerife by their wooden bowls, respectively Fig. 19n (La Dehesa, juniper), Fig. 19m (handle like a scallop or fish-tail) and the beautiful Fig. 19l (San Miguel).

No complete pot has been published for Lanzarote. Verneau's notes on the sherds associated with the *casas hondas* (Masdache), the collection in Tenerife's museum (Fámara, Haría, Zonzamas) and Dug Godoy's preliminary note (1972, Zonzamas) show the decoration was broadly similar to that of Fuerteventura's pottery. A technical study (Rosenfeld) of Zonzamas sherds collected by Zeuner's group requires further comparable investigations to become of value.

Understanding, then, has to come primarily through the vessels of the other four islands. The picture which will emerge is of a likely common basis in Fuerteventura (and thus probably Lanzarote), Gran Canaria and Tenerife: an ovoid form and an incised decoration built on the straight stroke. Ovoid vessels with incised ornament have been made in N.W. Africa since pottery first reached the region as a Neolithic characteristic. Gran Canaria had also a completely-different style, ranging widely in shape and painted in various colours; this is the pottery with the geometric designs which have been already encountered in the painted caves, idols and stamps. Palma's pottery will be seen to be distinct, consisting notably of shallow bowls with inverted rims, the decoration of incised festoons made of concentric semicircles; the straight-line ornament, different in overall pattern from that in the eastern province, is placed at the recent end of Hernández's sequence.

Fuerteventura's pots, to give a little more detail now, have as their simplest form a truncated ovoid (Fig. 17a), plain or incised with

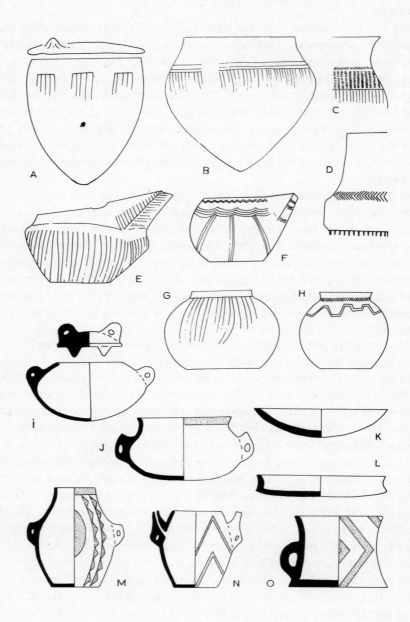

Figure 17 *Pottery (heights given). Fuerteventura (sites unknown): plain ovoid with travertine lid (a, about 75cm), shouldered (b, about 70cm, and c) and collared (d) ovoids, milking pots (ef, 19cm, 16cm), showing simple (abeg) and advanced (cdfh) decoration. Gran Canaria painted ware (after González): globular, Arguineguín (i, 9cm), globular, Gáldar (j, 10cm), bowl, Sta. Brígida (k, 4cm), bowl, Gáldar (l, 3cm), barrel-shaped, Gáldar (m, 30cm), double-spouted, Gáldar (n, 14cm), cup, Gáldar (o, 11cm)*

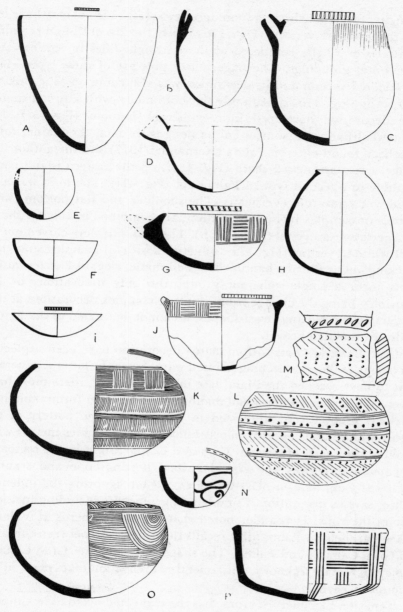

Figure 18   Pottery (heights given). Tenerife (after Diego 1971): plain ovoid,
Las Cañadas (a, 41cm), handled ovoid, Cañada de las Mostazas (b, 23cm),
spouted globular pot, simple decoration, Arico (c, 19cm), handle-spout,
Cañada Blanca (d, 15cm), globular, La Guancha (e, 14cm), bowl, Cañada de
la Mareta (f, 9cm), scoop, simple decoration, Arico (g, 6cm), pear-shaped,
south of island (h, 33cm), bowl, Cañada de la Mareta (i, 5cm), lugged,
Cañada de Pedro Méndez (j, 25cm). Palma bowls (after Hernández 1977,
except m): straight-line decoration, site unknown (k, 13cm), line and dot,
Barlovento (k, size not given), line and dot, Fuerteventura (m, 4cm),
meander, Roque de la Campana (n, 3cm), festoons, site unknown (o, 14cm),
straight-line, La Cucaracha (p, 11cm)

hanging fringe-like lines; a shouldered type (Fig. 17b, c) may have led
to the collared version (Fig. 17d), with the decoration becoming
partially or wholly composed of short straight lines in vertical and
horizontal groupings. The huge butter pots are of these types. The
shouldered version and its decoration was also common as a milking
pot, *tofio* (Fig. 17e, f)—suitably flat-bottomed—with a broad spout;
the decoration developed into exuberant festoons (Fig. 17f, h),
somewhat like the favourite Palma designs. In fact, the plainer *tofio*
has been found once on Palma (Hernández 1977) and the author has
come across an incised sherd (Fig. 18m) on the eastern island comparable to a second type of Palma pot (Fig. 18l). The *tofio* was also
made on Lanzarote (Verneau). The shoulder and flat bottom, with
simple or complex incised decoration, are combined in another shape
of Fuerteventura vessel (Fig. 17g, h). The pots' lids were carved out of
soft white travertine (Fig. 17a), sometimes with an included stone left
sticking out as a lifting handle. The well-made, elegant Fuerteventura
pots form a single coherent group, the only innovation—or in-
cursion—being the change from simple to complex decoration: as this
occurs on the existing vessel-shapes, it cannot be treated as the sign of
a drastic social upheaval.

Gran Canaria's pots with indented decoration have been neglected
in favour of the eye-catching painted ware. Since the latter is generally
felt to have reached the island late in its prehistory, there must have
been common and widespread manufacture of earlier forms—plain or
incised, grooved and impressed in decoration. The pottery of the
central mountains appears poorly known. Jiménez notes incised ware
around the coast, at Arucas, Guía and Gáldar, right in the region of
the painted pottery; he also described herring-bone and stabbed
patterns from San Nicolás. González, all but ignoring the indented
ware, says its decoration is simple and geometric, including incisions
along the rims. Hernández noted that impressed sherds at Valerón
have parallels on Palma; this recalls the other links between this area
of Gran Canaria and Palma. The shapes of the earlier Gran Canaria
pots will remain unknown until scientific excavation takes place in the
mountain caves.

Tenerife, like Fuerteventura, has the truncated ovoid as its simplest
shape (Fig. 18a), this becoming rounder (Fig. 18e) and also more
bowl-like (Fig. 18f). A vertical or angled handle was very common,
often partially perforated lengthways to avoid cracking when drying
out (Fig. 18b). Bowls with pourers or pourer-handles were also
standard pots (Fig. 18c, d). Some pots have two solid or two pourer
handles, others one of each. All shapes also existed with only small
lugs as handles (Fig. 18j). There were also very shallow bowls (Fig. 18i)
and scoops (Fig. 18g). A single pot of particular interest is a bag-

shaped vessel marked 'S. Tenerife' (Fig. 18h)—its distinctive form
recalls one from Ain Hanish, W. Sahara.

Tenerife's indented decoration is partially similar (Fig. 18c) to the
simpler work on Fuerteventura. Diego (1964a) lists numerous incised-
pottery sites, spread all over Tenerife. The western island also had an
unemphatic 'advanced' stage of decoration seen only on sherds (Diego
1971); this consisted of groups of small indentations, circular
and crescentic, and perhaps a somewhat-similar development to the
short straight-stroke compositions in the eastern island. Although
indented ornamentation was never popular on Tenerife (nor is any
other decoration known), there was a distinctive aspect, the illustrated
incising or toothing of the rim: this occurs on examples of all shapes of
pot and thus suggests a unity and continuity for the craft on Tenerife.

The only useful dating evidence on Tenerife comes from Pellicer's
Arena Cave (1971, 1976), reported sealed soon after the second
century AD. On the surface there was an unperforated lug exteriorly
like that on Fig. 18c, a feature still being made at the time of the
conquest (Diego 1971). The upper levels produced sherds from large
hemispherical pots, some with pinched lugs, in shape much like Fig.
18j; there was also the spout of a *tofio*, better known from Fuerteventura and, again, implying a common origin for the people of
different islands. There were however no sherds from conical-based
pots. The radiocarbon dating for the pottery levels was second-century
AD.

Palma's commonest shape of pot is a broad rounded bowl with
inturned, even angular rim. The incised decoration covers most or all
of the pot. It is of two kinds. The straight stroke: unbroken horizontal
lines between which there may be vertical or oblique lines or stabbed
dots and dashes (Fig. 18k, l). The festoon made up of concentric semicircles, around the upper half of the bowl, perhaps with wavy
horizontal lines filling the zones between the festoons (Fig. 18o). A
more globular pot, similarly festooned, is held by Palma's museum
whilst the Roque de la Campana cave (Diego 1970) yielded much the
same shape of vessel with an incised meander over its lower half (Fig.
18n). As noted, the straight-stroke decoration is the same as elsewhere
in its elements but different in their composition; similarly, festoon
work occurred also in Fuerteventura but again the overall result is
different. As on Gran Canaria and Tenerife, a good number of the
rims of these Palma types bear straight incised strokes. Two other
peculiar forms have been found on Palma: a single, grooved *tofio* and
two funnels, these covered in ornament, one incised, the other
grooved, the themes as on the pots.

Diego has produced a relative sequence of Palma pottery, based on
his 1956 Belmaco Cave work (still unpublished) and his investigation

of Roque de la Campana Cave (1970, excavated pre-1956). As far as can be made out, the earliest pot-type is held to be plain, red or greyish, conical. Of intermediate age is a shallow 'bell-shaped' vessel (with lugs at Belmaco), fawn or reddish, the decoration grooved; this is contemporary with the spirals and associated engravings. Lastly, a hemispherical pot, black, with incised decoration. The intermediate and latest forms also have decorated rims. No illustrations have been published: no accessible Palma pots are 'conical' nor clearly 'bell-shaped'. Yet so little stratification has been recorded in the Canaries that this data has to be given.

Hernández (1977) considers the shallow bowls (Fig. 18k, l, referred to as 'semi-circular') with incised straight-stroke decoration to be the most recent Palma type. Next in his sequence come those bowls, both shallow and deep ('globular'), with grooved festoons and, once, an incised meander (Fig. 18n, o). The earliest type, he feels, is a shallow, angular-cornered bowl ('cylindrical'): one he illustrates has grooved vertical lines meeting on the circumference of a circle placed in the middle of the base, another has, in addition, broken horizontal lines between the vertical strokes (Fig. 18p); it is not clear how common (and thus representative) this type is, but there are none in the island museum.

The same excavator linked Palma's pot-types to the island burial practices. His 'earliest' bowl (Fig. 18p), is found with the cremation rite. The 'latest' (Fig. 18k, l) occurred with plain burial; so too, though less often, did the 'intermediate-age' form (Fig. 18o).

One of the most interesting aspects of Palma's vessels is the occurrence amongst their decoration of the concentric circles and, once, of a meander such as typify the island's rock engravings. Both Diego and Hernández have seen such pots as of intermediate age, providing a hint as to the period of currency of the 'art'; the only other evidence on this is the incised quern, itself not earlier than the Christian era.

The second major grouping is that of the Gran Canaria painted ware. The commonest pot is in a variety of barrel shapes with degrees of neck and bellying (Figs. 17m, n). Spouts were common (Fig. 17n); there was also partial perforation as in Tenerife. Typical also were flat bowls (Fig. 17k, l). It was rare for a pot not to have one or two handles; these often have holes, either for hanging (Fig. 17i, j, m, n) or large enough to take the hand (Fig. 17o). Lids were highly evolved: holed lugs on top with more protruberances (Fig. 17i) or a rim-groove, underneath, to stop the lid from slipping off.

The painting is basically red, this wholly or partially covering the vessel; red with black is also common; red with white and all-black are each rare. The designs are complex: primarily the triangle (Figs. 16, 17), to a lesser degree right-angled and curved forms. However, the triangle is often itself part of a composition, this in turn either a triangle or a chevron; it is obvious that the triangle fascinated the potters. The basal decoration, satisfyingly symmetrical, consisted of circles enclosing star-shaped designs (Jiménez: heavenly bodies). According to González, no lids were painted. As on Tenerife and Palma, tiny versions of the pots are found, use unknown.

González's distribution map shows the painted ware to occur right around the coast but not in the mountains. However, a walk through the highlands suggests this may be a *lacune de connaissance*, though it may be comparatively-rare there. An important link with the large tumuli came when the Agujero tomb, probably used over a long period, yielded a red-ware pot (Fig. 16g).

Various workers (Zeuner 1966, Crawford, González 1973) have seen similarities between the painted ware and the pots now made by the Berbers of the Maghreb. Their toothed or fringed triangle occurs on the island pots (Fig. 16c), though woven cloth—believed the origin of the decoration in Africa—did not reach the Canaries. The geometric non-representational aspect again suggests Islam. Zeuner drew attention to the pots' possible imitation of the hammer-dents and shine of metal vessels, also suggested by the sharp profile of the cup-shaped forms (Fig. 17o); this sub-division might be the result of late pre-conquest trading or other contact with N.W. Africa, then copied by the island potters, apparently not averse to change at this time. The preferred fourteenth-century Catalan origin has already been discussed.

Alcina (1958) considered the pourer-handles of both Gran Canaria and Tenerife (the catalogue of the latter's museum lists spouts from Palma too). He draws comparisons with Iberian and Mexican pots going back to the end of the second millenium BC. Alcina did not discuss the presence of the device as part of two (perhaps three) markedly different Canary pottery groupings. The symbolist Jiménez sees male and female sexual representations in the various spouts and handles of the Gran Canaria ware.

The potters' techniques have been reconstructed by the four authors and by Zeuner (1960), drawing on their observations at some of the archipelago's remaining workshops. On Gran Canaria, these are or were until recently at Agaete, Atalaya, Guía, and San Bartolomé; on Tenerife, at San Andrés, Candelaria, San Miguel, Arguayo and La Victoria; on Lanzarote, El Mogón; Hernández does not name the workshop he studied on Palma; on Gomera, Chipude still has potters; on Fuerteventura the author visited the last potter, in retirement, at Sta. Inés. It seems that, out of all these workshops, the only one to have been recently making pots of notably pre-conquest shape was that of Fuerteventura. The potter, her features close to the

Cromagnoid pole, was photographed holding her last, undecorated *tofio* or milking pot (Mercer 1973, plate on p. 144). Some of these workshops may still be in existence.

The early historians coincide in that pot-making — at the time of the conquest at least — was specialist work on the two main islands. The potters were women, as up to the present everywhere in the Canaries; Marín said the nuns of Gran Canaria were amongst them. The earth, collected from special quarries (Sta. Inés: yellow soil at Majuelo) was sieved and then ground on one or other type of quern. The grogs have been little studied; Marín says the *harimaguadas* mixed in sand, Diego has identified volcanic ash and vegetable matter, this including bracken-fronds and grass-stalks. Large amounts of clay are nowadays kneaded with the feet. Construction of the pot was by the coiled technique — without a wheel, that is. Smoothing was with a spatulate tool, such as the bone artefacts described in the next chapter. On Fuerteventura, the potter used a hollow-edged scrap of iron for the convexities and varied pieces of sharp-edged wood for the concavities; on Palma a knife is now used, on Gran Canaria a bamboo scraper. After a few hours drying, the pot was given a first burnishing with water-worn pebbles.

At this point at least the painted ware had special treatment. Sedeño's notes (1484) show that it then existed alongside a coarser ware, such as cooking pots. González suggests the 'hammer dents' were made with the spatula. The colour appears to have been applied as a slip before firing or as a paint afterwards. Zeuner said the red soil used was probably that of old land surfaces baked by later lava-flows; an alternative was one of the roterde soils of the laurel forests. Finely ground, the soil was mixed with water (Jiménez: fat added to help adhesion and to bring up the colour), this now replaced by paraffin (Zeuner, on Atalaya). The paint was next applied to the pot. Once dry again, the pot was burnished a second time, producing a glaze-like finish. The last Canary workshops all give their vessels a bath of red ochre but the techniques used produce a coarser finish than that of the ancient Gran Canaria painted ware.

Lastly, the firing, the pots having been shade-dried for perhaps a week. The Fuerteventura potter used to arrange her vessels on four stones, in a line, then covered them with wood and set the whole 'bonfire kiln' alight. The pots emerged a rich red-chestnut, with black smudges and bars where burning wood had lain against them. Hernández (1977) notes a sandy ravine-bed as chosen, on Palma, for a similar firing technique; however, the resulting, oxidized pots are quite unlike the ancient island pottery in appearance, as has been noted generally. Marín describes 'a hole in the ground covered with sand and a great fire on top' for Gran Canaria. Herrera refers to ovens of stone and mud on Gomera. Diego says that, on Tenerife, caves were used in addition to open-air firing; the pots were placed with their mouths downwards.

Looked at overall again, the archipelago's known pottery appears most likely to fall into three groups. A founding implantation, in the four easterly islands at least, of vessels based on the ovoid and with incised decoration; perhaps a different original type on Palma, in need of clarification. Development on the opening types, again peculiar on Palma. A late phase, the painted ware, on Gran Canaria. There is no precise dating evidence for any Canary pottery. Amongst Zeuner's unfinished projects was to get an age by remanent magnetism for the Tara idol; thermoluminescence dating would be possible on suitably-preserved sherds. The bulk of the Canary pottery can be parallelled by vessels made over the last two millenia in N.W. Africa; the red ware of Gran Canaria may be of Berber or even N.W. Iberian inspiration.

CHAPTER ELEVEN

Men's Tools and Weapons

The main work of the men was to look after the flocks; crop-growing was only a seasonal task. Those men who lived on the coast, upon the poorer land, supplemented the family diet with fish. Specialization is recorded only in cave cutting and carpentry. Each man was able to make and use a wide range of tools and weapons.

Metal artefacts, never found if occasionally suspected, could not have been made in the Canaries for lack of ores. In the Maghreb the Berbers anyway used their Neolithic tools into the Roman period. In the interior of the Maghreb, metal-working has always been greatly in the hands of the negroes.

BONE AND HORN TOOLS

Two described uses of horn have been as the working end of the digging tool in the eastern province and as a fish-hook in the central islands. Its third use was as a reinforcement for the tips of the shepherds' travelling poles (Pl. 16), described shortly.

Skin-working required bone points for piercing, these usually made on goat metacarpals and metatarsals; on Palma and Tenerife at least the tips were protected by tubes of bone, pig on the second island. The sewing was done with needles made out of bone splinters; fish and palm spines were sometimes used.

Spatulate tools from Gran Canaria, Tenerife and Palma may have been used for softening skins as well shaping the pots. Siemen's comparison (1969) of these to the bull-roarers of Australia and elsewhere simply underlines how little is known of the pre-conquest rituals; the bull-roarer, on a cord, is swung around the head to make a mysterious noise during initiation ceremonies—the Canary spatulate does have a hole in one end, not yet explained and unlike, say, the bone points. A pendant is always a last-resort explanation—bone was used as an adornment.

Torriani wrote of the use of goat-bone in the quarrying of dwellings, on Gran Canaria, into the tuff and the earth. Possibly, as in primitive Europe, the shoulder blades were used as shovels.

THE DOMESTIC USE OF WOOD

The professional carpenters were on Gran Canaria. The archipelago's wood-working techniques, unstudied, depended greatly on stone tools with perhaps some use of fire in the preliminary stages of large-size work.

Torriani noted 'little doors of palm-wood' worked with stone axes (adzes?), on Gran Canaria; there were also the partitions and the panelling. An adze would also have been used to make the archipelago's bier-planks (Fig. 12e). Those from Guarazoca (Hierro) may have been first split off with a wedge; one was fire-hardened on one face and inscribed on the other. This is one of the sites where the use of a metal tool has been proposed, on a plank and an associated goat-skull; the C14 age, about 900 AD, would lead one to expect the cuts to be due to sharp stone tools. On Gran Canaria there were also the planks for the tumuli cists to be roughly hewn, together with the occasional dug-out coffin — and, the largest work, Torriani's otherwise unrecorded dug-out boat.

More delicate carving was done with small sharp stones. Nothing is known of this work in the two eastern islands. The other five all had wooden pots (Fig. 19l, m, n), on the two largest with spoons, Tenerife a ladle too; bark lids were made on Gran Canaria. On each main island the women had wooden combs, one poorly decorated with lines of dots; on Tenerife they used wooden needles. Apart from its wooden fish-hooks, Gomera has produced wooden buttons — square, round and oval — recalling those of Tenerife in shell. It seems worth noting that, on Gran Canaria, most of these small wooden finds are from the mountains.

Craft rather than art usually describes the Canary woodwork, this rarely transcending the everyday plane. The milking tray (Fig. 11g) from Gran Canaria, on the well-worn sex and libation themes, is a novel improvization on the natural shape of the raw wood. Still not understood is the Palma boomerang-like tool (Fig. 19j), some 50cm long; four are known, thought to have been found with burials in a cave at Bajamar (Breña Alta). Diego (1968b) sees them as a parallel to Tenerife's añepa (Fig. 19e, f, i, k), an insignia of rank in his view. Siemens (1969), searching Canary prehistory for musical instruments, suggests the Palma artefacts were for banging together in pairs. He cites an Egyptian relief of 1350 BC (Luxor Temple, Tutenkamen) showing a line of musicians beating together similarly-curved sticks and, not least, wearing ostrich feathers on their heads, in turn suggesting a Saharan origin; similar objects were used in this way by the Australian aborigenes. The unemphatic handles suggest that only the curved ends could have been clapped together. Neither the ancient writers nor the present Palma music-making contain any trace of these

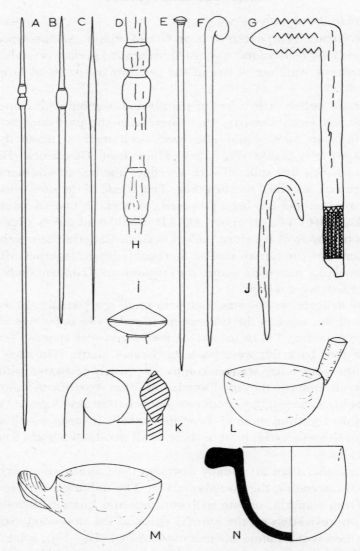

Figure 19   *Wooden artefacts. Tenerife:* banot *lances (abdh), plain lance (c),* añepa *insignia (efik), between 1m 50cm–2m 50cm. Gran Canaria: club (g, 1m). Palma: 'boomerang' (j, 60cm). Bowls: Tenerife, Gomera, Hierro (lmn, each about 12cm in height)*

artefacts (Chapter 22). Nobody has explained the sharply-bevelled edges running right around the tools: these should be examined for silica gloss and other traces of the cutting of vegetable stalks, since they may have been bracken sickles — or even post-conquest imitations of metal tools used by the European settlers, being thus for reaping grain crops. A wooden instrument said to have been in pre-conquest use is the flute; examples have not survived but it was probably in fact a later European importation.

Worked sticks, very important tools, fall into many types, extending into the next section. The simplest are preserved on Palma: three in the museum and two more, recently found with incised pottery, by Hernández (1977), in a burial cave in the Bco. de Gallegos. Averaging 70cm in length, slender, occasionally with a slight curve at one end, polished by use, their function is unknown. The present writer, having on the third attempt climbed the unpleasantly-steep, loose and slippery base of the Roque de Idafe (Pl. 6a), found one of these sticks, carved in hard juniper, at the top. Prodded into the soft face of the mountain, it proved an ideal tool for the descent. Left at the bottom, it is available for those wishing to try it out on an ascent. Experimental archaeology, even involuntary, is still rare in the Canaries.

Heavy sticks would have included — at least on the two main islands — digging, threshing and fish-killing tools. The universal implement, surviving everywhere still (Pl. 16), was the shepherd's travelling pole; a response to the vast steep ravines and ridges, the pole was used both to speed up journeys and to keep up with the flocks. Nevertheless, there are few of these poles in the museums, collectors perhaps ignoring them in favour of the more distinctive weapons. The Gomera pole (Herrera) was 2m 50cm long, made of the heart-wood of an old beech (*Myrica faya*); it was fire-hardened, being thus darkened. The chroniclers often referred to the poles: called *Tezzezes* in the two eastern islands, they were made of pine heart-wood on Tenerife (Azurara), painted yellow (Torriani) and polished with goat-marrow (Darias) on Hierro. Diego (1968b) illustrates two peculiar examples from Campanario Cave (Tenerife): the tips are reinforced with twisted goat-horns, a common feature, but the upper ends terminate in short forks, use unknown. The modern poles seen by the author are either plain or tipped with a metal spike.

Abreu described how the Hierro people used the poles 'to assist them in travelling the country . . . very rocky, so as frequently to oblige them to leap from one stone to another, which they did by the help of these poles'; on death a man would be buried with his pole at his side. The tool was used in descents, the shepherd lunging forwards and downwards and, according to Herrera (on Gomera) then sliding down the shaft at the same time as he swung in a half-circle, a shock-dissipating technique.

WOODEN WEAPONS

It is clear from the chroniclers that the islanders, when attacked, used their pointed poles as very effective lances. Torriani describes how the Gran Canaria men also fought with them in duels.

On Tenerife there was, however, a wooden implement made

primarily as a weapon. At its simplest this was a double-pointed lance with a bulge, to help gripping, towards the back end (Fig. 19c); a Balos engraving shows a man who may be wearing feathers on his head and holding a plain lance. More evolved versions had a single (Fig. 19b) or double (Fig. 19a) pommel. The length was at least 1m 75cm. The early writers recorded that some of these lances had notched tips which broke off in .he wound; possibly this means they were fitted with wooden or stone barbs, these deliberately loose.

Tenerife's museum has five examples of another type of lance: the distinguishing feature is one end's continuation into a 'whorl' (Fig. 19f, k) or fitted disc (Fig. 19e, i). The discs are incised with circles whilst just below one there is a ring of goat-horn. These implements are not fire-hardened nor do they have reinforced tips. Torriani wrote that when an island king and his court were travelling 'there was carried ahead a slender rod, well carved, called the *añepa*'. The impractical nature of the museum items supports the idea that they were the *añepa* insignia. Two came from Campanario Cave, together with the two fork-ended staffs and the plain lower end of the fifth. They lay together on the surface of the minute cave (50cm high at the most and just long enough for the staffs)—one visualizes the hiding, perhaps in time of war, of the insignia of a ruler.

A Sahara-alphabet inscription on Hierro may read 'Spare me the javelin', perhaps a prayer before a local combat. These weapons, flung with great force and accuracy, were slender double-pointed rods, fire-hardened like the travelling poles and the lances. Sedeño (1484) referred to the Gran Canaria people's short throwing weapon of matured pine and, since he fought against them in the conquest, he should be a reliable source; Abreu said this 'dart' was called a *susmago*. Though records are particularly confused on this, it seems that some javelins were fitted with slivers of wood which produced a whistling noise when the weapons were in flight. This may have been a late pre-conquest attempt to imitate the hiss of the crossbow bolt, known to have been associated in the islanders' minds with its deadliness; alternatively, the javelins may simply have been barbed, like some lances, and have made a noise incidentally whilst in the air.

A short stout weapon was the mace or club, usually an undistinctive piece of wood such as a specimen in the Tenerife Museum. The early travellers recorded these, Verneau adding—a century ago, source unknown as so often with this enthusiastic worker—that the clubs were also fitted with projections, in this case of obsidian or other stone. To this can be compared the magnificent and fearsome Fiji-style mace (Fig. 19g), a metre long, from Gran Canaria (Guayadeque). Its teeth are carved out of the body of the wood. The weapon has an incised geometric decoration (Fig. 16d) at the gripping point; linked by this to the painted caves, pottery and the rest, it comes from the mountain region.

Wooden swords and shields are also recorded. Abreu says these were imitations of the invaders' weapons. The swords, of fire-hardened pine, 'cut like steel'. The shields were roundels of dragon wood (Tenerife); Sedeño described chequered emblems (Gran Canaria), incised or painted in red, black and white . . . the colours of the painted ware, clearly showing it to have been current at the time of the conquest. Some Canary men used only their skin cloaks, wrapped round their forearms, as shields.

Diego (1961a) studied the manufacture of Tenerife's wooden weapons. Pine heart-wood was the main material, followed by juniper and one of the laurels (*Apollonias barbujana*). *Cneorum pulverulentum*, linked to the burial rituals, was sometimes used for javelins; so too was the wild olive (*Olea europea* var. *cerasiformis*). Diego said the weapons show the use of an adze and of lengthways scraping; the workmanship is better than on the travelling poles.

Two aspects of the weapons have been linked to N. Africa. Tenerife's functional lance has been compared to the Roman *soliferreum*; this also had a swelling or pommel towards the rear end and was, in fact, barbed at the point. A similar weapon apparently occurs in black Africa. Secondly, the Sahara's earliest inscriptions are accompanied by representations of men carrying round shields and javelins—and, as in the Balos engraving (Gran Canaria) and the chronicled dress (Lanzarote and Gran Canaria), wearing feathers on their heads.

HEAVY STONE TOOLS

The Canaries are generally poorly supplied with rocks suitable for making high-grade tools—but, anyway, wherever good raw material was available, the islanders' techniques were too limited to take advantage of it. In summary, all probably used basalt, 'quartz keratophyre or altered quartz trachyte' (Mineralogy Department, British Museum) and pumice; phonolites on Gran Canaria, Tenerife and Palma; obsidian on Tenerife, with a very small amount worked on Gran Canaria and Palma; another volcanic glass, blueish-black, on Gran Canaria; red, yellow, brown and green glasses on Fuerteventura. Chloromelanite (jadeite) tools are said to have been found on Gran Canaria and Gomera; imported, the nearest source of the stone is the Swiss Alps (Benítez).

The use of stone has already been encountered: carved idols, a few body ornaments, the grinding stones and cheese-making blocks, a single stamp or seal, the pot lids of travertine. This section will describe the heavy core tools, following these by the flake industry.

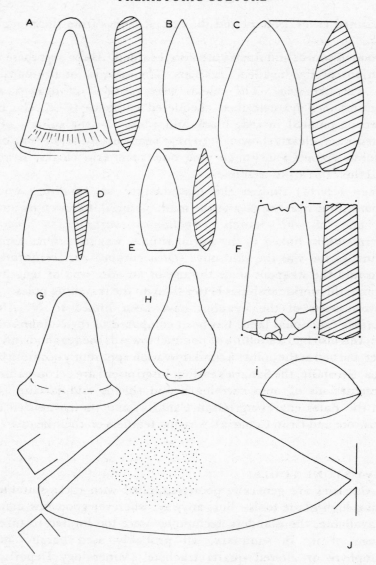

Figure 20 *Heavy stone tools (approx. lengths). Polished axes: triangular, Gomera (a, 10cm), almond, Arucas (b, 15cm), rectangular, Gáldar (d, 5cm), squared edge, Arucas (e, 7cm). Axe-shaped tools: pounder, pumice, Lanzarote (c, 11cm), ends lost, Gran Canaria (f, 10cm). Pounders: Gran Canaria (g, 10cm), Palma (h, 9cm). Grinding ball, Tenerife (i, 10cm). Adze, Gran Canaria (j, 22cm)*

The jadeite implements are five polished axes, usually described as dark green though their exterior is black, presumably a patina. Four are from Gran Canaria, one from Gomera. There are four different shapes, significantly: two are elongated-almond (Figure 20b from

Arucas, the other perhaps from San Lorenzo); another differs in that it has a squared off cutting edge (Fig. 20e, Arucas); a fourth is rectangular (Fig. 20d, Gáldar); the fifth is triangular (Fig. 20a, Gomera). This very variety is against both their manufacture in the islands and their importation by closely-associated immigrants. Found long ago in vague circumstances, they are so alien to the Canary stone age as to make one wonder whether they may not be post-conquest importations; similar axes occurred in the Mediterranean Neolithic and, as charms and in other guises, were widely collected by people of the pre-scientific age. On the other hand, the shapes and patination would be acceptable in the Neolithic of the W. Sahara (Mercer 1973). However, only thin-section work (under way by Zeuner, 1961) can really hope to locate the origin of a stone axe, made in a few widespread shapes.

Nevertheless, there are three locally-manufactured tools worth looking at in relation to the polished axes. One (Fig. 20f) is from Gran Canaria and, unluckily, its ends are lost; it appears to have been shaped by percussion but not polished. Another (Fig. 20c) comes from Lanzarote (Yé, Haría) and is a shaped pounder made of pumice; a rather similar tool has also been found on Tenerife (Tegueste). The axe-shapes of these tools confuse rather than clarify the picture.

The palm-wood doors of Gran Canaria were worked with 'sharp axes of hard stone, held between two pieces of stone, these well joined and tied together'; Torriani compared the tools to some in the Escorial Palace, near Madrid. Sedeño said wood was worked with stones held in horns, 'like adzes'. The Museo Canario has a number of massive triangular tool-heads, in basalts and phonolites, many badly damaged by use. The best (Fig. 20j) is adze-like, with one corner pointed, the second chisel-edged, the third being rounded off; a deliberate hollow in the middle may be part of Torriani's fastening method, though Zeuner (1961) said this was to help hold the tools in the hand. Some of the tool-heads are carefully worked all over by percussion but not polished; others are simply crudely flaked to shape, without hollows. It is likely that the coarser tools, the most common, were used as picks for cutting caves: Torriani said this was done with hard, shaped stones, in addition to the goat bones.

Zeuner (1961) gave the archaeological data on these unusual tools. The seven wood-working adzes fell into two size-groups (lengths about 24cm and 18cm) and were found at Gáldar, Tirajana and Agüimes. At the last (Roque 'Acuario', Los Corallillos), the tool was associated with a good flake industry (core, flakes, bifacial discoid, these types of artefact to be discussed shortly) and poor red-painted pottery. The coarse, tuff-hewing picks, ranging between 29–17cm, have been found with flakes and the same pottery and appear limited to Gáldar.

Parallels in N.W. Africa should be sought for these distinctive tool-heads.

Heavy chopping tools, lacking character, were probably common in all islands; most would have been used without handles. Those collected are simply flaked cobbles; Diego (1968a) features one resembling the Asturian pick but does not say how many more have been found on Tenerife. Pounders were also common, some showing careful and even distinctive shaping: Figs. 20h (Palma) and 20g (Gran Canaria). There is a mortar and pestle in the Museo Canario.

Pestles with stone balls in them have been found (Gran Canaria) suggesting grinding was the function of some at least of the unassociated balls (Gran Canaria, Tenerife) usually assumed to have been missiles. Carefully-rounded balls are unlikely to be used in this way, other perhaps than for hunting birds; the *bolas* and also a single-leather-encased ball on a thong have been suggested as weapons, without evidence (Diego 1968a). The enigmatic 'ridged' balls of Tenerife (Fig. 20i, possibly Arona) are probably just rubbers, worn consistently on one hemisphere; they may have been used in the small-scale preparation of valuable substances such as poisons, perfumes and spices. The Guarazoca burial cave (Hierro) yielded a good specimen. Other polished roundish stones, probably beach pebbles, may well have acquired their gloss from burnishing pottery.

Espinosa, amongst the texts on the use of stones in fighting, discussed in the next section, was the only one to refer to the throwing of 'rounded' stones. Naturally rounded stones without any signs of domestic use have certainly been found on prehistoric sites—the author noted two, about a kilo each, in a Fuerteventura cave. Small lava bombs were also collected.

The final category is the abrasive rubber, made of pumice. Some have carefully-made handles. Shapeless, holed pieces of pumice are common (Lanzarote, Tenerife, Palma). Tenerife has produced a well-made lozenge-shaped tool; a tiny hourglass perforation in this weak rock could not have taken a haft. On Gran Canaria there are preserved a set of flat discs, mostly of pumice, use unknown; some have edge-battering and centre-pitting, one thickish specimen has a groove around its outer face.

THE FLAKED-STONE INDUSTRY

A thorough study of the Canaries' flake industry has yet to be made. The island archaeologists, seemingly without experience outside the archipelago, have seen a wide range of Iberian or N.W. African forms in the Canary material; recently the claims have been replaced by statements that the industry is 'atypical' and thus nothing can be expected of it, a parallel attitude to the ancient assertions that the island sites had no stratification and thus did not merit controlled excavation. The only specialist who has worked on the stone tools was Zeuner, his death ending the work—nothing remains except the unillustrated and greatly garbled transcript, from a tape, of the clearly interesting paper he read at the 1963 Panafrican Conference in Tenerife (1966). The worker who wishes to study the stone tools is hampered in two ways: official collectors have only picked up the specimens they considered of interest and there is also a marked reluctance to allow handling of museum collections, essential in the case of stone industries. Consequently the author studied instead material *in situ* on open-air working floors in remote zones of Fuerteventura, Gran Canaria and Tenerife.

The archipelago's only good raw material is the obsidian of Tenerife. This is found in its natural state in Las Cañadas and over a zone running down to the north coast at San Juan de la Rambla. The most inaccessible source is perhaps on the eastern flank of Mña Guajara (Pl. 7a), the highest point of Teide's crater; the black obsidian occurs as massive boulders in a crumbling cream-coloured volcanic deposit. Concentrations and single artefacts were found on Guajara and elsewhere around the crater rim and in the interior lavafield. Most artefacts are still a fresh, glossy black in aspect; some are dulled, perhaps by grit-blasting; a brown skin on a number appears to be a travertine-type deposit. Perhaps untouched, a working floor was located halfway up the crater's inner wall, just behind a group of eroding pinnacles between the Guajara and La Grieta summits (Pl. 7b). In all some 350 pieces were examined in Las Cañadas, informative in spite of their limited quantity. The associated pottery was plain apart from the island's typically notched rims. In some cases the artefacts were close to caves or to the remains of improvised shelters (Chapter 8). Overall, these were the vestiges of the way of life of the shepherds of these high pastures.

The obsidian artefacts show there was a basic knowledge of stone-flaking in Tenerife. Regularly-worked cores with striking platforms can be found (Fig. 21a); the abundance of raw material may account for their rarity—there was no need to work economically. Flakes suggesting core-rejuvenation occur, both parallel to the platform and (Fig. 21b) a tip with converging facets. There are many flakes (Fig. 21c, d) and even a rare blade (Fig. 21e); the punch technique was used. Many sharp edges show use; trimming looks likely (Fig. 21d, inverse on one edge, and Fig. 21e). The recognizable shapes amongst the secondarily-worked tools, fell into two types only. Three or four 'scrapers' (Fig. 21f), probably mainly used in working wood and skins. A great many *éclats écaillés*, crude bifacial tools like chisel-heads (Fig. 21h, i).

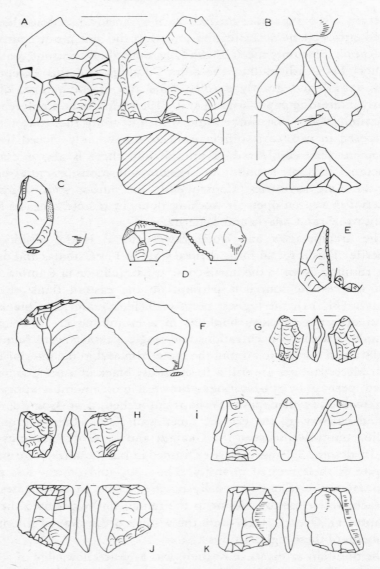

Figure 21 *Artefacts of volcanic glass (72% life). Tenerife, obsidian, black: core (a), core tip (b), flake (c), trimmed flake (d), trimmed flake with scaled bulb (e), scraper (f), éclats écaillés (hi). Gran Canaria, dark blue: éclat écaillé (g). Fuerteventura, yellow-brown: éclats écaillés (jk)*

When, at the beginning of this century, archaeology first recognized the *éclat écaillé*, a paper was devoted to them (Bardon & Bouyssonie). These *outils écaillés par percussion* were considered a deliberate tool, prepared or used with a bipolar action, or both; they could be of modern chisel or gouge form; there might be as many as four working edges and a geometrical shape. The hammer-anvil stone which sometimes accompanies the *éclat écaillé* has been collected on Palma but not apparently on Tenerife; it is a flattish cobble, round or oval in plan, say 5–10cm in long axis, with battering around the edge and pitting in the middle of the flat faces.

The museums also have struck obsidian found on Palma and Gran Canaria. A site in the latter's mountains was found by the author to hold both this black glass and also a softer blue kind, perhaps chemically related or even simply obsidian altered by peculiar weathering: amongst the 50 small pieces were half a dozen *éclats écaillés* (Fig. 21g). On Fuerteventura (Malpaís Grande), the author found the various brightly-coloured glasses, unknown then in the Canaries (examination by P. Rothe and H. Hausen): again the only recognizable tool was a number of these splintered chisel-edged splitters or wedges (Fig. 21j, k).

The *éclat écaillé*, seemingly a typical tool of the closing phases of at least the European stone-flaking period, has often gone unnoticed even where, in quantity, it was the most important tool in an industry. Though perhaps simple enough to have been a local development, its equivalents should be sought in N.W. Africa.

Over the rest of the Canaries, the obsidian had to be replaced by coarser rocks such as brown basalt, weathered black, by the trachyte, grey, and by phonolite, yellow-green to dark olive. The basalt shatters naturally into prismatic flakes, these needing no more than picking up to provide an average cutting tool; in the two eastern islands these were called *tafiagues*, on Tenerife *tabonas*.

The museums hold few examples of true flake-tools in these rocks; Gran Canaria has produced a set of discoidal knives, rounded flakes with secondary flat-flaking. It may be that the flaking of the coarse rocks was most developed in the eastern province. On Fuerteventura there certainly occurred cores (Fig. 22a), flakes and scrapers (Fig. 22b), the techniques not distinguishable from those used elsewhere on the obsidian. In Gran Canaria a mountain site was located at which, in addition to cores, scrapers, choppers and a long, neatly saw-edged flake, there was a type new to Canary prehistory. These (Fig. 22c, basalt; Fig. 22d, trachyte) are bifacially-flaked ovates of highly-standardized workmanship; the first has been made or used so as to remove its minor edge-protruberances, giving it a neater circumference. The tool was very common at this site. Painted pottery also occurs there but, without excavation, nothing can be said about its relationship to the ovates.

The author has come across this new tool on the adjacent Sahara coast and, in the standard work on the region (Almagro), the type is placed within the Sbaikian facies, its centre the south of the Algerian department of Constantine. The origins of the Sbaikian may lie in the

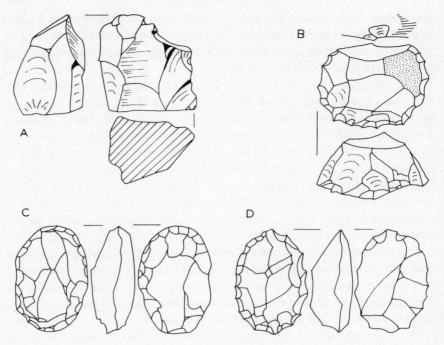

Figure 22   *Heavy flake-industry (43% life). Fuerteventura: trachyte core (a) and scraper (b). Gran Canaria: basalt (c) and trachyte (d) ovoids*

regional Acheulian or Mousterian industries. Not firmly dated, the Sbaikian's relationship to the Oranian and Capsian of the Maghreb (Chapter 5) is unclear. The bifacial ovate continues into the Sahara Neolithic (Alimen), pockets of which are known to have lasted, in cultural backwaters, into the last two millennia. It is from such a region that the new tool is likely to have reached the Canaries. However, this somewhat-Solutrian tool had a wide distribution (unlike the Sbaikian facies), being found in the European stone age, including in Iberia.

This new Canary artefact may have been a tool, a weapon-head or a missile — though for one reason or another none of these appear to have certainly been its function. Almagro, for example, considered the Sahara specimens to have been javelins tips. The ovates, however, lack points and have instead been flaked to an almost double-bevelled cutting edge right around — suggesting that contact with the subject might be made at any point. This in turn suggests a missile; the shape may have been aerodynamically suited to horizontal flight, the cutting edge hitting the victim. The objection is that such a stone would be painful to throw — but in a desperate combat it would be even more painful to be hit by it.

Looking for explanation to the early chroniclers of the way of life of the fifteenth-century stone age people of the Canaries, one reads everywhere that thrown stones were their main weapons. Torriani said that, with a single hit, a Gran Canaria man would break a palm branch, a feat beyond a musket ball—stone-throwing was also a favourite sport. There is a good description as part of a passage on Gran Canaria duelling. A licence was needed from the island council and approval from the chief priest. The scene was a raised place, with spectators. The combatants began each upon a small flat-topped stone and at a distance one from the other. First they threw three 'round' stones at each other, then got down and attacked with three 'thin' or 'sharp' stones held in the fingers of the left hand, and with the usual staff, held in the right. There might be intervals for food and counsel. Either the loser or the authorities might shout *gama, gama*, 'Enough, enough!'. The two men then made up their quarrel.

Gomera merited extra space in Abreu and Torriani by the way in which the islanders trained themselves in *avoiding* thrown missiles. The children had balls of earth flung at them, either moving aside or stopping them with their hands; as they became older, stones were thrown instead and, finally, javelins were used, just as in war. Abreu added another element: 'The natives were . . . very active and dextrous in attacking and defending, and excellent slingers of stones and darts (javelins)'. Having described the evasion training and how 'they used to catch the stones and arrows as they flew in the air', he adds that 'on reaching to manhood, they threw them (? stones) out of slings'. He thus twice refers to the use of slings, the only evidence and, since these are not mentioned in the many reports of the use of stones in the conquest battles, he must be considered wrong.

In summary, stone-throwing was a highly-developed skill and it would not be surprising that the islanders should have prepared missiles, such as the flaked ovoids, to supplement and improve on their collections of naturally-shaped stones. The cutting stones used for duelling would have been those also noted by the early historians as tools for scarifying, bleeding, shaving, killing and cutting up animals and so on.

Two parallels to the chronicled stone-throwing practices are found on the adjacent Sahara coast. James Riley, shipwrecked there and caught by the nomads, in 1815, wrote that level with the Canaries there was a feared tribe whose men were said to throw three-kilo stones so as to kill a man at 50 yards. Secondly, the Oulad Delim tribe—Arabs who entered the coastal desert in the fourteenth century—had very recently two comparable sports. In one, a circle of men try to hit one in the middle, his place being taken by whoever he hits; in the other, two men joust with sticks. As with the similarities in the two region's fishing techniques, it is hard to decide whether these similar cultural facets are due to a direct connection or are simply local developments fostered by a common N.W. African ancestry and habitat.

An important N.W. African element, dateable, is lacking. It was described in Chapter 5 how Neolithic traits were reaching the western coast of N. Africa from about the opening of the fifth millennium BC, some dying and disappearing during the second, others continuing into this century. Known at its most developed as the Neolithic of Capsian Tradition, the distinctive features of its stone industry — for example the arrowheads, with of course the bow — are lacking in the Canaries. This is seen by the author as further clear evidence of late immigration. The first islanders would have stemmed from peoples who had greatly replaced their ancient expertise in the use of stone by the comparatively-newly introduced metal tools. Finding themselves lacking ores on the islands, they would have been forced to re-expand their old techniques — obviously not entirely forgotten — and perhaps develop new aspects too.

The stone age in the Canaries generally ended in 1496, with the fall of Tenerife. The next seven chapters will describe the invasion of the islands and widespread destruction of the ancient culture by the Europeans of the fifteenth century.

PART FIVE
THE CONQUEST

CHAPTER TWELVE
Reconnaissance and Raiding

Pliny's report was followed by a thousand years of silence. It is known that Moroccans such as Ibn Fatima and Mohamed ben Ragano sailed down the coast in the thirteenth or early fourteenth century; the latter period saw the apogee of Merinid power, with Moroccan pirates raiding the Canaries.

The development of the map, compass, rudder and quadrant encouraged late-Medieval European explorers to venture southwards on the 'Sea of Darkness'. The Genoans and Castillians were active on Morocco's west coast (Safi) by the middle of the thirteenth century. In 1291, the Vivaldi brothers left Genoa for 'East India' by the Atlantic route, never to be seen again; a few years later Marco Polo set off eastwards. In 1336, Lancelotto Malocello reached Lanzarote, named after him, returning to spend about 20 years there from 1365; killed by the islanders, he was by then a vassal of the king of Portugal. The first known map of the Canaries, the planisphere of Angelino Dulcert, made in Mallorca in 1339, shows the Genoan arms upon the island of 'Lanzarotus Marocelus'. Below is 'La Forte Ventura', unclaimed, with Isla Lobos marked 'Vegi Marini'. Aided by the new rudders, the sailing ships tacked to and fro, E.N.E. and N.N.W., back to Europe (Mauny 1960).

The first surviving chronicle is that of a military expedition sent out from Lisbon by the king of Portugal in 1341. It consisted of Iberians, Florentines and Genoese, with one of these, Niccoloso da Recco, as the leader. They took with them siege engines and horses—perhaps the first time the latter had been seen by the islanders and recalling their Balos engravings (Pl. 5b). The chronicle, preserved thanks to Boccaccio, refers to five islands.

One of the eastern pair was visited: 'A mass of uncultivated stony land, but full of goats and other beasts, and inhabited by naked men and women . . . like savages'. Here the expedition obtained the greater part of their loot of skins and fat.

Gran Canaria was probably the next to be raided. The Europeans were met by a great number of islanders, all nearly naked. Their 'prince' and leaders wore well-sewn goat-skins coloured yellow and red. The people wanted to communicate, speaking a soft tongue, 'their pronunciation rapid and animated like Italian'.

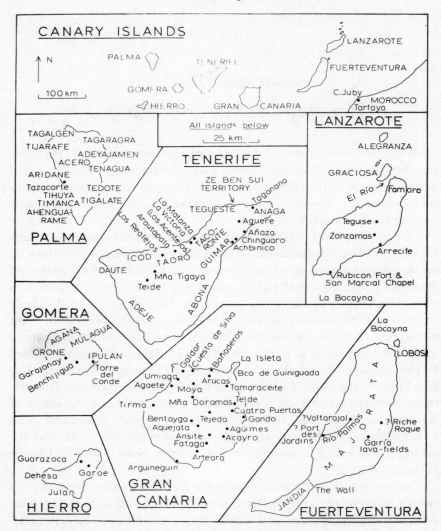

Figure 23 *Fifteenth-century territories (capital letters), settlements and other sites*

Four islanders swam to the boats—and were kept as slaves. This is the first recorded example of the trust and treachery henceforth to become commonplace in the Canaries. And, since the islanders were to be the first people to be conquered and colonized by Europeans, here were the small beginnings of a cycle not yet gone full circle. The captives, young, were described as handsome, robust, courageous and very intelligent. They had long hair, to their waists, and wore the yellow and red aprons of vegetable fibre. Uncircumcised, these men at least were thus not Moslems—though 'they absolutely refused wine'. 'They sang very sweetly, and danced almost as well as Frenchmen.

They were gay and merry, and much more civilized than many Spaniards', recorded the expedition. These islanders could make nothing of money, spices, metal weapons, gold rings, carved vases. They showed 'remarkable honesty and faithfulness' and always shared everything amongst themselves.

The northern coast of Gran Canaria, better cultivated than the southern, held little houses, fig and other trees, the palms however without fruit, and gardens with cabbages and other vegetables. A landing party put to flight 25 naked men and then broke into their houses; these were 'handsome' and 'made with much skill of square stones, covered with fine large pieces of wood . . . as clean inside as if they had been whitewashed'. The booty was limited to dried figs in palm baskets 'like those of Cesena'; corn finer than the Italian in its whiteness, length and thickness of grain; barley and other cereals. *Gofio* flour was mentioned. A temple was found, the only ornament being a stone statue of a man, wearing a palm-leaf apron, holding a ball; the figure was added to the loot. The island was considered well populated and cultivated.

Recco's ships then circuited the western islands, remarking their forests and streams. Tenerife's Teide peak was apparently smoking and the mariners were afraid to land; although there were of course volcanoes in the Mediterranean islands, they mistook the mountain's emanations for the raising and lowering of a great mast and lateen sail. Then, with its cargo and its stories, the expedition returned to Europe.

The Canaries were now known to offer slaves; the skins, fats and oils of goats, seals and fish; dragon-tree blood; and orchil, the dyer's lichen most in demand in late-Medieval times, the secret of its use at one period limited to the Italian family of Roccella, hence its name. There followed—over a century and a half—a series of squabbles between the nobility of Europe for the 'legal' possession of the Canaries. The first 'grant' was made to the Infanta Luís de la Cerda in 1344 by Clement VI, the Avignon pope—but no effective action was taken. The British were perhaps the only W. Europeans not interested in the Fortunate Islands: their unawareness was such that upon hearing of the grant to the Infanta, England's embassy in Rome 'immediately dispatched an express to their court, to prevent their conveyance, imagining there were no other Fortunate Islands than those of Great Britain' (Glas).

Practical action now became concentrated in the hands of the rich, hard-headed Mallorcan merchants. Four licences, granted in 1342, have been recently studied (Sevillano). The vessels were *cocas bayonesas* and their task was the conquest of the 'recently discovered' archipelago in the name of Jaime III, king of Mallorca. It was about this time that the already-mentioned Mallorcan-Catalan expedition reached Gran Canaria; landing at Gando, it was defeated and had to leave behind a number of men. These prisoners lived there for a long time, marrying island women and producing children. They are known to have introduced new elements into the island dwelling-styles and, it is inferred, brought in other Mediterranean cultural characteristics. Two priests among them 'built two neat hermitages in which they placed three images'. Abreu says that after many years a famine occurred. The people were forced to kill all but the first-born of their own children. The Europeans, some perhaps accused of homosexual approaches to the islanders, were all killed, with their numerous progeny, because of this and of the lack of food. Abreu rounds off the incident by saying that the infanticide brought a plague — the latter certainly usually followed a famine in the post-conquest Canaries — reducing the islanders, 14,000 in number, by two-thirds.

The 1352 expedition of Arnau Roger, under the now-united crowns of Aragon and Catalonia, had colonization and religious conversion as its overt and currently-respectable aims. *Et ad fidem ortodoxam reducendi*, another element in the European colonial cycle had taken up position. In 1352, one Bishop Bernat was charged with founding 'a Seat, Cathedral and City' in Gran Canaria. He did go as far as to equip himself with interpreters from amongst the islanders enslaved in Mallorca but no more is known. In 1394 the incumbent of the still-unconquered island, a Dominican, was living in Mallorca. The strength of all-justifying religious zeal was not to be felt until the next century.

Roger carried with him a dozen Canary people who had been caught earlier, taken to Mallorca and there baptized, redeemed from slavery and taught Christianity and Catalan; they were seemingly returned on the orders of Pedro IV, more clement than his successors. The *Catalan Atlas* of Abraham Cresques, 1375, shows accurately enough the five easterly islands but not Palma nor Hierro. It also depicts one of the Mallorcan adventurers, Jaime Ferrer, in his boat; this *coque* is a simple vessel, with neither superstructure nor even deck, driven by a lateen sail (Mercer 1976, Pl. 5).

About the middle of the century, the 'Francos', probably Mallorcans, sold a number of islanders in N. Africa. Ibn Khaldun recorded that, once they had learned the language, they described their home customs. They kept goats and grew barley, dug their land with horn tools and fought by throwing stones. These islanders also prostrated themselves before the rising sun.

The second half of the century saw many attacks on the Canaries, so that the French conquerors wrote, in 1402, that Lanzarote 'used to be heavily populated but the Spanish and Aragonese and pirates have caught so many of the people . . .'. The Castillians had reached the Moroccan Sus by 1353. Verlinden cites two cargoes of Lanzarote people, 330 in all, including their king and queen, sold in 'Andalucia' and San Lucar de Barrameda in 1385 and 1393 respectively. The first Castillian landfall may have been by accident in 1382: a ship, under Francesco López, was blown southwards from W. Iberia, landing eventually at the mouth of the Guiniguada (Las Palmas) in Gran Canaria. Well received, the thirteen sailors spent seven peaceful years there, living off the flocks granted to them by the islanders. In exchange they taught Christianity and Castillian. Suddenly all were killed. If the story sounds suspiciously like that of the Catalans and Mallorcans, it is also distinct in many details. It seems that one of the Castillians managed to write a denunciation of the islanders and, when the French arrived in 1402, a young man swam out to their ship with it tied round his neck.

CHAPTER THIRTEEN

The French Invasion: Lanzarote

European colonialism moved into its first full action in 1402, almost a century before Columbus. The little-known conquest of the Canaries, begun then by the French and finished, in 1496, by the Spanish, followed a general pattern which was to be played out all over the world. Nor, as will be seen, was it a miniature version of the later invasions — the two main islands were very difficult to conquer, far harder than say the Inca kingdom. Had medieval Europe taken as much interest in the simple islanders of the Canaries as it was to do in the riches-laden kingdoms of America, then a *leyenda negra* of appropriate enormity would now exist. Nor was there an equivalent to Bartolomé de las Casas, neither to defend the islanders or to publish the behaviour of the *conquistadores*; there was certainly Juan de Baeza, a Franciscan who reached Fuerteventura in 1416, but he concentrated on improving the islanders' standards of living. This and the following chapters bring together not only the chronicles of the conquests but also the last decade's research by Spanish workers into the resulting despoliation, slavery and deportation of the islanders — not subjects to be found in the pages of Spain's history books.

The French invasions of 1402–4 were planned by Gadifer de la Salle and Jean de Bethencourt. The campaigns were carried through by La Salle, being in the main written up, somewhat partially, by his own priest, Boutier. The 1420 catalogue of the library of the Dukes of Burgundy: '*Item, ung aultre livre nommé* Livre de Canare, *escript en parchemin, de lettre de forme, à une histoire enluminé d'or, commençant ou II fueillet* Et pource, *et ou derrenier* Les gens, *couvert de cuir rouge à II fermouars de laton*'. Discovered by scholars only in 1889, this MS is now in the British Museum. In 1404, La Salle was entirely ousted by Bethencourt — who, having spent most of the campaign period at the Castillian court, had used the time to obtain the title of 'Lord of the Islands' in exchange for his acceptance that the Canaries' ultimate sovereign should be the Castillian king. A second MS, lost, covered events up to about 1480. Bethencourt founded his own dynasty in the islands: about 1490, one of his descendants, Jean V, wrote out a third manuscript of the conquest, based on the two preceding works but clumsily falsifying the respective contributions of the two leaders in order to show Bethencourt in a more favourable light. This manuscript, now in Rouen, has been the one most used by students of the islands, hence Bethencourt's historical prominence. However, the present summary is based primarily upon the original manuscript of Boutier.

Both this and the narratives of the Spanish conquests of the last quarter of the fifteenth century show that the islanders, defending their lives and land, were usually trusting and humane, whilst the invaders were a merciless rabble of adventurers, masking their greed and personal aggrandisement under the banners of Christianity. The pope gave out the usual indulgences to those who supported or went on the expedition. Like all conquests, it was a succession of diverse forms of evil and suffering. Upon this foundation is built the history of the Canaries and, to understand their present, it is necessary to bear in mind the way in which the indigenous people were incorporated into Spanish society. In 1978, as this book is written, the founding of Las Palmas five centuries earlier is being celebrated . . . it is likely that if Schwidetsky were to parallel her 1956 study of Tenerife's capital she would equally find the Cromagnoids commonest in the outskirts and poorer quarters of Las Palmas.

THE VOYAGE AND FIRST LANDINGS

The coloured frontispiece of the original manuscript (Pl. 12) shows the Frenchmen's boat, La Salle's property. The vessel, a single-master with a superstructure, appears transitional between Jaime Ferrer's simple craft and the *coques*, with three masts and a superstructure, of which the first illustration known to students of early navigation is the ship on the 1466 seal of Louis de Bourbon. Standing on the superstructure in the stern, La Salle is shown with plume, sword, shield and his own flags, Bethencourt with plume and sword only; the latter's lesser role is underlined by a note that he had not got the full use of his limbs. One of the two chronicler-priests, presumably Boutier, can be seen above the anchor flukes. The picture has many other details of historical interest — the Christian banners, a serpent-like trumpet, armour, crossbows and lances.

La Salle (1355–c.1422), a soldier and adventurer, is described by Boutier as from the region of Thouars in the ancient province of Poitou, or near the present Poitiers, just inland from the west coast of central France. Bethencourt (1362–1425) was a Norman courtier-landowner from the region of Caux; his estate was at Grainville-la-Teinturière, a village of dyers, and the lost 1482 MS noted of Fuerteventura's orchil lichen that 'this plant will be of great value to the lord of the country'.

The expedition, 280 men, set sail from La Rochelle on 1 May 1402.

La Salle's choice of men was no better than his choice of partner, so
that the expedition was to be a catalogue of internal conflicts from
which he was to emerge both without profit or a place in history and
barely with his life. It is to La Salle, for his leadership and daring in
the reconnaissances, for his determination to survive and go on with
the conquest in the midst of treachery and an absolute lack of supplies
and reinforcements, for his merciless extermination of the islanders
once his rebellious henchmen had made peaceful annexation impossible—for all this, it is to La Salle if to anyone must go the doubtful
honour of the title of first conqueror of the Canaries.

At the Cantabric port of Vívero there is a dangerous quarrel
amongst the crew, already divided into two factions. At La Coruña,
the French find a fleet led by the Scots 'Count of Crawford'.
Bethencourt, going ashore, opportunistically joins in the stripping of a
captured ship. In spite of being chased, the French get away with an
anchor and a ship's boat—or *batel*, the name used in the falsified MS
for the otherwise-undescribed craft of the Gran Canaria islanders.
Reaching Cádiz they are accused of piracy, La Salle is arrested and
stores are refused them. Whilst he is away and though Bethencourt is
aboard, the crew mutiny, led by the master-mariners from Harfleur:
morale has dropped as, without provisions, the men fear they are
going to their death.

Only 63 men left Iberia and, after three days becalmed, reached the
Graciosa sound (Fig. 23)—El Río, a favourite anchorage at all
periods—in a further five days, in July. La Salle reconnoitred the
interior of Lanzarote twice, only the second time managing to make
contact with the people. A pact was agreed between the two Frenchmen and the island king by which, in exchange for protection
against other doubtless similar adventurers, the Europeans could
build a fortress—the first 'protectorate' in the current cycle had come
into being. The fortress was constructed at the southern end of
Lanzarote, about a kilometre from the now-abandoned settlement of
Papagayo and three times as far from the Torre del Aguila, a later
defensive tower (1741). The ruins of the Rubicon fortress, with the
nearby vaulted wells and the site of the conquerors' chapel to San
Marcial, have recently been located, buried in the sands. The fortress
consisted of two rectangular rooms each 2m 50cm high at the centre
of their vaulted ceilings (Fig. 24).

Little more now remains of the islanders of 1402 and their way of
life. Slave-catching had by now reduced this 'handsome' and once-
numerous people to about 300; the French are to kill 50 more and—
since at this point they have 80 imprisoned—they probably shipped off
most of the rest to Europe. The men were naked but for the knee-
length capes which hung down their backs; the women dressed in

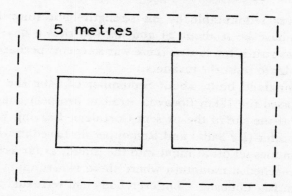

Figure 24   *Rubicon fortress, 1402, Lanzarote (plan)*

ground-length skin tunics. Most women had three husbands, each in turn a month at a time; the next in line spent the month as servant to the woman and her current husband. The women produced many children, 'as white as ours', but, having no milk, fed them with their mouths; as a result the women usually had greatly enlarged lower lips. These customs appear peculiar to Lanzarote.

The island, in native speech, was called 'Tyterogaka'. There were many settlements and good houses, with good crop and pasture land; barley was grown in quantity, salt was copiously available. The island lacked trees but there were shrubs for fuel; one, unburnable and yielding a medicine, would have been *Euphorbia balsamifera*. The reader will recognize a few of these notes, used in the archaeological chapters — they are given again here both to provide the contemporary background to the scenes of conquest and to show up the aspects of the islands in which the Europeans were most interested.

The line of Lanzarote patriarchs can be traced from a quarter-century earlier, the monarchs then Zonzamas and his wife Fayna; their stronghold has been described. In 1377, a Spaniard, Martín Ruíz de Avendaño, was blown on to the island; he was hospitably received by the king and queen, to the extent where, after his departure, Fayna gave birth to a fair-haired girl, Ico. The succession passed to a legitimate son, Tiguafaya, but in 1399 he, his queen and 70–170 islanders were caught by Sevillian slavers. Another son, Guanarame, had by now married Ico, his half-sister, but, being himself killed in battle, Ico claimed the throne for their son, Guadarfrá. This was challenged by one Atchen on the grounds of her own illegitimacy and Ico was submitted to a trial: immured in the smoke-filled Zonzamas Cave with three women servants, she was the only one to survive, thanks it is said to breathing through a wet cloth. Guadarfrá was accepted. The French, arriving in 1402, frequently fought an island

king who was redoubtable by his strength—but since Ico herself
should only have been about 24 and her son thus a boy, either the
date of Ruíz's visit is too late or there was a regent, perhaps chosen as
military leader to resist the invaders.

Their stronghold built, about September of 1402 the French expedition crossed the 12km Bocayna Strait to prospect Fuerteventura,
anchoring off the site of the present Corralejo. Leaving Bethencourt
aboard, 'Gadifer (La Salle) and Remonnet de Levedan with some of
their companions set off at night into the island, as far as they could,
until they reached a mountain where there is a running spring, six
leagues from Isla Lobos . . . but everybody had retreated to the other
end of the island . . . Gadifer and his companions stayed there eight
days, until lack of bread forced them back'. Yet another mutiny has
occurred in their absence—again with Bethencourt aboard—and La
Salle's party are only allowed aboard on condition that the dissidents
can take the ship and go home to Europe.

So, still in September, the ship sails away northwards, with
Bethencourt aboard. The chronicler-priest notes in disgust that the
mutineers took away most of the wine and the best of the cross-bows—
clearly considered the essential stores. Although Bethencourt is to send
supplies by Christmas to La Salle and his few men, it is not to be until
1 July 1403 that relief reaches them.

On arrival in Cádiz, Bethencourt has the mutineers imprisoned.
Then, refusing a good offer for the ship, he sends it off to Seville—and
it is lost on the way, during a very short journey, it seems. The captain
of another vessel, the *Morella*, offers to take supplies out, but
Bethencourt refuses, being perhaps unable to pay. It had been agreed
with La Salle that, in order to get support, Bethencourt should place
the ultimate sovereignty of the Canaries with whoever offered the best
terms and it is to such negotiation that he now devotes himself.

TREACHERY YET AGAIN

Presumably now reduced to no more than about two dozen men, La
Salle takes a party across to Isla Lobos (N.E. Fuerteventura). The aim
was to hunt the seals to get skins to make shoes for the expeditionaries,
since 'for lack of these there was not one of them who could go
anywhere or do anything'. But goat skin would have been as good or
better and it was probably as much goods tradeable with passing ships
which were sought: of the seals, 'their skins and fats would yield 500
ducats annually'.

Lobos (Fig. 23), triangular, consists of little but a red volcanic cone,
122m, falling straight into the breakers at the angle of the two shorter
sides; just in from the longer coast there is a marshy salt-water lagoon.

After a few days, La Salle sends Remonnet de Levedan back to the Rubicon for supplies, because Lobos was 'a desert island and without water'; the 11 who stayed behind had food for two days.

However, the temporary commander of the fortress, Bertin de Berneval, had meanwhile worked out a plot with the Gascons amongst the expedition. A Spanish slave-catching boat, the *Tajamar*, has anchored off the north of Lanzarote, causing the islanders to turn to their pact with the French for protection. Bertin tells them to group themselves together for safety and he will see they are all right. This way he catches two dozen of them and, presumably marching overland, hands the islanders to the slavers, with whom he has made a prior agreement. However, the Lanzarote king, 'daring and strong, broke his bonds and freed himself from his three guards, one of whom, a Gascon, chased him; but the King turned on him furiously and gave him such a blow that the others let him go; and this was the sixth time that he escaped from the hands of the Christians, by his courage'.

Aware that La Salle would not accept this abduction of the islanders, Berneval had left orders that his leader's boat should be seized when it came into the Rubicon fortress from Lobos. Berneval's henchman, 'the Bastard of Blesy', takes it from Levedan at sword point. About to depart for Europe, the mutineers have already begun to destroy the expedition's stores. Berneval soon arrives overland, with 30 Spaniards off the *Tajamar*. After a huge and deliberately wasteful meal, they finish off the stripping of the fortress, piling up both La Salle's boat and that of the *Tajamar* — which seven more Spaniards have brought round — with the remaining supplies and the arms. Berneval wrecks all he cannot carry off, pouring the last barrel of wine on the ground. The Spaniards, in the meantime, are raping a number of French women whom Berneval had handed to them, and whom, since they were from Poitou, can be assumed to have belonged to La Salle's party. Levedan's pleas to be allowed to send food to the seal hunters brings a spate of abuse from Berneval 'whom Gadifer trusted as none other'. 'If he wasn't older than me', says Berneval, 'I'd kill him myself. But, as it is, if he gives any more trouble I'll have him drowned, that'll show him how to hunt seals'.

On Lobos, La Salle's party was soon out of drinking water. 'Each night he put a strip of cloth out on the ground to soak up the dew, then squeezed it out and drank the drops'. Perhaps hunger was less of a problem: the seals, the birds on the brackish lagoon, the crabs and limpets, these would have kept the well-armed and resourceful band alive. There was little danger from the Fuerteventura people, without boats. However, watching hopefully, La Salle may have seen his own boat and another, unknown, set off in the opposite direction, to the north: Berneval and the Spaniards taking their loot up to the

Tajamar, anchored in the Graciosa strait.

Levedan is not yet defeated. He sends the two priests and two squires overland to Graciosa, 60km. Arriving before the small boats, they enlist the sympathy of the captain of the *Morella*, the Spanish vessel which had been offered to Bethencourt in Seville. In fact it had arrived before the *Tajamar* and had also been approached by Berneval — but the captain had refused his proposals, saying it was treachery. His first action is to send a man overland back to the Rubicon with oars — this sailor and four of La Salle's loyal men cross to Lobos in a little boat which Berneval had not thought worth taking. After a hard voyage they bring their comrades safely back to the fortress.

Berneval's boats, in the meantime, have reached Graciosa. One was La Salle's property, both were piled with loot, including 'two hundred bow-strings . . . and several crossbows . . . and a great quantity of thread for making crossbow cords, and all the arms, of which there were a lot . . . and they even had to damage a cable we had . . . the Spaniards took off two dozen arrows; and they broke into two of Gadifer's coffers'. But the priests and squires, supported by the *Morella*'s captain, go aboard the *Tajamar* and confront Berneval and his gang of French mutineers and Spanish accomplices. An acrimonious exchange ensues, with Berneval claiming he is only taking away his own property. At length he is forced to relinquish the boat and also tosses one of the expedition's interpreters, 'Isabel the Canary woman' — able to denounce him in Seville — in after them, literally. They fish her out and row indignantly away.

But Berneval has not finished yet. He gets those who helped him in the mutiny onto the shore, under a pretext — and then, with a last shout of 'Sort yourselves out as best you can, for you'll not be coming with me', disappears northwards aboard the *Tajamar*, with the expedition gear and the captured islanders.

The abandoned mutineers now become suddenly penitent — superficially at least — and persuade one of the squires to set off overland to ask La Salle's pardon. Once he has gone they simply seize the much-disputed boat from the remaining trio and set off for Africa. 'As for them', wrote the chronicler-priest, 'they went off and drowned themselves five hundred miles away and of the twelve only two escaped and these were made slaves'. According to this writer, the boat itself was miraculously washed back up, at the very point from which it was taken, in August 1403 . . .

Berneval, aboard the *Tajamar*, reaches Cádiz, only to be denounced by La Salle's trumpeter, Cortille, and imprisoned. The herald writes to Bethencourt, still in Seville — who does nothing. By now he has passed the sovereignty of the Canaries to the king of

Castille, taking entirely for himself the title of 'Seigneur des isles de Canare' and one-fifth of the value, the *quinto* duty, of all the merchandise exported in the future. La Salle was not mentioned. The king also provided immediate funds of 20,000 maravedis. Bethencourt entrusted these to one Enguerrand de la Boissière — who absconded not merely with this money but also with the sale money of the boat from the wrecked expedition vessel, with a golden collar given to La Salle by the Duke of Orleans . . . and, for good measure, with Bethencourt's wife.

WAR WITH THE ISLANDERS

It comes as no surprise that the people of Lanzarote who had begun 'with demonstrations of friendship, as was their custom,' should henceforth distrust the Frenchmen. Little more than twenty of these now remained, at once reduced by two during an attack by the surviving islanders led by their escaped king.

The Europeans now bring in a new tactic, to become standard practice in the colonial era. Along comes a Lanzarote man called Afche *'qui vouloit moult estre roy'*; he was probably Atchen, the man who had challenged Ico over the passing of the throne through her to Guadarfrá. La Salle agrees to catch the existing king and replace him by Afche. The latter had in mind also to kill the Europeans once he was in power. La Salle and 20 Frenchmen make a surprise attack, at night, on the accepted king and 40 of his men, in a house near Arrecife. The islanders knock a hole in the back wall and some escape, but most are caught. La Salle takes the king, chained at the neck, to the Rubicon fortress.

Now Afche *'se vesti comme roy'* and agrees to the baptism of his subjects. The 'divide and rule' tactic was safely past its first stage.

Needing barley, the French collect up a quantity in *'un vieu chastel que Lancelot Maloisel avoit jadis fait faire, quant il conquist le pays'*. This fortress was a fair way from the Rubicon and, on their way back, a party of Frenchmen are ambushed by Afche and his faction, surviving with difficulty. Simultaneously, the first king escapes from the Rubicon, taking with him his *'fers et la chayne'* — and has Afche caught, stoned and burned. The day after, those French left at Lancelot's old fortress hear of the ambush of their compatriots, seize an islander and, taking him up on to a high place, cut off his head and stick it on a pole for all to see.

'And henceforth there was war between us . . . and we have taken and killed a great number of their people and have caught women and children'. There were many prisoners in the fortress, the rest hid in their caves. The French now spend all their time catching islanders, hoping to exchange them for supplies with passing ships. La Salle's expressed aim is to kill all the fighting men and baptize the women and children. The chronicler-priest records with satisfaction how 80 islanders were baptized at Easter 1403.

CHAPTER FOURTEEN

The French Invasion: Fuerteventura and Hierro

At last, in July 1403, a Castillian boat brings four pipes of wine and 17 sacks of flour, though Bethencourt seems to have had little hand in sending these supplies. 'We have lived on a little barley . . . which the islanders had reserved for sowing, but we keep up such attacks that they have not been able to work their fields'. The Castillians refuse a French request for the transfer of the captive islanders to 'Erbanne', or Fuerteventura. 'There was no food left in Lanzarote, as a result of which many died'.

Allowing only La Salle, four Frenchmen and two islanders aboard, the Castillian boat now sets off on a three-month looting circuit of the archipelago, primarily seeking animal skins. Making a landfall in the west of Fuerteventura, La Salle considers the 'Port des Jardins' (the present Puerto de la Peña) as a likely future harbour and then takes a party of 34 men up the watercourse towards the Río Palmas valley.

Soon 21 Spaniards turn back, La Salle going on with 'only two archers'. The defile into the valley 'is so impregnable that a single man could hold it against all comers, for it is not more than two stone's throw long and only three or four fathoms wide'. There are in fact the ruins of a well-hidden pre-conquest settlement amongst the over-looking hummocks of the Risco del Carnicero (Mercer 1973), but the Mahohs took no action. La Salle and his men 'had to remove their shoes in order to cross the marble stones, so smooth and slippery that one has to go on all fours and, even so, those at the back had to support the feet of those in front with their lances, and then these pulled the others up after them'. On the further side of the pass they found 'a flat and beautiful valley, a very pleasant place, where there must be some 900 shady palms, and streams . . . running down from the middle, and the palms are in groups of 100 to 120, the tallest like masts, more than 20 fathoms high, and so green, so thickly fronded and so laden with dates that they are a pleasure to see'. Doubtless, as at present, the valley was well cultivated, but the crops would have been harvested before the July heat. La Salle and his gang now 'ate in the delicious shade, upon the fine green grass, near to the running streams, and rested a little, because they were very tired'.

Then they set off again, up a great slope — the western cordillera — and La Salle sends three men on ahead. At once these 'met their

enemies'—the phrase leaves little doubt of the relationship expected
by the Europeans. 'Pietre le Canare', an interpreter, chases three
islanders and caught a woman and 'surprised two more in a cave, one
of whom had a child at the breast, which she strangled for fear that it
would cry out'. From the top of the cordillera La Salle sees a badland,
un mauvais pays, the Gairía lava-fields of the central plain.

> 'So he ordered that some of his men should beat the whole of the badland;
> and they spread themselves out wide apart, as only eleven had stayed with
> Gadifer. It fell to the Castillians who had not deserted to come across a
> group of people, forty-five or fifty in number, who attacked the Castillians
> and kept them off until their women and children had escaped. The rest of
> Gadifer's men, who were spread out quite a way ahead, heard the shouts
> and came as fast as they could, and the first to arrive was Remmonet de
> Levedan on his own, who attacked them; but they utterly surrounded him,
> and if it hadn't been for Jennequin d'Auberbouc, who arrived at that
> moment and threw himself at them and forced them to retire, Remmonet
> might have been killed. Jeuffroy d'Ansonville also arrived, bow in hand,
> and never more needed, and between them they put them to flight. But
> Gadifer, who had been far ahead in the badland, and who was coming
> with all speed, with three more men, went straight for the mountains
> where they were going, and was about to cut them off, when night fell, and
> he got so near that he spoke to them, and only with great difficulty could
> our men recognise each other, as it was so dark. And it took them all night
> to get back to their base, without having captured more than four women'.

The chroniclers gave their general impressions of Fuerteventura.
The few inhabitants were 'very tall, both men and women, and very
firm in their beliefs. It's difficult to catch them alive; and they are so
built that, if one turns on his captors, they have no choice but to kill
him'. 'The people are completely naked, especially the men, who only
cover themselves with a hairy skin, tied at the shoulder. The women
wear one in the same way, and two more, one in front and one behind,
held in at the waist and reaching to the knees; their shoes have no
heels; they have hair which is long and curly, cutting it across the
forehead, as do the men'. It is here that the chroniclers refer to the
division of the island by the Jandía wall'. Thirty thousand goats might
be taken every year from the island; there was plenty of salt, with good
sites for making pans. Compared to the other Canaries there was little
woodland; the French note a shrub which gave a balsam (*Euphorbia
balsamifera*) and say there are many other species, including the date-
palms and also olives and mastic trees. The springs ran so strongly that
in four or five places it would be possible to set up water-driven
grinding mills—with which the present day watercourses and dropping water-table are in sorry contrast. 'The land is very rich in birds:
herons, bustards (Houbara), river birds with a different plumage to

ours, big pigeons with their tails marked with white, and ordinary pigeons, always taken by the hawks, and quails, larks and numberless others'. The Egyptian vultures 'are always amongst the people and clear up all the filth'.

The islanders themselves come more to life in Abreu's and Torriani's histories. There were 4,000 fighting men, obviously an exaggeration, divided between two kings, Ajose and Guise, just then in conflict over gazing rights. On Fuerteventura the elite were probably the bravest, at this time notably Mahay and Altihay. Of the two mentioned witches, the mother settled differences between the two chiefs, the daughter, was in charge of undescribed ceremonies; they were also seers—one prophesy was that an invasion would come . . . they counselled submission.

THE RECONNAISSANCE OF THE OTHER ISLANDS

The ship next anchored in 'a great port' between Telde and Agüimes, on the east coast of Gran Canaria. Five hundred islanders gather, coming out to the vessel in groups of 10 or 12: 'they brought figs and dragon's blood in quantity to exchange against fish hooks, old iron tools and sewing needles'. Establishing the trading ideals of the future, the Europeans 'obtained dragon's blood worth 200 doubloons (*doubles*) when everything they gave in exchange was not worth two francs'. La Salle sends Pietre to the king, five leagues away (? Gáldar). However, after a couple of days of trading, enlivened by an ambush in the middle, the Spaniards insist upon leaving. The chronicler mentions here the 'testament' of the 'Castillians' who had recently (1382–9) spent seven years on Gran Canaria, as encountered in the last chapter; their deaths are here ascribed to the islanders believing they had sent letters 'against them' to their distant countrymen, perhaps seen as an invasion plot.

Gran Canaria *'est la plus renommée de toutez'* with fine people, the women in particular beautiful. At this point the island is thought to hold 6,000 *'gentilz hommes'* apart from the common people. The men wear palm-leaf shorts, the women skins. Most are tattooed. Their hair is tied back, much as in a plait. Domesticated animals were plentiful—pigs, goats and sheep—with savage dogs like wolves, only smaller. The islanders grew wheat, beans and other cereals, with the north best for cultivation. They were excellent fishermen and marvellous swimmers. The chroniclers described great woods of pines, firs (? junipers), dragons, olives, figs, date-bearing palms and other species.

La Salle had gone there 'with no other objective but to study the island, its government and organisation, and to examine the anchorages and routes to the interior, there good and safe providing one is well organised. And he sounded and measured the ports and coast wherever the vessel could get near . . .'. La Salle also considers the 'towns' of Telde, Agüimes and Arguineguín, suggesting the last as particularly suitable for a harbour and fortress. Ideally, he would like to get together a hundred archers and as many foot soldiers, then fortifying at Telde, until 'with the aid of God, he has put the whole island under his control and into the Christian faith'.

The ship steers clear of *'l'isle d'Enfer'*, Tenerife. The only information recorded is that the island has 'many people, small in stature, the bravest of all . . . and never attacked or carried into slavery'. There are great woods — only the dragon trees are specified — and running streams.

The expedition reaches Gomera at night. Some islanders had fires burning on the shore (fishing?) and the Europeans catch a man and three women. At dawn they attempt to stock up with water but the islanders have by now marshalled themselves and drive away the marauders. Many people live on Gomera, speaking 'the strangest of all the languages of these parts, with their lips, as if they had no tongues. And here they tell how a great prince, for no crime, had them put there and ordered that their tongues should be cut out. And from the way they speak you can believe it'. Again they single out the striking dragon trees for mention — indeed, the sixteenth-century Hieronymous Bosch was to include one in his 'Garden of Delights'.

Next a storm forces them to *'l'isle de Fer'*, Hierro — the western limit of the known world until, almost a century later, Columbus left its waters for America. The French priests look speculatively into the distant haze. 'They say that . . . to the south, eleven leagues away, there is the Island of Kings, inhabited by a red people' — perhaps showing that contact had already been made, across the mid-Atlantic, with the native inhabitants of the Americas.

Hierro, in 22 days hunting, yielded only four women and a child, there being few inhabitants 'because each year there are captures . . . as recently as 1402 four hundred were taken'. Both sexes were handsome; the men carried long lances, though these did not have metal points. Crop land was plentiful, yielding beans and wheat in abundance — and wine could be produced, as it has in fact been since. There was good pasture, used by pigs, goats and sheep. Though the coasts were unapproachable, inland there was a beautiful highland, well wooded with laurel and pine; most of the 100,000 pines were so thick 'that two men together could not get their arms around them'. It rained often and there was good abundant water. Hierro also had fruit trees and many birds — falcons, hawks, larks and quails. The chronicler was intrigued by 'a species . . . with the plumage of pheasant, the size of a parrot and a crest . . . like a peacock, and which flies but little', clearly the hoopoe. 'And there are lizards as big as cats', suggesting the larger species were by now common only on Hierro. La Salle is handicapped by lack of an interpreter and decides to send back to Seville for a native of Hierro — the chroniclers note elsewhere that the Canary Islanders are '*de diverses loys et de divers langages*'.

Reaching Palma, '*l'isle de Palmes*', they anchor in the mouth of a ravine with a running stream. The island is noted to be well peopled but, being '*très forte*', has been little raided. There follows one of the references to the lack of crops on Palma. The French consider this island the most attractive of all the Canaries.

The ship now sailed straight back to the Rubicon. 'Here they found us all in a good state and with over eighty prisoners . . . amongst whom there had been many deaths; and we had our enemy in such a state that they did not know what to do and some come every day to give themselves up, so that few have not been baptized, especially of those who could do us harm. And we have entirely succeeded in our aims, as far as Lanzarote is concerned — and it had 200 fighting men when we arrived'. They had made a desert and called it peace.

THE INVASION OF FUERTEVENTURA

The Castillian boat left Lanzarote for Europe on 9 October 1403. Jeuffroy d'Ansonville was aboard, his job to send supplies by Christmas. Inevitably, nothing is received but on 25 January 1404 the French again catch the elusive king and 18 of his men — and his stores provide a month's food. The king eventually asks for baptism for himself and his entourage, to the satisfaction of the chronicler-priest, who now fills many pages of the MS with details of the religious instruction given to the islanders, who 'live in part like animals'.

Clearly little happens for many months and further pages are devoted to a description of Africa taken from a well-known fabrication of the period, the travels of a mendicant friar. La Salle's conquest plans are also described. The chronicler notes that the subjection of the Canary Islanders will be easy '*car il sont gens sans trait*', that is without bows — the Europeans were always to be at least a step ahead in arms. The bow, wrote the priest, is particularly effective out here as it is too hot to wear much armour.

On 19 April 1404, Bethencourt at last returned to the Canaries. Worn out by fighting and hunger, La Salle's party record that 'for the last two and a half years (*sic*) we have been sleeping on the bare ground, with no more bedding than our torn, worn-out clothes, being brought to a low state'. However, Lanzarote has certainly been conquered, the symbolic end considered to have been the final capture of the king; the islanders, noted as originally three hundred, are mostly dead or imprisoned, enslaved locally or in Europe — though, justifyingly, those still alive are all baptized.

The meeting of La Salle with Bethencourt has to be imagined. The latter, doubtless well-fed, in good clothes and accompanied by a herald, squire and strongly-armed retinue, would have produced the documents showing he was the 'Lord of the Isles' and entitled to the *quinto* revenue on all goods exported — 'even on those on Gadifer' wrote the chronicler in disgust in the margin. La Salle, ragged, gaunt and tanned, would have been further enraged to see how Bethencourt now kept the bulk of the replenishments for himself: wheat, sent by a friend of La Salle, and mattresses, blankets, cloth, including fustian, and several pipes of wine. Henceforth the two men and their bands are on openly hostile terms.

Lanzarote is clearly worked out as a source of profit and a scramble now begins to exploit Fuerteventura. Three months appear to have been spent on further reconnaissance and raids, the prisoners being sent across to Lanzarote. Then each faction begins its fortification on the southern island. An extra incentive is that the 'King of Fez' is said to be planning an attack, claiming that the archipelago belongs to him if to anybody. Such claims by more local but less effective powers were often left to incubate off-stage during the colonial period, then coming forward to join in the polemics of the moment of decolonization. A related parallel has been Morocco's several attempts to annex the western Sahara ('Spanish Sahara' from 1884–1975). The latest invasion has led to the war with the Saharauis at the time of writing; there is also a linked and developing debate around the future relationships of Spain, the Canary Islands, the Saharaui people and Morocco. This is discussed in Appendix One.

Bethencourt's fortress, Riche Roque, is described as 'on the steep slope of a mountain, above a spring, almost a league from the sea'. An Inquisition document of the fifteenth century places the fort a league from the east coast anchorage of Pozo Negro where there is indeed a spring called 'Fuente Roche', though no ruins have yet been found (Serra and Cioranescu). However, in the nearby Bco. de la Torre (Ravine of the Tower) at El Junquillo, the ruins of a round fortress (Fig. 25), surely European in construction, have been disinterred (Jiménez 1965); according to the report, it was built upon a pre-conquest settlement. The archaeological commissar collected European artefacts as well as the usual island small finds. The imported material consisted of pieces of iron from pikes, sabres, daggers and other weapons; copper plate; nails; coins possibly from the late fourteenth or early fifteenth century. The plan should be compared

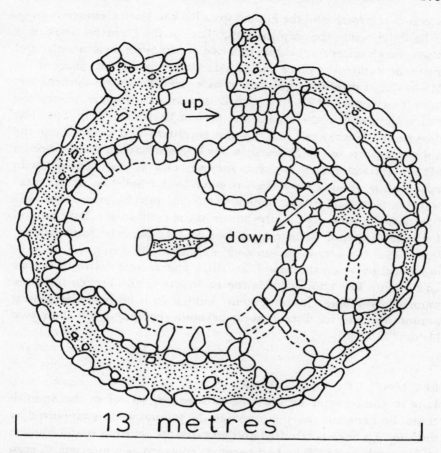

up →

down

13 metres

Figure 25   *Fortress, Bco. de la Torre, Fuerteventura, possibly French, 1404*
(foundations)

with those of Norman towers of the early fifteenth century.

Before starting his fortress, La Salle again tries Gran Canaria,
possibly feeling he would rather not be on the same island as
Bethencourt. He sets out on 25 July 1404, the *barge* getting caught in
a violent storm and eventually making land at Arguineguín. Pietre the
islander now re-appears with the son of Artamy, the king. Lured by
them into the shore on a promise of water and the gift of some pigs,
the French are ambushed 'in a shower of stones, so that all were
wounded'. La Salle's son, 'Hannibal the bastard', though hit, seizes an
oar and gets the boat out to sea . . . all except one, who protected
Hannibal with a shield, had dropped hopelessly onto the floor of the
boat. This gives a further idea of the effectiveness of the stone-
throwing on Gran Canaria. The islanders claimed they had 10,000
fighting men but La Salle said he had never seen more than 700–800
men together. Either way, it must have been clear that Gran Canaria

was also 'très forte' and the French went back to Fuerteventura.

La Salle brings the ship in at the 'Port of the Gardens', making a tower 'two leagues from there, in a fine open region, near a wood and a stream, calling the place Valtarajal'. Unluckily the next sheet of the MS has been torn out, probably to hide details showing Bethencourt in a bad light. The later, pro-Bethencourt chronicle places the Valtarajal tower in the area of the present Betancuria (Fig. 23). The now-ruined Torre de Lara, on the cordillera and overlooking the approach route to the Betancuria bowl, might have originally been a Mahoh fortress (Serra and Cioranescu); now at least European in appearance, it may have been re-built by La Salle as an advance-warning post. The village of Betancuria (Pl. 14b) became the island's first post-conquest capital, the houses of the early settlers built around La Salle's fortress. Bethencourt, soon to take over the whole island, was to have the settlement named after himself. The architecture is the most distinctive on the island, recalling the ancient farms of France and Spain. The church holds the remnants of the French invaders' banner. Now both the settlement, hidden in a bowl in the central mountains, and its distant small harbour rest quietly on their past history.

BETHENCOURT TAKES OVER

Late in the summer of 1404 the two leaders set off to the Spanish court. Bethencourt, having prepared the ground well, is supported by the king. La Salle is rebuffed and now disappears from island history; by his death (c. 1422) he had become renowned as a mercenary, even being once classed alongside Du Gueschlin.

From this point, events have to be seen through the later, pro-Bethencourt MS; this is a long work but contains little beyond marvellously hypocritical panegyrics on the 'King of Canaries', the title to which Bethencourt soon upgrades himself.

La Salle has left his fortress in the hands of his son, Hannibal, but the latter's men are outnumbered ten to one by Bethencourt's faction. The Norman's first attempt to take over Valtarajal was probably halted by the islanders breaking into Riche Roque, unaccountably left unguarded, as soon as he has set off; they burn the Frenchmen's chapel and wreck the fort, carrying away supplies and also some cannons, these an example of the inventiveness of the 1490 MS. Henceforth Bethencourt frequently provokes Hannibal's party; he uses threats to take away over 30 of their prisoners and, soon after, forces them to give up a number of island women also at Valtarajal. The two bands, in conflict, do still act together when attacked by the islanders.

The people of Fuerteventura fight back throughout 1404. After one ambush the French 'retreat to their quarters with their heads bleeding and their arms and legs broken by the stones . . . they can throw and handle a stone much better than a Christian can. When they hurl one, it is like a shot from a crossbow'. To deal with the Mahohs, the French arm the Lanzarote people with bows and arrows: '*tous les habitans de l'isle Lancelot se prennent à estre archers et gens de guerre . . . contre ceux d'Erbannie*'. Several Lanzarote men die in the daily battles. The Fuerteventura people conscript all men over the age of 18 as 'the war has occasioned them great losses'. Although 'they have the strongest castles to be found anywhere, they've left them for fear of being cornered' — the Mahohs have only unsalted meat and fear a siege. At one point Hannibal and his band kill a giant nine feet tall and capture a flock of a thousand goats. Some of those taken prisoner are transferred to Lanzarote, being put to repair the springs and reservoirs tactically destroyed by La Salle; others, including children, look after the flocks taken over by the French.

In January 1405, Fuerteventura's two kings send a single emissary to announce their capitulation. The chronicler-priest describes the baptisms of the kings — as Louys and Alfonce — and of their subjects. Henceforth all newly-born children are to be christened in the chapel of 'Our Lady of Bethencourt'. A second island had fallen to the Europeans.

COLONIZATION

Bethencourt at once returns to Normandy. Many people there offer themselves as settlers and the King of the Canaries, after a three-day feast at his mansion, sails back with almost 200 *colons*. Mostly single men, it is clear that many will have taken island women as wives, thus ensuring at least a partial survival of pre-conquest physical and cultural characteristics. The chosen *colons* sound to fall into two social classes. Many are artisans and labourers, brought to oversee the enslaved islanders — the chronicle's last word on the latter is that they are now 'beginning in earnest to work the fields, to plant and to build', though without saying for whom . . .

The other type of immigrant, led by various close relatives of Bethencourt, is most experienced in dressing up, pageantry, playing music and feasting. Landing on 9 May 1405, their splendour awes the islanders, according to the pro-Bethencourt MS. Four or five dozen of them, in silver lace, they come ashore, with banners and standards flying, to the sound of 'trumpets, clarions, drums, harps, rebecks, bassoons and other instruments' (Major's translation). Bethencourt has his own personal valet, groom, cook and other servants and rides on a mule. The immigrants are the first *gentils hommes* or *hidalgos* of

Canary society. Obsessed with their ancestry (Pl. 15a), dishonoured by work yet—with notable exceptions—increasingly poverty-stricken, they will live by taking part of the produce of one or more pieces of land worked for them by the ancient islanders and the other members of the lower social class.

TREACHERY ON HIERRO

On 6 October 1405 Bethencourt sails with three ships for Gran Canaria. His MS records that, blown eastwards on to the Sahara coast, he takes the chance to carry out manhunts there . . . Serra and Cioranescu say this journey was another invention of Jean V. One way or another Bethencourt does at length reach Gran Canaria and has several meetings with King Artamy (in fact already killed, at Agüimes in 1403, another example of the unreliability of this MS). An imprudent foray at Arguineguín by 45 Frenchmen—intoxicated perhaps by the clarions and rebecks—results in the deaths of half the party, including Hannibal, Jeuffroy d'Ansonville, Guillaume d'Auberbosc and Jean le Courtois, this last Bethencourt's own lieutenant. This disaster, incidentally, allows the Norman to take over La Salle's fortress.

Having made 'grosse guerre' against Palma for six weeks, killing a hundred, the ships turn their attentions to Hierro. The island lived in peace under a single leader, Añofo according to Torriani. The only status criterion was the size of one's flock the richest man being the leader; he received voluntary tributes from the rest.

Landing on the island, the key move by the French is to send Augeron, dubiously both a native of Gomera and the brother of the Hierro king, Armiche (French MS), to decoy the islanders to a peace meeting. This is successful, the French catching 112 bimbachos (Beni Bachir), as the people called themselves. 'Monsier de Bethencourt kept thirty-one for himself, prime amongst them the king, and the rest were shared out as booty and sold as slaves'. Not only was this financially rewarding but, in the approving words of the chronicler-priest, it provided dwellings for the immigrant colons. Bethencourt soon settled 120 householders on Hierro, the chronicler's logic allowing him to praise this too, since 'but for these people . . . Hierro would have been left utterly deserted'. The island had several times been depopulated already, it seemed.

This clearance of Hierro has been underlined when discussing the significance of the recent anthropological work. Marín said Bethencourt brought in French and Flemish from Fuerteventura. Soon sold to the Spanish, Hierro then received many Iberians. Darias said that, amongst the long lists of Europeans names in Hierro's early post-conquest archives, the few indigenous ones were all from Gomera and Tenerife. In the eighteenth century, he noted also, there were many negro, morisco and mulatto slaves. If any original islanders survived, hidden in the mountains, they would have been swamped, physically, by the immigrants.

EARLY ADMINISTRATION

The two eastern islands were shared amongst the Norman settlers, the only detail being that 'it was reasonable that they should be better off than the islanders'. The ex-king of Lanzarote, seemingly by now in European-style clothing, beseeches the French for a place to live, with land — and Bethencourt graciously allots him 300 acres, their produce to be subject to the *quinto* tax. Nor may he build a fortress — only the French nobles are allowed these. The Fuerteventura kings get 400 acres each.

About to leave the Canaries for ever, Bethencourt appoints his nephew Maciot as governor, his administration to be according to 'the customs of France and of Normandy'. Only a fifth of the *quinto* revenues seem to have gone to public works, the rest being shared between Bethencourt himself ($\frac{1}{5}$), Maciot ($\frac{1}{5}$) and the church ($\frac{2}{5}$).

On 15 December 1405, the King of the Canaries leaves his subjects. These, apparently unconsolable, cried: 'Alas! What will happen to our country, lacking such a wise and provident Lord, one who has put so many souls in the way of salvation'. Happily, they were not totally abandoned. On reaching Iberia, Bethencourt has his entourage dressed in fresh livery and then goes up to see the Castillian king at Valladolid. Having explained the conversion of the Canary Islanders, *tout par beaux et bons moyens*, he asks the king to get the pope to send out a bishop. Next Bethencourt rides his mule to Rome, his title making a great stir there, to receive the pope's personal congratulations. However, according to the thorough study by Serra and Cioranescu, these lengthy description of Bethencourt's activities on his final return to Europe are falsifications by his biographer.

Maciot de Bethencourt has himself knighted once his uncle leaves; the new governor is 'all goodness . . . beloved by all, especially by the natives'. A bishop soon reaches the islands; churches are being built under Bethencourt's final commands. The Frenchman died in 1425.

CHAPTER FIFTEEN

The Subjection of Gomera

Between the last events extracted from Bethencourt's MS, c. 1405, and the invasion of Gran Canaria in 1478, there is little coherent information on life in the Canaries. Brief, eye-witness summaries came from the Portuguese: Azurara (1443) and Ca da Mosto (1455). As it was during this period that Gomera was taken over by the Europeans, many details of the annexation are unknown.

Maciot de Bethencourt, the 'beloved' governor of the conquered islands, acted so despotically that, in 1414, the Queen of Castille sent out Pedro Barba de Campos, with three war caravels, to replace him. Maciot ceded the title to the three islands, together with that to Gomera, to Barba — though the Canaries 'belonged' by European law to his uncle, Jean, still alive in France. Then Maciot went to Madeira and sold the islands a second time to Prince Henry the Navigator of Portugal . . . and, subsequently, also to the Spanish Count of Niebla. This horse-dealing brought both endless law-suits in Europe — the details of which were of little importance to the islanders — and also 60 years of conflict between the crowns of Castille and Portugal. The background sequence of international events, given first, is better known than the actions on the tiny island of Gomera.

HENRY THE NAVIGATOR IN THE CANARIES

The Portuguese Infanta's ambitions encompassed all the Atlantic islands, both for their own sakes and as bases from which to invade Africa. His first ships were probably in Canary waters by 1415 (Beazley, in Azurara). In 1424, he sent out a fleet under Fernando de Castro, with 2,500 foot-soldiers and 120 horsemen, to try to improve on his paper title to the islands. The year before, Maciot, unblushingly trying to take over Gomera on his own account, had been caught by the leading Castillian claimant — attempting himself to gain control of the island — and imprisoned on Hierro. The Portuguese now rescued him and, together, they were soon again manoeuvering for control of Gomera. As a result of these and later European invasions, the islanders became divided into factions. However, soon both the cost and a complaint from the Castillian throne caused the Portuguese expedition to return home. About this time Henry was starting the colonization of Madeira and the Azores.

Azurara's notes were made during the return journey from a slave-catching expedition in 1443 against the W. Sahara. The ships were now 20–30m caravels, with three masts carrying lateen sails. The Portuguese land on Gomera to enlist the help of two island leaders, Bruco and Piste, for a raid on Palma. These men had earlier been at the two Iberian courts. Henry had treated them the better; and he had sent them back wearing clothes—the ending of the distinctive aspects of local culture seems to have been a colonial policy from the beginning of the cycle. The Portuguese reach Palma at dawn and attack some shepherds; several, together with one of the marauders, fall to their death during the chase. Stones were still the islanders' main weapons, supported by their horn-tipped staves. 'And it was a beautiful thing to see . . . the Christians engaged in capturing the Canarians'. The Portuguese, aided by the Gomerans, abduct 17 including a big woman who is a regional 'queen'. The Europeans then betray the Gomerans themselves, taking away 21 islanders—but Henry, afraid it will turn Gomera against Portugal, sends them all back . . . in clothes, of course.

Azurara gave figures for the 'fighting men' in each island: Lanzarote 60, Fuerteventura 80, Hierro 12; Gomera 700; Gran Canaria 5,000, Tenerife 6,000, Palma 500. The contrast between the conquered and the unconquered islands is significant . . . and the figures for the former presumably included Europeans too.

In 1446, the Infanta got a fresh mandate from the Portuguese crown to take over the Canaries and enforce a *quinto* tax for his own benefit. Lanzarote, earlier 'purchased' from Maciot, was taken over in 1446. The behaviour of the Portuguese, together with changes such as the currency, brought revolt by the established European settlers, forcing the incomers to leave the island in 1448. Parallel to this an energetic protest was being made by the Castillian claimant, Fernán Peraza—then busy establishing himself on Gomera—and in 1454 the Portuguese king again told the Infanta to withdraw, at least from the conquered islands. Henry died in 1460.

In 1468 yet another Lusitanian expedition set out, under Diego de Silva, to be again halted by diplomatic protest across Iberia. This venture concentrated, as will be seen, upon Gran Canaria. In 1477 there was a battle on Gomera between the Portuguese and the Castillians, each with their island faction. A year later, during the eventual conquest of Gran Canaria, the Portuguese landed a large force in alliance with the islanders against the Spanish. The international dispute was only settled by the treaty of Alcaçovas, 1479: the Portuguese were to have Africa from Cape Nun to the Indies, whilst Granada and the Canary Islands went to the Spanish.

GOMERA

The fourteenth century had brought the usual raids and reconnaissances by European slavers and missionaries. The clearest story is
of a 1384 expedition, led by a Galician, which was cornered by the
island king, Amaluige, on a high rock called Argodei, a word said to
have meant 'fortress' in the island speech. The Europeans surrendered
but were then allowed to go free — and, it is said, the islanders began
their conversion to Christianity at this time. Following Amaluige's
death, the island's four regions — Ipulan, Mulagua, Agana, Orone,
each with its own leader — were often in conflict, a division to be used
to their own advantage by the Europeans.

In the 1420s came the incursions of Maciot de Bethencourt and the
Portuguese. The Frenchman apparently occupied the Orone region
(now Arure), in the west; a local ruler was baptized, changing his
name from Unchepe to Maciot. By 1424 there was a chapel on
Gomera officially at least; it was dependent on the bishopric of
Fuerteventura. For the next two decades there was unresolved
competition between the French-Portuguese alliance and the
Castillian claimants, with the islanders divided behind them. About
1446 Fernán Peraza obtained the title to the Canaries and soon after
began building the Torre del Conde (Pl. 11b), now part of the port
and capital of San Sebastián (Ipulan). From this point at least there is
a permanent European presence.

Azurara (1443) gives an impression of the Gomerans just before
Fernán Peraza's definitive occupation. The inhabitants went naked,
saying 'that clothes are but sacks into which men put themselves' —
Henry's policy must have had little effect. Sexual relations were easy-
going; the men left their wealth to their sister's sons. Strangers were
lent married women as a mark of hospitality. The Gomerans lived in
caves and huts; they had goats and pigs, grew a little barley and
collected roots. Fighting was done with javelins. They spent much
time singing and dancing. Government was by a leader supported by a
number of officers, suggesting a re-united island. The Gomerans
believed in a god but followed no divine laws.

Ca da Mosto (1455) wrote just after Peraza's installation. Referring
to the inhabitants of the four 'conquered' islands, he said: 'They have
not been subdued in the mountains, for these are very high with many
strong places, which the whole world could not reduce, except by
siege. It is the same in all the islands held by the Christians'. Tenerife's
museum has a cross-bow labelled 'Benchijigua', Gomera's highest
settlement. In spite of the continuing hostilities, valuable cargoes were
already leaving for Europe, especially great quantities of the orchil
lichen. Azurara remarked that the unconquered islands too 'have
dangerous fortified places'; he put Tenerife's population at 15,000

and Gran Canaria's at 8,000–9,000, but Palma had 'few' people. These three islands were regularly raided at night in search of slaves.

HERNÁN PERAZA AND IBALLA

The early historians concerned themselves more with the tedious intrigues and marriages of the claimants to the Canaries than with the lives of the islanders. These were subjected to a series of local despots, with the records enlivened occasionally by a knife-thrust or large-scale revolt by the abused and desperate survivors of the pre-conquest people.

One example will suffice. Gomera passed from Fernán Peraza, by way of Inés Peraza, to Hernán Peraza. In 1477—on the eve of the opening of the conquest of Gran Canaria, described next—the new owner had to fight and defeat the islanders of the Mulagua region (now Hermigua) and their still-present Portuguese allies. The next decade saw intermittent revolts on Gomera (notably in Agana, now Vallehermoso) with Peraza's harsh retributions in turn increasing the dissent. In 1486 he was besieged in the Torre del Conde and had to be relieved by two caravels under Pedro de Vera—who had by now conquered Gran Canaria. Two hundred Gomerans were deported to Vera's island.

Peraza's end came in 1488. His affair with a Gomera woman, Iballa, has become a part of Canary folklore. An island leader, Hupalupa, opened a new rebellion, assembling his men—by whistling—at Benchijigua. They caught Peraza in Iballa's cave, in the Guahedún region, and, in spite of his lover's defence, he was speared by an islander, Hautacuperche. Peraza's wife, Beatríz de Bobadilla—later to add to island folklore by becoming the mistress of Columbus—was now besieged in the little tower in her turn. A bolt from a cross-bow killed Hautacuperche and, perhaps seeing Vera's ships again on the horizon, the islanders retreated and entrenched themselves up on the Alto de Garajonay, above Benchijigua and the island's highest point. Apparently they had originally made a pact with the Castillians but now they announced that 'the vessel (gánigo) is broken'; Alvarez (1959) associates this with a Berber custom of sealing a treaty by drinking milk together.

Pedro de Vera, fresh from his subjection of the far more difficult Gran Canaria, soon defeated the Gomerans, executing or deporting to Spain a good number, including most of those he had transported to Gran Canaria after the 1486 revolt. Gomera could be said to be finally pacified.

CHAPTER SIXTEEN

The Spanish Invasion: Gran Canaria

This island resisted the Europeans for three-quarters of the fifteenth century. Bethencourt's 1405 expedition against it was utterly routed. Twenty years later, Fernando de Castro and his Portuguese assailants were hardly allowed to set foot on the island. Azurara's notes (1443) are the first information since those by the French. His estimate of 5,000 'fighting men' implies a population of around 20,000.

This book has now reached the point at which the history of the Canaries becomes acceleratingly detailed. Some of the archaeological material will be seen in use, here and there, in the descriptions of the conquests of the three main islands. And, in fact, seen for the first and last time in an active role in island life. It may be that archaeological material not mentioned in the fifteenth-century histories—for example, the spiral engravings—had only an early role in Canary prehistory.

Little had changed, according to Azurara, in weapons, dress, food and daily life. However, as on Gomera, there are signs that the islanders had lost their early illusions about the more materially-based way of life of the Europeans: the people of Gran Canaria mock at those who prize clothes and they disdain metals, wrote the Portuguese. Nevertheless, some were not too proud to beat fish-hooks out of the Europeans' scrap-iron, with stones. There were now two kings—the French had reported a single monarch—but effective rule was still in the hands of the council of 190–200 nobles. The islanders had a god, dispenser of reward and of punishment; some called themselves Christians.

Azurara described three institutions. The bride-fattening, believed to help child-bearing: the women became so bloated that 'their skins are wrinkled like ripe figs'. Children were suckled by nanny goats. Secondly, the nobles' right to the first night: the fattened maidens paraded naked before these gentlemen, those who were judged *too* fat having to go into the sea and swim it off. Only after having lain with the nobles did the women go to their new husbands. Bernáldez (1479) said the women had the right to chose amongst the nobles. Thirdly, the Portuguese confirmed the lowest-level butcher caste: the islanders thought it 'a great sin to kill or skin an animal'; nobody would eat with the butchers nor would the women have relations with them. In fact, the work was preferably given to a captive Christian if available.

The Venetian Ca da Mosto (1455), in the service of the Portuguese, also left relevant notes. Taking several paragraphs from Azurara, he adds three unattributed details which, though usually said to refer to Tenerife, appear from the MS more likely to relate to Gran Canaria. First the men and women painted their bodies with green red and yellow designs, using herb-juices: this is in line with earlier evidence. Secondly, polygamy was normal. Thirdly, the installation of a new leader was marked by a ritual in a deep valley followed by a voluntary human sacrifice, the subject throwing himself down from a height; the leader was henceforth under a great obligation to this person's family. Ceremonies in the mountains were very much a part of Gran Canaria life, whilst the probability of the custom applying only to the installation of two coastal-based leaders, the *guanartemes* of Gáldar and Telde, meant the practice was not too demanding in numbers . . . Tenerife, as will be seen, had nine leaders.

Abreu gives details of the way Gran Canaria's leadership evolved into the hands of the famous islanders who were to oppose the Spaniards in 1478–83. Late in the fourteenth century, rule had been by numerous tribal chiefs. At Gáldar, probably in the Painted Cave, lived the virgin Antidamana (Andamana), a mediator of great wisdom. Conflict with some chiefs led her to marry Gumidafe, a noble, and together they conquered the island. It was their son, Artemis, who had been king, based at Gáldar, when the French had arrived; he was killed in the Agüimes skirmish in 1403. His two sons divided the administration between them: Egonayche Semidan at Gáldar, Ben Tagoyhem at Telde. A joint council, held at Gáldar — as Artemis' court had been there — consisted of a dozen nobles, *guayres*, half from each province, chosen for their 'prudence and valour'. Many of these figure in the conquest annals: Adargoma, Tazarte, Doramas (Gáldar), Maninidra, Autindana (Telde). Conflict led to rupture between the two *guanartemes*. The dividing line of their states ran roughly south-west from Tamaraceite (perhaps from the present Las Palmas towards Tejeda, Fig. 23).

HERRERA'S ATTACKS, 1461–76

The first European to make any serious impact on Gran Canaria was Diego García de Herrera. His interest in the Canaries came from his marriage in 1445 to Inés Peraza, the holder of the title to the four small islands from the death of her father, Fernán, in 1454. One of his first tasks was to impose his rule on the two eastern islands: having ejected the Portuguese, the European settlers did not want any form of imposed local government. This rebellious spirit had also crossed the Bocayna Strait to Fuerteventura; here it may have brought revolt by the descendants of the pre-conquest islanders.

In 1461 Herrera's first Gran Canaria expedition left Lanzarote, taking the Bishop of the Rubicon, and landed in the region of the present Las Palmas. Persuading the Gáldar and Telde *guanartemes* of their peaceful intentions, the Spaniards then held a unilateral ceremony taking over the island. A formal document of annexation was drawn up, the triumphant news sent back to Europe. However, attempts by the bishop to take over his new flock in 1462 and by Herrera to land again in 1464 were met with derision and hostility. Such 'treaties' are of course endless in the history of European colonization.

In 1468 came the Portuguese expedition under Diego de Silva, in continuance of the claim acquired by Henry the Navigator half a century earlier. By now Herrera had a fort, garrisoned, at Gando. Silva besieged and took this over. The Castillian throne complained to the Lusitanian crown and, aided by Silva's marriage to Herrera's daughter, the Portuguese changed their role to that of supporters of the Spanish in a major attack on the Gran Canaria islanders. Landing a further thousand men at Gando, four-fifths of them Portuguese, Herrera and Silva marched on Agüimes but were driven back; by now the islanders were using wooden swords and shields, copied from weapons taken from the Europeans (Viera).

Silva and 200 men next tried a night assault, by sea, on Gáldar, but were cornered by the *guanarteme* — best known as Tenesor Semidan — with 600 islanders. The Portuguese took refuge in the town's place of justice, a round unroofed area enclosed by a high wall. After two days' siege, Silva asks Semidan to let them go back to their ship.

The island leader thereupon makes one of the many gestures which — paralleling the trusting simplicity of the shepherd class — demonstrate the magnanimity of character of the nobility. Coming forward alone, Semidan tells the Europeans that nothing he can say will stop his men from killing them — but that he is willing to appear to be captured by Silva and then be used as a hostage to allow them to reach the shore. In the event Semidan goes so far as to persuade the islanders to befriend the Europeans in exchange for his 'liberty' — and even entertains them for a couple of days at Gáldar. Viera: 'The memory of this strange event (in which Diego de Silva suggested to Hernán Cortés the way in which — through the person of Montezuma — he would be able to take over Mexico) lives on in Gran Canaria'.

The return to the boat was made by way of the Cuesta de Silva, below the common granary described in an earlier chapter. The temperamentally-suspicious Portuguese, seeing the appalling steepness of the route by which they were being taken, felt the agile islanders intended after all to despatch them—but Semidan gave his arm to Silva to reassure him, the other islanders likewise helping down the other *conquistadores*.

The present author attempted this track in 1977 but found an essential section had just been blasted away in the course of the building of the new bridge across the enormous Bco. de Moya. In fact, many of the Canaries' prehistoric tracks are disappearing: damage by nearby development is common but so too is lack of upkeep, as pastoralism diminishes and the spread of vehicles causes the precipice-face paths to be abandoned.

Once Silva had set sail, the Gáldar *guayres* agree amongst themselves that Semidan must be a secret Christian and so prepare his assassination. On the first day of the next *sabor* or council, they hide their clubs, fitted with sharp-edged stones, under the palm branches which strew the floor of the meeting place. But Semidan has heard of the plot and, in a scene suitably Shakespearian, asks his *guayres*: 'Where have you hidden your weapons? Get them out and kill your leader!'

In the meantime Silva had returned to Gando to find Herrera preparing an attack on Telde. This too was beaten off, by the *guanarteme* Ben Taguayre, soon reinforced by Semidan; unlike the Tenerife *menceys* a decade later, the *guanartemes* did ally against the common invader. Viera affirms that Silva had tried to dissuade Herrera from this further aggression and, also, that he stopped the Gáldar *guanarteme* from being taken prisoner, in each case out of gratitude. The Europeans again left the island, this still unconquered.

Soon Herrera was back at Gando, laden with presents and with a Trojan horse in the shape of the Rubicon bishop. There was a meeting with the two *guanartemes* and their high priests or *faycanes*. The Europeans proposed peace, trade and the construction of a chapel. This was accepted by the islanders subject to their being given 30 Christian hostages under the age of 12. Herrera obtained a monopoly of the orchil in exchange for agreeing to pay its collectors. Prisoners were also exchanged.

In fact, the Spanish, aided by the trusting islanders, built another fort (or rebuilt the old one, Viera being confused over this incident); it was carefully called 'The Oratory'. The 30 hostages were in fact Canary children from the conquered islands and thus expendable. Herrera, with the bishop, went back to Lanzarote, leaving orders that the garrison, under Pedro Chemida, should take every opportunity to weaken the island by dividing it into factions.

The Spanish force rapidly became hated for its behaviour, the abduction of some women of noble birth leading the islanders to decide to throw the Europeans off Gran Canaria. Headed by the *guayre* Maninidra of Telde, they fell on two marauding bands and killed all 40 Spaniards. Then they dressed themselves in the dead men's clothes and, driving a flock of animals ahead of them — in imitation of the return of a successful foraging raid — approached the fort around midnight. Behind them came many more islanders in their ordinary dress. The Spanish were misled, opened the door . . . and most were slain — 50 of them, with half a dozen horses — whilst the fort was burnt and then demolished down to its foundations.

It can be seen that the islanders, once alerted, were astute campaigners. It is said that, on one occasion, afflicted by Herrera's attacks, the inhabitants of a village made it look abandoned by placing well-fed seagulls, their legs tied together, on their roofs — and then fell on their decoyed and scattered adversaries.

Nevertheless, the trusting island people could always be won over by an apparent change of heart. Pedro Chemida was now their prisoner and, in January 1476, he persuaded a great meeting, led by the two *guanartemes* with their *guayres* and *faycanes*, to send a deputation to Herrera to ask him to re-establish the trading treaty. Delegates were drawn, one each, from Telde, Gáldar, Agüimes, Tejeda, Aquejata (Aguacata), Agaete, Tamaraceite, Artebirgo(?), Artiacar (Arteara?), and Arucas — presumably administrative divisions, perhaps based on the founding tribes' lands. The treaty re-activated, Herrera began to plan yet again the annexation of Gran Canaria.

However, by now his typically despotic conduct in the conquered islands had again raised a powerful faction against him amongst his own countrymen and, in 1476, he and his wife, Inés Peraza, had to go to Castille to justify themselves. Since 1474 the ambitious Fernando and Isabel had been ruling in Spain and these decided in 1477 that, Herrera clearly being unable to conquer the remaining Canaries, their subjection should become the concern of the crown. Herrera and his wife were given the title of 'Counts of Gomera' — hence the present name of the tower on the shore at San Sebastián — and were confirmed in their title to the four islands. A cash indemnity helped Herrera (d. 1485) in his remaining expeditions — man-hunting on the coast of the W. Sahara, the details of this outside the present work (see Mercer 1973, 1976).

CONQUEST, 1478-83
The Catholic kings at once sent out an expedition: 600 foot-soldiers, 30 horsemen, together with many mercenaries attracted by the prospect of obtaining land and other wealth. The leaders were a general, Juan Rejón, his second-in-command, Alonso de Sotomayor, and the bloodthirsty prelate Juan Bermúdez. The expedition sailed

from Spain on 28 May 1478 in three ships, landing on the Isleta isthmus on 24 June.

On their way to rebuild and garrison the old Gando fortress, the miraculous advice of St. Anne, in the shape of an old peasant woman, leads the Spanish to fortify themselves instead on the banks of the Bco. de Guiniguada, near their landing place. The structures are a tower and a store protected by a great wall of stone and tree trunks. The many palms roundabout led to its name, the camp of Las Palmas. In 1978, this enormous city is celebrating its five-hundredth anniversary; the cathedral is dedicated to Sta. Ana.

The two island leaders, in midsummer 1478, were Semidan and Doramas. This Gáldar *guayre* had first rebelled against Semidan and then forcibly taken over the leadership of Telde when Ben Taguayre had died leaving only infant sons. Two thousand islanders united under Doramas, with another Gáldar *guayre* as his lieutenant, now marched on the Spaniards. The battle speech by Doramas was worthy of that by another 'barbarian', Calgacus, facing the Romans before the battle of Mons Graupius in N. Britain. Other legendary islanders who fought at Guiniguada were Tazarte and Maninidra. The Spanish infantry was led by Alonso de Lugo, then still a captain — but soon to become the most notorious and commanding figure in the Canaries — whilst Dean Bermúdez headed the Christian cavalry.

The battle was won by the Spanish, their first victory. Decisive were the terrifying horses, the cannon and the backing of the fortress. Adargoma was speared by Rejón, on horseback, and, caught and baptized, was taken to Spain. He became just another of the many recorded examples of the exhibition of Canary 'savages', often still in their skins, in S. Europe. Preferably they were encouraged to show off their great agility and dexterity or, like Adargoma, their famous strength; his name meant 'shoulders of rock'.

The fort finished, the Spanish now began the second phase, incessant raids which laid waste the fertile north and east and forced the islanders to retreat to the mountains. During this early period there was a renewed Portuguese threat, since the Iberian crowns were still in disharmony. Seven caravels anchored at Agaete, making a pact with the islanders that the Spanish should be attacked by sea by the Portuguese and by land by the local people. However, Rejón and his men ambushed and killed many of their fellow Iberians and the project failed. After this, according to Viera, Rejón became 'less generous in his way of fighting the islanders, laying waste their crops and fig-trees, taking their flocks and catching their children'.

Little progress was made during the next eight months. Supplies were low, due to a maritime blockade by the Portuguese, and the Spaniards record that they carried out foraging expeditions twice a

week. The poor morale led to internal conflict: Rejón against Bermúdez and Pedro del Algaba, the governor. The lengthy intrigues end
when the general, confirmed in his post by the crown, sends the dean
back to the Rubicon, on Lanzarote, and executes the governor. Rejón
is also in conflict with Herrera, to the extent even of bombarding
Arrecife, the port of Lanzarote.

During this period there was only one major battle with the
islanders. The Spanish land at Arguineguín and attack Tirajana — no
easy march — only to be totally routed on the return descent by the
faycan of Telde and his men. The Europeans lost 22 dead and 80
prisoners, with 100 wounded. The islanders, soon embarrassed by
their captives, decided to burn them alive; this was when the head
of the nuns, mother(!) of the *guayre* Autindana, obtained their release
instead, to avoid divine punishment. As the rout occurred on 24
August, the attacked settlement has since been known as San Bartolomé de Tirajana; to the islanders, the stronghold was probably
'Ansite' (Pl. 8b, Fig. 23).

The illegal execution of the governor led the Catholic kings to send
out Pedro de Vera in August 1480. Vera, aged forty and from Jerez in
Andalucia, had already an evil bloodshedding reputation. He took
over the Las Palmas camp and sent Rejón back to Spain as a prisoner.
To be the eventual conqueror of Gran Canaria, Vera at once behaved
as his predecessors: announcing an attack on Tenerife, he enlisted 200
of the Gran Canaria men who had become allies of the Spanish but,
once on the sea, the ship set off for the Spanish peninsula. The
watchful islanders immediately mutinied and forced a landing on
Lanzarote, swimming ashore in their haste to leave the slavers; here
they fared little better, Herrera taking them to fight and die in his
African man-hunts. Back in Las Palmas, many 'pacified' islanders
returned to the mountains on hearing the news.

The turning point in the invasion may have come with the death of
Doramas. The Telde *guanarteme* came and challenged the Spanish,
drawing up his army on a hill at Arucas. Daring any one of the invaders to meet him in single combat, he successfully despatched the
first contender, Juan de Hozes, with a javelin (*susmago*). However,
Vera himself then at once charged him on horseback — the fairness of
this is not questioned in Spanish history books — and killed Doramas
with his lance. The ensuing battle was won by the Spanish. The
guanarteme, baptized whilst dying with water out of a helmet, was
buried in the mountain which has his name, many of his subjects
suffering captivity in order to be at his interment.

Vera now turned his attention to the mountain fortresses. The front
line of these, seen from Las Palmas, were in the heights of
Tamaraceite, Moya and Gáldar (Fig. 23). Leaving Lugo with 500 men

and 10 horses at Las Palmas, Vera sailed round to Agaete and there began a stronghold of stone and adobe. The aim was to attack from both east and west. Two further assaults were also made in Tirajana, the first unsuccessful, with 25 attackers killed, but the second temporarily dislodging the islanders. Probably it was the food-stores and flocks which were sought, since such incursions achieved little else except reconnaissance and a psychological victory, hardly worth so many deaths . . . unless these were of renegade islanders, comparatively expendable.

Doramas was replaced by a Telde *guayre*, name unknown; Viera gives him much the same name as Doramas' predecessor. The new *guanarteme* had once defeated Doramas in single combat. His first action was to give himself up to the Spanish, asking for baptism. After a period at the fort, during which he studied all aspects of its organization, he returned to the mountains and began a series of attacks. These, though carefully planned, never succeeded in taking over the fort. On one occasion 'Ben Taguaya' himself scaled the wall at night and killed the best horses—the islanders greatly feared these animals, their impact soon to be repeated under Pizarro, in America.

Once again the invasion was interrupted by internecine conflict: General Rejón returned with four armed ships and a mandate from Queen Isabel for the conquest of Palma and Tenerife. Vera refuses to let his predecessor land on Gran Canaria and so Rejón takes his 300 men and 20 horses away to attack Palma. Unluckily driven by the wind on to Gomera, he has to land at Hermigua. Hernán Peraza, remembering the Lanzarote conflict between Rejón and his father, Herrera, sends a force to catch the *conquistador*—and the latter is killed in the struggle. There are obvious parallels in the factionalism which was to divide the Spaniards in the Americas early in the next century.

Rejón's widow at once returned to the court, her denunciation leading to the arrest in turn of Hernán Peraza. Queen Isabel freed him on two conditions. First, that he should add himself, with a company of his Gomerans to the conquest of Gran Canaria. Second, that he should marry the beautiful Beatríz de Bobadilla . . . in whom the king, Fernando, was in his turn showing too much interest.

The 1482 campaign against the northern strongholds of Gran Canaria proved successful. Lugo, from Agaete, took Gáldar; Peraza had brought 80 Gomerans and 13 horses together with 70 Lanzarote men sent by his father. Vera attacked Moya and Arucas, linking up with Lugo at Los Bañaderos, as it has since been called, on the north coast.

At Gáldar, Lugo took prisoner the ancient Tenesor Semidan, asleep in his palace, with four *guayres*, including Maninidra of Telde and 11 servants; the settlement yielded huge spoils to the invaders. Semidan and the nobles were taken to Spain and displayed, still dressed in skins, in the main cities of the south. At Toledo, Semidan was dressed in silk and scarlet cloth and baptized 'Fernando Guanarteme'; the first name was that of the Castillian king, the second was subtly designed to retain his title as far as the islanders would be concerned . . . for, his thinking re-oriented, the Gáldar leader was at once returned to Gran Canaria to play a key role in the final encounters. The Spanish crown generously promised him a zone of poor mountain pasture, Guayedra, on the Agaete coast.

Simultaneously, the Spanish monarchs sent out reinforcements: 300 men from Viscaya and Burgos. The Holy Brotherhood also decided it should be represented, adding two companies of light horse (55 men each) and one of arquebusiers (150 men). The five ships sailed from San Lucar de Barrameda.

The sight of the new contingents dismayed the islanders, becoming aware of the inexhaustible supply of men and arms against them. Semidan had been replaced by his nephew, Ben Tejui, with Tazarte — another renowned figure — and Hecher Hamenato as military leaders. The Spanish at once send 'Fernando Guanarteme', magnificently apparelled, to describe to the islanders the splendour of the Catholic kings, the power of the invaders . . . and to promise them freedom and all other rights if they will capitulate. The complex emotions which result when the islanders recognize and hear their old and revered leader have to be imagined . . . though dismayed, they totally reject his embassy.

Fernando returns to the Spanish and gives them full details of the organization of the islanders, including a description of their main fortress, Bentayga (Pl. 1a; the reader is reminded that some, perhaps all, of these high rocks were also places of worship). Vera besieged Bentayga, in the central mountains, for 15 days, his eventual onslaught repulsed by javelins, stones and tree trunks. The Spanish marched back by Tirajana and Acayro; this, incidentally, shows the latter fortress was probably the present 'Roque Acuario' near the Balos site, in the south east (Fig. 23).

Vera then turned his men towards the weaker fortresses. The stronghold of Titana (site unlocated by the author) was taken next, using islanders; looted and abandoned, it was at once re-occupied by the local people. Sendro (near Telde) was attacked from two sides, one force actually led by Fernando Guanarteme and made up of 500 Christianized islanders; they defeated Aytami, the Gáldar *faycan*, and his 2,000 men. Next it was the turn of the Amodar (unlocated too) — two women flung themselves over the precipice rather than be taken by the invaders — and then of Fataga, on the penetration route from the southern tip of the island.

Aytami, in fact the uncle of Fernando, now counsels surrender and soon crosses to the Spanish side; baptized, Gáldar's high-priest will in due course fight against Palma and Tenerife. One of the military leaders, Tazarte, throws himself off the Risco de Tirma, invoking the name of this sacred peak; it overhangs the west coast, between Agaete and San Nicolás.

Elsewhere the islanders continue to resist, however. Vera orders an imprudent attack on Ajódar (unlocated), a coastal fortress, only to lose most of his force of 200 bowmen, under Miguel de Muxica. Fernando Guanarteme is sent to cover the retreat, his authority alone saving the last Spaniards.

On 8 April 1483 Vera and 1,000 men again laid siege to 'Ansite', the final action (Pl. 8b, Fig. 23). In it were gathered 600 men, 1,500 women and many children, led by Ben Tejui of Gáldar, and the *faycan* of Telde. Again Fernando Guanarteme goes to them with sumptuous regalia and valueless promises. The majority decision is to surrender — also crying out '*Atis Tirma*', Ben Tejui and his lieutenant leap off the summit of the fortress.

The current Lanzarote bishop, Juan de Frías, brought along specially for the eventual capitulation, organizes a 'Te Deum' on the spot. The eighteenth-century historian and prelate Viera, if he had sometimes expressed reservations about his countrymen's actions on Gran Canaria, affirmed that though the conquest was to lead 'almost to the islanders' disappearance from the world, there's no doubt that this was more than compensated by the knowledge they gained of the true religion'.

CHAPTER SEVENTEEN

The Spanish Invasion: Palma

Following the information in the chronicle of the French conquerors, there are no notes on Palma until 1443. Azurara then confirmed the islanders' reliance on meat, milk and wild plants, adding that they did not fish; their fighting staves had horn tips at each end, one sharper than the other; they were led by chiefs—the bravest, according to Torriani— and had no god. This Portuguese had a low opinion of the people, 500 in number. Like most chronicles, his impressions can be seen to disagree in part with other evidence. Ca da Mosto did not visit Palma.

Maciot de Bethencourt is known to have attacked Palma, in search of slaves, in the 1420s. The 1443 raid by the Portuguese and Gomerans has been described. Soon after this, Fernán Peraza, having established his authority over the newly-acquired lesser islands, also decided to attack Palma. About 1447 he sent three warships there with 200 Spanish arquebusiers and 300 Canary men, these armed in their own way; his son Guillén was put in command. The expedition landed in the Tihuya territory (Fig. 23), probably at Tazacorte in the centre of the west coast, an anchorage favoured by invaders. The chief of Tihuya was Echedey and he now put his brother Chenauco in charge of defence; a lesser role was taken by Dutinmara, lieutenant of Tinaba, ruler of the north-eastern lands of Tagaragre. The Spaniards imprudently marched inland, to their doom, unable to cope on the difficult terrain with the stones and boulders hurled at them. Trying to marshal his force, Guillén Peraza was killed.

This defeat led to attacks, for loot and revenge, by the Europeans of Gomera and Hierro. The territories assaulted are recorded by name with their leaders: Tenagua, under Atabara, Ahenguarame under Echentive, Tigalete under the brothers Tariguo and Garehagua. In the attack on the last they caught a sister of the chiefs and, when she later attacked her personal captor, he killed her. Eventually a trading pact was concluded between the islanders and the Europeans. But one day Garehagua found himself face to face with his sister's killer—and transfixed him with his javelin instantly. As the Gomerans would have said, 'the pot was broken', fighting began again. The Europeans attempted to catch a huge, handsome woman called Guayanfanta but the first to reach her found himself seized and bundled towards a precipice . . . but eight more slavers got to their comrade in time, breaking the woman's legs. The Palma women always had a reputation for strength.

The pact was re-established, to be a factor in the eventual conquest. Around 1488 a number of Palma leaders were baptized, in Gran Canaria—five years after this island's capitulation—resulting in the people of their territories becoming known as *bandos de paces*, groups who would not resist the Spaniards.

Alonso de Lugo now stepped further forward, to become the foremost *conquistador* in the Canaries. In 1489 Pedro de Vera had been relieved of his governorship of the Canaries, having been denounced by the current bishop for the atrocities he had committed against the Gomerans in retribution for their killing of Hernán Peraza; however, the Crown also wanted his help against the Moors at Granada, an event coming to play a part in developments in the Canaries. Lugo came from the city of his name, in Galicia. In the conquest of Gran Canaria he had been the captor of the Gáldar *guanarteme*, a prisoner of great strategic value; subsequently Lugo seems to have continued as governor of the Agaete fort and region. In 1491 Columbus was preparing his first voyage; in 1492 he was to pass through the Canaries, his last sight of land being Hierro. Around Granada the troops of the Catholic kings were besieging the Moors. As a young man Lugo had distinguished himself against these and he appears to have been at Granada in 1491. However, without waiting for the siege to be successful, he obtained the Crown's permission to conquer the two remaining Canary Islands. His mandate included taking over the zone from Cape Guer to Cape Bojador on the adjacent African coast, soon to be allowed to Spain under the Treaty of Tordesillas (1494).

Funds were raised by going into partnership with two merchants, one Florentine, the other Genoese; presumably Lugo offered them a share of the *quinto* tax, agreed with the Crown to come to him as a return for his leadership in the conquests. Lugo recruited part of his force in Seville, attracting men with promises of slaves, flocks and lands. In 1491 he sailed from Cádiz in two ships, his weapons including cannon. On Gran Canaria he added many islanders, including Gomerans, bringing his contingent up to 900 men.

Amongst those who willingly set out, intending to share in the spoils and, if needs be, to fight the still-free Palma people, were Fernando Guanarteme and the Gáldar *guayre* Maninidra. This use of Gran Canaria men against Palma was sanctioned by the Crown. Ever since Vera had conquered Gran Canaria, 10 years earlier, it had been official policy to limit the resident islanders to 40, these being the retinue and family of the collaborating Fernando Guanarteme;

however, many had returned secretly, so that their use in the invasions of Palma and Tenerife would solve this problem by reducing their numbers again.

Lugo's two frigates, together with a supply boat, reached Palma uneventfully, anchoring at Tazacorte as usual, on 29 September 1492; Columbus was then over halfway to America on his first voyage. A fort having been built, Lugo began negotiations with the island chiefs. Palma may then have had 1,200 inhabitants spread over the dozen territories. Lugo offered peace, freedom and material gifts in exchange for recognition of Spain's authority and for conversion to Christianity; the ancient trading pacts and, above all, the earlier negotiations by an island woman, Francisca Palmesa, enslaved on Gran Canaria, are known to have been reassuring to the islanders. The four S.W. territories accepted at once, but Tigalete, under the two brothers, refused; the islanders lost the ensuing battle but soon reformed to harass the Spaniards from the north-east of the island. However, by the time winter came, all except one of the territories had effectively submitted to the invaders.

Eceró, believed to have meant 'strong', consisted of the great erosion bowl now called La Caldera de Taburiente; the terrain has been described in earlier chapters, with an illustration of the people's sacred rock, Idafe (Pl. 6a). The leader was the well-organized Tanausu. There are only two ways of getting into the bowl: the great ravine (Axerjo, now Bco. de las Angustias) and the notch in the south-east arc of the rim (Adamacansis). In the spring of 1493 Lugo unsuccessfully tried first the high pass and then the watercourse; Palma men carried him and his officers during the second expedition.

Lugo now resorted to the Spaniards' second customary tactic — treachery. Tanausu had said he would only discuss a peace treaty once Lugo was off his land, so the Spaniard — leaving a part of his men hidden in the bowl — lured Tanausu down onto easier terrain and then attacked him from two sides. The islanders were defeated and their leader captured. Lugo's treatment of the Palma people, in spite of his promises, will be described later. Thus ended the conquest of Palma, on 3 May 1493.

CHAPTER EIGHTEEN

The Spanish Invasion: Tenerife

Tenerife, the last island to fall, had been raided but rarely in the course of the century. The Guanches—this name, one interpretation being 'sons of Teide', is correctly used only of these islanders—would at least have noticed the increasing presence of sailing ships in the archipelago.

Azurara saw the Guanches as comparatively well off and civilized—a state achieved in spite of the absence of the advanced cultural elements found on Gran Canaria. He recorded all the main crops and food animals—wheat, barley, sheep, goats, pigs—and said the dwellings were both caves and huts. Wives were not shared. Tenerife was divided into eight or nine territories (Fig. 23), then regularly at war with each other; the usual fire-hardened pinewood lances were described. Each territory had its chief. The latter kept his predecessor's remains near him, unburied; his own successor threw the penultimate relics in a pit, replacing them by the latest remains; the disposal of a set of relics was marked by the bearer saying 'May he go to salvation', or so we are told. And the Guanches had a god, according to Azurara (1443).

Ca da Mosto (1454) heard stories about Tenerife, several disagreeing with Azurara's notes, others expanding on these. The Guanches—estimated at 14–15,000—greased their bodies with a mixture of goat fat and herb juices, their skin garments not adequate alone against the cold of winter. They did not have huts, he said. The position of chief was not inherited but went to the strongest. They had no Christian faith nor god: 'Some worship the sun, others the moon and stars, with strange idolatrous fancies'.

The historical sequence leading towards the invasion period begins prior to Azurara's passage. Tenerife was then ruled by Ben Zenuria, his seat perhaps Adeje. At his death, his nine sons divided up the island. The succession ceremony, putting together Torriani and Espinosa, involved only one ancestral bone, presumably because the dead king's relics had in fact been divided amongst his many heirs. The event took place in the *tagoror*. A territory's new leader, or *mencey*, made his oath whilst holding the bone over his head. The elite, including his family, followed suit, with the words: 'By the bone of he who made thee great'. The relic, wrapped in skins, went everywhere with the *mencey*. The line of succession was from the leader to his brothers and only if these had no issue then to his own sons; the elite had a degree of choice over the succession, however. The most powerful of the first nine *menceys* was Tmodat of Taoro, with 7,000 fighting men (Abreu). This territory was to lead the resistance to the Spaniards.

RELIGION, THE SPEARHEAD

Tradition, enshrined in the work of the priest Espinosa, tells how, in 1390–1400, a wooden image of Mary carrying Christ appeared on the shore in the N.E. Territory of Güimar. Could this be the Virgin and Child statue made by the two priests amongst the Mallorcans and Catalans caught on Gran Canaria late in the fourteenth century? Abreu refers to this image specifically, also saying that one of the two hermitages was at Agaete (opposite the Güimar coast). His story was that the priests met a peculiar death, being thrown into a pit in the mountains. However, their clothes were later washed up on the shore, so it was thought by the islanders that there must be an underground tunnel to the sea. But perhaps the statue had in fact been thrown in the sea (which had brought the priests and their religion in the first place), to float across to Tenerife, whilst it was its vestments which had been washed back onto the shore.

The image at once demonstrated its supernatural powers to the Guanches and so it was placed in the Güimar chief's cave, Chinguaro. About the middle of the fifteenth century, Fernán Peraza organized a raid on Tenerife; his son's death in the assault on Palma was noted in the last chapter. Amongst the captives taken back to Lanzarote was a seven-year-old boy, christened Antón Guanche. Seven years later, touching at Tenerife on a voyage to Gomera, the boy escaped. Recognizing the image and being by now well instructed in Christian teachings, he soon formed a cult to the Virgin, around the statue, with himself as priest. The image was given its own cave, Achbinico; in the 1970s the shrine has become a 'basilica' in the nearby Bco. de Candelaria. As a result of this cult, the pre-conquest people of Güimar were henceforth to feel more in harmony with the Spanish *conquistadores* than did those of the other regions.

Military incursions were carried out by Diego de Herrera in 1464, parallel to the attempt by this 'Lord of the Isles' to take over Gran Canaria, as described. On Tenerife the Europeans' favourite anchorage has always been Añaza, now Sta. Cruz. Herrera's three ships landed 400 men but these had hardly started inland before the sight of the gathered islanders sent them hastily back aboard. Two interpreters were despatched to the nine *menceys*, demanding subjection. Having held a *tagoror*, the islanders sent back a non-committal message of friendship. The Spanish thereupon marched up to Aguere, now La Laguna . . . Herrera cutting down branches, turning over the soil and moving boulders—to the good-humoured astonishment of the Guanches—to indicate his possession of Tenerife. As on Gran Canaria, an official document was drawn up, purportedly accepted by the chiefs of the nine regions, together with the leader of the enclave, within Tegueste, called 'Hidalgo Pobre' or the Poor Nobleman by the invaders. The Spanish standard-bearer cried out three times in a loud voice: 'Tenerife for the King of Castille and León and for the noble knight Diego de Herrera' . . . only Antón Guanche, amonst the islanders, seems to have taken any notice of the charade. There was however a more practical aim: to have a form of claim to use against the Portuguese, should these attempt the conquest of Tenerife.

The Guanches' friendship had however been gained. Yet, soon after, Herrera's son, Sancho, stole the image in Antón Guanche's charge, taking it to Fuerteventura . . . later returning it because of its miraculous manifestations of disapproval at the sacrilege. This oddly impolitic act did not affect relations, since the islanders had not even noticed the disappearance of their image because, as the ecclesiastical historians put it, the illuminations, fragrances and celestial music in the cave had continued unabated.

Sancho de Herrera and 80 men obtained permission to build a fort at Añaza, provided each side agreed to submit any aggressors to the other side's justice. A Spanish foraging party soon stole a large flock of animals, beating up their shepherds: duly handed over, the aggressors were reproached by the Anaga chief and then freed. Such conduct continued until, one day, five Guanches in revenge assaulted a Spanish soldier: in turn given over to the European justice, the islanders were at once garotted. The *mencey* of Anaga, incensed, attacked the fort with 1,000 Guanches, killing many Spaniards. Sancho de Herrera and the other survivors hastily embarked in the middle of the night and went back to the eastern islands.

About 1490, Pedro de Vera's successor as Gran Canaria governor, Francisco Maldonado, equipped two ships and set off to conquer Tenerife—this was a time when, in Spain, any gentleman might see himself in the role of knight errant, with the adventures of Don Quijote soon to be written. Landing again at Añaza and marching on Aguere with only part of his men, he was confronted by a force ten times as great but, believing them perhaps to be sheep, attacked at once and suffered a bloody defeat, only being saved from total annihilation by the arrival of the rest of his men. A hundred of the invaders were killed, both Spanish and islanders. Maldonado, judge as well as governor, used to say afterwards: 'No more litigation with the Guanches of Tenerife'.

LUGO'S FIRST EXPEDITION REPULSED

The opening stage of the conquest began on 30 April 1494; Viera's account is by far the most detailed and so his chronology has to be followed, even though it is clear that this cannot be exactly correct. By now the veterans of the successful siege of Granada — over in January of 1492 — had become available for further exploits against the heathen. The success of Columbus' exploration was a further spur to conquest. The Spaniards' experience and superior weapons (Viera includes fire-arms) and endless supply of men would sooner or later outweigh the problems of logistics, the difficult terrain and the Guanches' strength, agility and clearly outstanding command of such weapons as they had developed. And, above all, the Spanish placed success before scruples — the Guanches were but beginners in the art of treachery. By the time Lugo appeared, the islanders seem to have felt the end was near. The soothsayer Guañameñe had told Ben Como, leader of Taoro, that Tenerife would soon be ruined. Ben Como, the most powerful of the *menceys*, had recently deemed it wise to make a treaty with those of Tacoronte and Anaga, ending 30 years of strife which had followed his marriage to a woman each of the other two leaders had claimed.

Lugo arrived at Añaza with no less than 15 brigantines carrying 1,000 infantry and 120 horsemen; their weapons included cross-bows and artillery. In an action by now becoming familiar to 'primitive' peoples in America as well as Africa, Lugo landed with a huge cross in his arms, 'after a few steps fixing it in the sand and adoring it with the greatest humility' (Viera).

Setting up a camp in spite of some Guanche harassment, Lugo at once sent Fernando Guanarteme, with 70 kinsmen, on a successful mission to persuade Ben Eharo, the *mencey* of Anaga, to leave them in peace. The small territory of Tegueste was then raided by the Spanish. In one incident they caught a shepherdess with a child and carrying a *zurrón* full of *gofio* on her back: a few days later her captors tried to baptize the boy but she preferred to throw herself and her son into the sea.

On 4 May Lugo felt able to leave the fort and march on Aguere. About half-way up the 10km slope they were met by the Guanche army. Significantly, in view of the whistled language of Gomera, the Tenerife people not only shouted but whistled when they attacked; this may well have been a form of communication, above the din, as much as for theatrical effect. The Guanche force, 400 men, was in fact that of Ben Como, accompanied by his famous lieutenant Tinguaro. Lugo made the usual promise: peace and freedom in exchange for submission and Christianity. Ben Como is said to thereupon have offered Lugo supplies—and asked him to leave, adding politely that he knew too little of Christianity to embrace it . . . and, uncompromisingly, that the *menceys* of Tenerife submitted to no man.

Ben Como went back to Taoro, the scene a few days later of the most famous *tagoror* ever held in Tenerife. Eight leaders attended, that of Güimar significantly absent. At first it was generally agreed that the island should unite to repel the Spanish—but, when Ben Como proposed himself as military head, the jealousies and fears of the remote, westerly *menceys* (of Icod, Daute, Adeje and Abona) overcame their commonsense. Saying each should defend his own land, these four leaders left for their distant territories. Those of the north-east, already threatened, joined Ben Como; Taoro alone was said to have over 4,000 men.

The *mencey* of Güimar now played the role of Tenesor Semidan in Gran Canaria; his collaboration with the Spanish was partly the result of the Christian shrine on his land and partly due to a very personal feud with Ben Como . . . and he would also have expected the invaders to make him chief amongst the islanders once they had taken over Tenerife. Añaterve el Bueno, as the Spanish henceforth called him, took 600 men and went to see Lugo at the shore camp; the invaders were then engaged in further fortification and in opening wells. The interpreter was, of course, Antón Guanche. Añaterve the Good agreed to vassalage, baptism, abstention from the Taoro alliance and a contribution of men and supplies.

Lugo, repeating his Palma campaign, settled in for the winter—though, other than in the higher lands, this season would seem to be the best for a military campaign by Europeans. Anyway, in the spring the Spanish again marched inland, camping at Aguere. In 1495 there was still a lake there, bordered in places by a dense wood, notably of *madroños* and *mocaneras*, the freshness of the basin attracting flocks of Canary and African birds; the Spanish settlement of La Laguna saw the lake almost entirely disappear, both silting up as a result of erosion due to intensive clearance and farming of the surrounding hillsides and being deliberately drained for health reasons—problems hitherto avoided by the Guanches' non-intensive settlement pattern.

Apparently the soldiery was loth to leave such a pleasant place—and indeed, marching towards the north coast, they were heading for Spain's greatest defeat in all the Canary campaigns. The aim was to attack Ben Como in his domain. The invaders made their way through the Tacoronte territory without opposition. Led on by the finding of some unguarded animals, they reached the valley of Arautapala (Orotova). Here, however, Lugo decided the Guanches' silence was too suspicious for safety and so ordered the return to Aguere. Entering the intricate Bco. de Acentejo, the Spanish found themselves hopelessly ambushed by Tinguaro and 300 Guanches. The horses were unusable, standard military formations impossible.

The battle lasted three hours. Tinguaro despatched Diego Núñez, one of Lugo's mounted captains, with a javelin thrust and then a blow of his mace. The *banot* or pommelled lance was also used by the Guanches. Boulders and tree-trunks, flung from above into the melée of horses, men and looted animals, were as effective as artillery fire. Lugo, too conspicuous in his red uniform, somehow found a moment to change it with that of Pedro Mayor, 'this good soldier having the glory of dying in his place' (Viera). After two hours of fighting, Ben Como himself arrived with a further 3,000 men. Lugo, maddened, attacked the Taoro leader from behind, wounding him, but Sigoñe, one of Ben Como's captains, at once threw a stone at the Spaniard, momentarily knocking him out. The story goes that he came round to find his horse killed under him and that he was surrounded by 50 Guanches . . . but survived. Indeed, Lugo was exceptionally good at survival: in 1499 he was to lead a Spanish force into a similar massacre on the African coast, being himself left behind as dead on the battlefield — and yet there too he survived (Mercer 1976). It is said that 30 Güimar men rescued Lugo at Acentejo.

The remains of the Spanish force fled in small bands in different directions. Some headed straight back to La Laguna over the central spine (now the Esperanza mountains), wisely avoiding the waiting Guanches of Tacoronte. A further 90 Canary men, with four Portuguese, had saved themselves by swimming to a rock out at sea; the Spaniards sent round some boats to collect them. Thirty invaders took refuge in a cave high on a hill, night then temporarily halting the assault by the islanders. In the morning, Ben Como offered them safe-conduct if they laid down their arms. This accepted, the Taoro leader received the reprieved Spanish with 'friendliness' (Viera), gave them food and, having them escorted by 100 men under Sigone, sent them back to Lugo. The reader may have noticed that the alternation of Canary magnanimity and European treachery is recorded in the annals of the *invaders* — so the contrast is unlikely to have been over-emphasized.

The Spanish settlement in the lower zone of the ravine is now called 'La Matanza de Acentejo' — the massacre of Acentejo. Six hundred invaders and 300 Guanches are said to have been killed, whilst the 200 of Lugo's men who survived were all wounded. For long after this, human bones and broken weapons could be found in the ravine. A painting by Jan Mostaert, in the Franz Hals Museum in Harlem, may depict the ambush, in spite of inaccuracies such as cows and monkeys and the bows shown, together with stones, in use by the attackers (Martínez).

Encouraged by the successful ambush, the Guanches now began attacks on the weakened fort of St. Cruz, at Añaza. The Güimar leader, the good Anaterve, now sent 300 men with provisions and medicinal herbs. Lugo, always short of funds, rewarded this by at once shipping off these islanders for sale in Cádiz and Seville. The Crown, probably judging this unlikely to further its conquest ambitions, ordered them to be freed; it is surprising that Lugo could be so impolitic as to risk the alienation of his essential and reliable ally. An attack by 400 Guanches from Anaga, under Jeyneto, was beaten off after heavy fighting—but the pressure on the wounded and exhausted Spaniards was too great and, on 8 June 1495, Lugo and the others sailed back to Las Palmas.

THE SECOND INVASION

Lugo's Italian backers, established in the Canaries, at once made a deal with a Spaniard on the Peninsula: he would send 600 men and 50 horses and 'once the costs of the venture were recouped, the captives, flocks and other spoils would be divided into two shares, one for the backers and the other for those who had fought'. This Spaniard approached Juan de Guzman, Duke of Medina-Sidonia; he was both a friend of Lugo and a descendant of the Count of Niebla, one of those grandees to whom Maciot de Bethencourt had sold the islands three-quarters of a century earlier. The Duke helped in the raising of the troops, mainly in San Lucar, a city under his jurisdiction. On 22 October 1495 the reinforcements left the Peninsula in six transport ships.

On 2 November Lugo again anchored off Añaza. This time he had 1,100 men and 70 horses. Amongst the many islanders in his force were Pedro Maninidra, Ben Taguayre and Alonso de Adargoma. Having prayed at his cross, still in place on the shore, Lugo set the men to rebuild the fort.

The island territories were still divided into the Taoro-led group and the unco-ordinated western lands, relations kept sour by the influence of Añaterve the Good, of Güimar, in pursuance of his personal ends. The new invasion brought an immediate call to arms in the north-east of the island: the official figures, repeatedly sceptically by Viera, were that Taoro raised ·5,000 men, Tacoronte 2,000, Tegueste 1,200, Anaga 2,600, with 250 men from the Hidalgo Pobre enclave. The Taoro lands—the Orotova valley—are of course the most fertile in the island and, in a wholly rural society, would certainly have been the most highly populated. However, if the alliance had really fielded 11,050 men, the whole island could have raised at least half as many again—implying a population of each least 60,000 Guanches. The usual estimate has been 15,000 inhabitants. Reducing the force which now opposed Lugo to a quarter, the Spanish were only out-numbered by about three to one, a disadvantage balanced by the fire-arms now carried in quantity by the *conquistadores*.

Ben Como sent two spies out down the Bco. de Tahodio, the ravine immediately east of the anchorage. Seen by four horsemen, one escaped by making enormous leaps with his pole-cum-lance but the other was caught and revealed that Ben Como planned to attack the invaders as they climbed the long slope inland. So, leaving Fermando Guanarteme in charge of the fort, Lugo marched up in the night, confronting a surprised Ben Como near the Aguere lake. The Taoro chief as usual rejecting Lugo's demands, the Spaniard fired his pistol in the air and his force discharged their muskets and crossbows against the Guanches. The reply, accompanied by 'horrendous whistlings', was a hail of sharp-edged stones and javelins. The Guanches threw back the crossbow bolts with devastating effect; in their simplicity they also imitated the twang of the weapons' cords on release, believing this would help produce the same deadly result. The historians like to see the invaders' victory, after two hours of indecisive hand-to-hand battle, as due to the arrival of Fernando Guanarteme with a mere 40 of his personal followers—in breach of orders and in spite of the opposition of the Spanish rearguard. There was jubilation when Fernando de Trujillo recovered a Spanish standard, lost at Acentejo, from the Guanche Tigayga.

The Acentejo victor, Tinguaro, was wounded and fled into the mountains to the east. Armed only with a halberd taken from the Spanish at Acentejo, he was pursued by seven horsemen. The first to reach him brought him to the ground with a blow of his pike. Tinguaro pleaded for his life—perhaps having in mind the clemency regularly shown by the Guanches to a defeated enemy—but the Spaniard killed him with a second blow. Tinguaro was Ben Como's brother and some Spaniards (and later Espinosa) insisted it was the Taoro leader himself whom they had killed. The body was taken to Lugo, the soldiers knocking it about and shouting: 'See now the terrible chief who caused us such damage at Acentejo!'. Lugo cut off the head and stuck in on a pike in full view of Ben Como and his men, these withdrawn to the wooded area of Aguere.

The Spaniards now went through the usual celebrations: a 'Te Deum' led by the horde of ecclesiastics detailed by Viera, a vow to build a shrine on the battlefield and so on. Similarly, it was recorded that 45 of Lugo's men were killed . . . against 1,700 Guanches. As soon as the invaders' supremacy became clear, Añaterve of Güimar, until then having kept away from the new Spanish force, now declared himself on their side, sending men, with provisions, to join the invaders in their temporary front-line camp at Aguere.

However, Lugo did not at once follow up his victory, again digging in for the mild Canary winter. His final shot had been to despatch Tinguaro's head to Ben Como with a message: 'This is the result of obstinacy—you can expect the same fate'. Ben Como is said to have replied with dignity. At Arautapala the Guanches of Taoro held a funeral lasting 15 days for Tinguaro; his head was mummified and placed in the burial cave of the Taoro leaders.

THE FRUITS OF WAR: PLAGUE, HUNGER, DESPAIR

Both sides now suffered. During the winter an unknown plague struck the Guanches of the Taoro league, with 100 dying each day at its height. Viera ascribes it to the laying-out in the air of the many bodies resulting from the Aguere battle, part of the corpse-preservation process, described earlier; he adds that the cold wet winter was also a factor. One note, that the island dogs ate so much human flesh that they became out of control, attacking the Guanches, so that these had frequently to climb up trees to escape, can be seen in another way: that it was in fact rabies which afflicted the Guanches, brought by European dogs. A psychological depression, as their end as a free people clearly approached, would have added itself to the disease.

The plague came to the Spaniards' notice when a raiding party of 500 men, foraging up in the mountains around the Aguere basin, were struck by the corpses and vacant dwellings. At length, in a cave, they found an old man, with three children, weeping over the body of his wife, just deceased. From him they learnt that the Tegueste flocks were out on the Hidalgo Pobre promontory. Their extended sortie to capture these alerted the Tegueste *mencey* and his ally Ze ben Sui, the leader of the enclave. On the way back the Spaniards went to collect the old man and this three children—only to find that he had killed them and, having run himself through with a pine javelin, was himself expiring. It is said that he told his frustrated captors that he had preferred these actions to slavery.

Expecting ambush, the Spaniards had scouts out ahead; behind these came five columns of infantry, between them the flocks, with the cavalry bringing up the rear. As the front column entered the pass through the peaks (Paso de las Peñuelas, now), a whistle was heard— the signal by the Tegueste *mencey* for the assault by his 1,200 men. However, the front three columns withstood this attack, those behind climbing the slopes and falling on the Guanches from above. At length the islanders abandoned the battle. The flocks had escaped but were recaptured by the Spanish down in the Aguere bowl.

One of the two leaders of the expedition, Gonzalo García del Castillo, attempting to catch Ze ben Sui, had his horse killed beneath him and was taken prisoner. The Tegueste *mencey* sent him to Ben Como by whom, a. usual, he was well treated. It is said he fell in love with the Taoro leader's daughter, Dacil, and that it was due to her intercession that Ben Como set free this Spanish captain.

Ben Eharo, the Anaga *mencey*, met his death in a similar skirmish. Amongst the invaders were a dozen soldiers who came from the same hamlet in Spain. They went about together and one day obtained permission to raid the eastern tip. From the southerly coast they took the Igueste ravine through to Taganana, captured a flock and six shepherds and, returning down the present San Andrés *barranco*, were attacked by 200 Anaga men under their *mencey*. Ben Eharo, seeing how few Spaniards there were, offered to let them go on their way—without the flock, doubtless—but, legend has it, the 12 *conquistadores* opened fire with their muskets and crossbows, then fell on the Guanches with their swords. The 200 islanders are said to have fled in disarray, all except Ben Eharo, who, eventually cornered, flung himself into the sea rather than be captured. Such incidents, though repetitious and perhaps exaggerated, are recounted for the clarity with which they show the character of the ancient Canary people.

If the Guanches were suffering from a plague, in the Spanish camp morale was also low, unexpectedly. This was the result of hunger— Lugo was again out of funds—and of inactivity, with quantities of soldiers deserting and embarking clandestinely, making for their homes. The problems of food and discipline were made the worse by the arrival of almost 2,000 adventurers from the eastern islands . . . the news that the conquest was almost complete had spread around the Canaries. These men, semi-official reinforcements, brought no supplies. The Guanches' remaining flocks were now up on the most inaccessible peaks—the Teide crater, for example, almost entirely above 2,000m in altitude. There were of course no crops. Añaterve el Bueno did give Lugo a further 1,000 animals, these lasting his hungry army a month. On top of this, the general had to fend off severe criticism both from his subordinates and from his backers over the apparent stalemate. For it had gradually become clear that Lugo did not relish an attack on Ben Como in his own territory—the *matanza* at Acentejo was not forgotten.

THE FINAL CAMPAIGN

During a council of war at the camp, one of Lugo's officers, Lope

Hernández de Guerra, offered to obtain funds to revictual the troops by going back to Gran Canaria and there selling his 'two sugar-cane plantations, his houses, slaves and animals'. These fetched 2,000 *doblas*, spent at once on more weapons, flours, hard-tack, barley and other supplies. These did not arrive too soon, since illness was breaking out in the camp, the daily ration down to a handful of barley and six dried figs, supplemented by the soldiers' own collection of bracken roots and other wild foods.

The appearance of the supply caravel on 1 December 1495 revitalized the Spanish army and, taking advantage of this, on the 24th Lugo marched on Taoro. The Bco. de Acentejo was passed without incident, the invaders entrenching themselves on the plain immediately to the west. Hernández went on a reconnaissance and, reaching a wood at about the present Sta. Ursula, was attacked by 15 Guanches, these 'whistling frightfully'. The Spanish captain turned his horse round and, luring them onto a flatter safer region, shot six with his pistol, driving away the rest with his lance — at least according to the early historians. One who had been trampled by the horse was taken back to Lugo and gave the information that Ben Como was to attack very early the next day; his 5,000 men would be divided into two forces, one under himself, the other under Acaymo, *mencey* of Tacoronte.

It was Christmas Eve and Lugo held the army on the alert all night. Bonfires were kept going all around the camp and, by their light, at midnight, three Masses were said by the *conquistadores*. At dawn the Guanches of the four N.E. territories appeared and, to match their tactic, Lugo divided his men also into two forces, the second under Hernández. After five hours of combat, Ben Como, an arm out of action, and Acaymo, his thigh pierced by a musket-ball, called on the Guanches to retreat. They crossed Bco. Hondo and disappeared across the Orotava Valley.

Instead of pursuing them, the relieved Spaniards apparently fell to their knees and sang a 'Te Deum'. The settlement on the site of this battle is now known as La Victoria de Acentejo; it is a few kilometres south-west of La Matanza. The Guanches are supposed to have lost almost 2,000 men . . . the Spanish a mere 64 dead.

Once again the invaders retired to their Sta. Cruz fortress on the southern shore of the northern end of the island, the expedition over on 4 January 1496. And, as before, Lugo's backers in Gran Canaria complained, going to the extent of declaring before a notary that 'there have been no lack of opportunities for ending the conflict but no advantage has been taken of these . . . that almost 2,000 men were sent from the neighbouring islands last year but it was not thought fit to use them . . . and, finally, that the outfitters find it impossible to send the further supplies demanded for this interminable conquest'. If the Moors could be thrown out of Spain, how could the Guanches keep the *conquistadores* at bay? The suspicion grows on the student of the island invasion that psychologically and in terms of terrain won no advance was being made by the invaders: it was only by a heavy cost of lives—the Spaniards poured men into Tenerife—and helped by the plague that they gradually reduced the finite Guanches numerically to the point where they could resist no longer.

This time by-passing the Gran Canaria company, Lugo sent direct to Medina-Sidonia and persuaded him to supply 30 barrels of flour, 36 bushels of chick peas, three tons of hard-tack, 20 barrels of wine, a ton of oil and other supplies. These came at the end of May but it was not until early July that Lugo again marched on the Guanches. The heat would have been at its height and, presumably encased in at least light armour, the Spaniards would have been at a disadvantage. Noting again the bodies of plague victims, the invaders crossed the Esperanza ridge, passed through Acentejo and, for the first time, entered the legendary valley of Arautapala (Orotava). Ben Como and the others of the Taoro alliance were now fortified up on Tigayga, the western wall of the valley, so there was no opposition. The Spaniards built a fort at the place now called Realejo Alto. On 24 July the Guanche force came down into the valley and took up position on the coastal flank of the Spaniards, at two musket balls' distance; their camp became the site of Realejo Bajo. Subsequent events are not clear. Viera wrote that, seeing the strength of the invaders' fortress, with 'the semblance of confidence shown by the soldiers and their determination not to leave their trenches', the Guanche leaders decided to negotiate a peace settlement. To his usual conditions, Lugo added that they should help him to subdue the rest of the island. The five Guanche leaders accepted this and, upon a missal, Lugo swore to respect his promises.

The general then deemed it politic to hold joint celebrations in which the Guanches were treated as equals of the *conquistadores*. The new subjects of the Catholic kings were given clothes. The Guanche women came out of their hiding places, to be treated, says Viera, with humanity and gallantry. The islanders' dexterity was happily channelled away from the arts of war into harmless games, in competition with the friendly Spaniards. And soon, out of the hills, down came Añaterve the Good and his men, to solemnly submit his domain and subjects to the Spanish and then in turn join in the merry-making.

After a few days, using the capitulated Guanches as cannon-fodder, Lugo began the mopping-up operation. In fact there were still pockets of resistance in Tegueste and Anaga, these islanders denouncing their old *menceys* for having treated for peace. During August and September a major campaign was fought against the people of Icod, Daute, Adeje and Abona. At length their respective leaders — Pelicer, Romen, Pelinor and Adjoña — met in a *tagoror*. Recognizing the mistake they had made in not joining the Taoro alliance, noting that its superior forces had been made to surrender and, above all, appalled to find its battle-hardened members now fighting against themselves, the western leaders also decided to ask for peace. Though numbers of their subjects in turn stayed behind to continue the resistance, on 29 September 1496 the four chiefs formally submitted themselves to Lugo at Los Realejos.

Tenerife was finally pacified, to use the colonialist euphemism for the last time. It was all over bar the 'Te Deum' and, in a scene which would have delighted Voltaire, this and a Mass were now sung by two canons, two licentiates, two Augustinians and four Franciscans. A church was dedicated on the spot. The Guanches were all baptized. Ben Como became Christobal; but modern historians (Alvarez 1959–61) are also amongst those who say that it was he, rather than his brother Tinguaro, who had been killed in the Aguere combat in November 1495, leadership of Taoro being then taken over by Ben Torey — who, in fact refusing to surrender to the Spaniards, flung himself over the Tigayga precipice. Ben Eharo of Anaga — who appears to have survived throwing himself into the sea in 1495 — became Pedro de los Santos. Añaterve changed his name to Juan de Candelaria. Viera gives a full list. Those who drew up this ecclesiastical game-book would have been none too scrupulous about whether the trophies were alive or dead. Ben Como's daughter Dacil was christened Mencía and married Gonzalo García del Castillo. This happy ending confirmed, as Pangloss and the early Spanish historians put it, that all was now for the best in the best of all possible worlds.

PART SIX

COLONIZATION, SLAVERY AND SURVIVAL

CHAPTER NINETEEN

European Colonization about 1500

In 1487 the Crown's Alms-Keeper, in Spain, recorded: 'Gave to Guanarteme, who was king of the Canaries . . . four *reales* to buy food'. Unluckily no written record has been left by the island people of life, seen from their viewpoint, in the aftermath of the 1478–96 conquests; this has to be pieced together from official government documents, legal contracts, law suits and so on. The islanders also figured prominently in the archipelago's early archives as breakers of the newly-imposed Spanish civil and religious laws. The records show the extermination of a people and its culture beyond anything effected by the Spaniards in the Americas: general enslavement, official large-scale deportations, total annexation of the land, destruction of the way of life, enforced acceptance of the Spanish beliefs and values. Only the inefficiency of the new authorities allowed the survival in the archipelago of a small proportion of the islanders and of their culture.

Few Europeans defended the islanders. The Spanish annexation was condemned from outside the Canaries by Bartolomé de las Casas and from within by Alonso de Espinosa; both these priests had by then seen their compatriots' behaviour towards the natives of the newly-conquered Americas. Possibly they had there heard about life in the Canaries, since many islanders served in the ranks of the later *conquistadores* — by sale, conscription and, doubtless, sometimes in preference to remaining in the Canaries. Columbus had passed through the Archipelago again in 1493, 1498 and 1502; Nicolás Ovando in 1502; Alonso Quintero, with Hernán Cortés aboard, in 1504; Pedrarías Dávila, on his way to Darien, in 1514; Francisco de Montejo, to conquer the Yucatan, in 1526; Hernando de Soto in 1538 — and many more. The hardy and intrepid islanders played a part in the conquests in the New World . . . the massive, perennial emigration from the archipelago to Spanish-speaking America dates from this period.

After the 1478–96 conquests the remaining islanders became divided into three groups. The bulk were slaves or, at best serfs, in the service of the new society. Many were taken, for various reasons, to the Peninsula. A third group was on the run in the mountains. The fate of these men, women and children will be examined in detail once the government and society brought to the islands by the Spaniards has been described.

In a newly conquered and colonized territory, direct government, wealth and social position are particularly concentrated. This chapter will show how Lugo established a personal dynasty and accompanying autocracy based on land-holding; the tardy and usually ineffective opposition to this by the distant Crown; the tightening control by the church and the Inquisition. It will be then understood how, against the immediate appearance of this complex and frightening gamut of despotic, legal and supernatural powers and punishments, the simple islanders had little chance of survival.

OFFICIAL GOVERNMENT

During the sixteenth century, by fires and pirate action, the early archives of Gran Canaria and Palma were destroyed, so that comparatively-little is known of the period after their conquests. Abreu relates that, following the fall of Gran Canaria in 1483, many soldiers left to take part in the campaign against the Moors in Spain; the troops of the Holy Brotherhood were sent back also. The Crown told Pedro de Vera to allocate the land to the *conquistadores*. Many *colons* soon arrived, mainly from Andalucia, bringing Peninsula agriculture together with sugar-cane from Madeira. Vera appointed a dozen of his senior officers to be the first *regidores*—government prefects and magistrates combined. The Canary bishop, Juan de Frías, at last moved his seat from the Rubicon to Las Palmas. In 1487 a ceremony in Salamanca incorporated Gran Canaria into Castille and, a dozen years later, the island was sent a body of laws, together with confirmation of many edicts made locally, in the meantime, by the governor.

Much more is known about events in Tenerife. On 5 November 1496 two royal decrees appointed Alonso de Lugo governor and chief magistrate of this island and of Palma, his other conquest, with the sole discretion to distribute land and expel people. Lugo and his troops spent nine months at Los Realejos, using the fort both as a base for subjugating the last pockets of resistance and, as will be seen, for rounding up Guanches for slavery and deportation. In 1497 he transferred his headquarters to Aguere, thus founding the city of La Laguna. On 20 October the first island council was held; Lugo had appointed six *regidores*, a lord mayor and a deputy governor, all of them *conquistadores*. However, real control was exercised by Lugo, to be relinquished only at his death in 1525.

The Canaries were now all incorporated into Spain; most national laws, in particular those relating to justice, applied throughout the archipelago. However, the Crown also owned directly Gran Canaria, Palma and Tenerife; the lesser islands belonged to the families already encountered.

LAND APPORTIONMENT IN TENERIFE

Ten years after the conquest the Crown sent the licentiate Ortiz de Zárate to investigate the allegations of malpractice by the administration in the allocation of land. Ortiz's preamble to his report states that 'the islands are not peopled as they should be, because many lands and properties have been given to foreigners rather than to natives . . . and to powerful people . . . some have appropriated more than they were allotted . . . including governors, justices and others . . . and have taken lands unjustly from those to whom they were given'. Ortiz drew up many lists. One gave the absentee land-owners; as well as Spanish, many were Portuguese and Genoese. Another showed the immense holdings by Lugo, his family and friends, and by the officials he had appointed. 'In Realejo a settlement was begun by fifteen people . . . planted with vines and orchards . . . but is now abandoned because the Adelantado (Lugo) took their water for his sugar-cane plantation'. The whole territory of Abona was given by Lugo to the Duke of Medina-Sidonia, recorded Ortiz. Next came a long list of people whose allocations had already been allowed them just long enough to clear them of stones and get them into agricultural production. Others had sold their lands in under five years, in contravention of the original regulations. The Crown attempted to right these wrongs — with little success, as will be seen.

With the reader warned, then, that the rules were treated with contempt by the authorities, the original principles on which the land distribution was based, in 1501, can be given.

a) Irrigable land in small plots, about 10 acres each (6 *fanegadas*), for which lots were drawn. Each foot-soldier had a right to one plot, each horseman to two
b) Unirrigable land in double-size plots
c) Soldiers to have preference over civilian immigrants
d) The original islanders not to be forgotten.

A total of 992 allocations was made, 50 being to islanders. However, 31 of these were to Gran Canaria men, including Fernando Guanarteme, Pedro Maninidra and Alonso Ben Taguayre; however, the first of these was recorded as killed in the conquest of the island — he is buried at La Laguna — so possibly false names were used to further increase the European elite's effective share of Tenerife. Many of these allocations were at Los Realejos, forming a colony of free Gran Canaria settlers . . . who now acted superiorly towards the enslaved Guanches, conquered with their help. However, many of these Gran Canaria men were soon to go with Lugo to Africa — and did not return. Only *nineteen* Guanches obtained allocations (out of the original 15–60,000 inhabitants), nor were any of these *menceys*, the significance of this explained later.

The full extent of Lugo's own holdings is unknown. After the fall of Gran Canaria in 1483 he had been given the Agaete region, with its port, developing it around a sugar-cane plantation. In Palma, in 1493, he allocated himself the Valle de los Sauces. On Tenerife, after 1496, he took over the Realejo region and areas of Tacoronte and Icod. It is also known that he settled his debts by allocating land to his creditors. Amongst Lugo's many other abuses of power was his refusal to allocate land for sugar-cane, to avoid competition with his own plantations.

The early *datas* or grants of land make informative and, sometimes, sad reading. Amongst the allocations was 'land which had belonged to the King of Güimar', 'land on the Teno road . . . which the Guanches used to sow', 'the place where Ben Ytono was born, between the two ravines', 'the ground at the head of the ravine into which Ben Torey threw himself'; this last does imply that Ben Como did die at Aguere and was replaced by Ben Torey. A Gran Canaria islander who had ingratiatingly called himself Pedro de Lugo got 'eight *fanegas* (about 13 acres) of arable and a cave'. However, the bulk went to men like Antonio Joven: 'I say you are an honourable and rich person and you are coming to live on this island, so I give you $1\frac{1}{2}$ *fanegas* so you can make a good house and a smallholding'.

CANARY SOCIETY IN 1500

During the fifteenth century the archipelago had seen few resident grandees: Jean and then Maciot de Bethencourt, the Perazas and Herreras, Beatríz de Bobadilla, then Pedro de Vera and finally Alonso de Lugo. The latter now followed Hernán Peraza, Fernando the Catholic and Christopher Columbus by falling for and in fact marrying Beatríz de Bobadilla — herself as great a tyrant as any of the previous owners of Hierro and Gomera — and, upon her sudden and unexplained death in Spain, Lugo did his best, unsuccessfully, to keep the two small islands from his stepson, the legitimate heir. Lugo's dynasty was to last several hundred years, his most direct heirs becoming governors and the rest of his relatives holding many important posts or marrying their incumbents. Lugo also gave prime lands to many rich Europeans, such as the Genoese Cristoval de Ponte and Domenico Rico Grimaldi, these marrying into his own family. Much Genoese capital was invested in the sugar industry.

The rest of the Canary nobility took shape around the first *regidores* and other important officials; some of these married the daughters of the ancient island leaders. These dignitaries at once became obsessed with lineage, in particular with the ostentation of a coat-of-arms and an illuminated 'Declatoria y Confirmación de Nobleza' . . . in Hierro the author was taken into the threadbare home of a living *hidalgo* to be shown the framed certificate of nobility in the hall. Above the door of a house in Sta. Cruz de la Palma there is a coat-of-arms (Pl. 15a) of particular relevance since it shows a pre-conquest islander carrying his weapons, a stone and a staff.

The land of the Canaries has continued to this day in the hands of powerful families descended from or purchasers from the leading *conquistadores* and early immigrant nobility. This is a subject which cannot be examined further here (for details on this aspect in Fuerteventura, see Mercer 1973). An idea of the contrasts in wealth can be gained from comparing the cave-dwellings—such as that allotted in 1497 to Pedro of Gran Canaria—still in use today with the vast and ornate houses built in the sixteenth century for the European nobility, notably in La Laguna.

URBANIZATION

The majority of pre-conquest families had lived in small settlements, probably each one usually a single extended family. The way of life, animal-rearing, made it difficult for population concentrations to develop, since this would have led to over-grazing of the neighbourhood or to a lengthy daily movement of the flocks. Only at Gáldar and Telde, on Gran Canaria, were there any number of islanders living together.

Again there is least information, on urbanization, for Gran Canaria. The early post-conquest rich lived at Telde, this having the double advantage of being already urbanized, to an unknown degree, and standing some way inland. The eastern islands in particular lived in fear of attack by European and Maghreb pirates. For this reason, the first capitals of Lanzarote (Teguise) and Fuerteventura (Betancuria) were in the centres of the islands. Late in the sixteenth century, another peak of Moorish maritime strength, Las Palmas still had only 80 houses but Telde had 300, according to Torriani, the fortifications consultant.

Tenerife, the most profitable of the Canaries for material exploitation, developed rapidly. Espinosa described La Laguna a century after the conquest: 'a place of many people, very rich . . . ennobled by grand and sumptuous edifices . . . inhabited by many knights, wealthy merchants and strong labourers'. In the town lived many Portuguese, French, Dutch and English. In 1592, La Laguna had 5,300 inhabitants and 950 houses. Torriani remarked that Tenerife was mainly populated by Portuguese, the union of the Iberian Crowns having taken place 10 years before his visit. The Daute territory, he noted, was now 'the great domain of a Catalan gentle-

man'. Other observers reported that Icod and Daute were four-
fifths inhabited by settlers from Portugal. The sugar industry,
modelled on that of Madeira, brought many of the Portuguese
workers. Lusitanian influence has been detected in Tenerife's architecture. Sta. Cruz had still only 200 houses, occupied by fishermen
and sailors.

Espinosa left suggestive notes on the remoter settlements of Tenerife
late in the sixteenth century. Orotava was 'peopled by the most
distinguished families which came to the island . . . very noble,
though somewhat haughty. Since the estates have been much divided,
they have not the means to support the pride they feel'. Similar gentry
were established in Garachico, Icod de los Vinos, Los Realejos,
Buenavista, Los Silos and, on the much less inhabited and developed
south side, at Vilaflor. Conversely, El Sauzal, La Matanza and La
Victoria were 'villages of labourers who maintain themselves by the
sweat of their brows' and Tagara (? Taganana) was 'built over the
rocks of Anaga . . . inhabited by people who live by the plough and
and spade'. Espinosa added that at Candelaria and Güimar, on the
south, there were Guanches, though 'there are few of them because
they have become mixed'. This Dominican, attached to the shrine
begun by Antón Guanche two centuries earlier, concluded by saying
that Tenerife, with 7,000 fighting men, had more inhabitants than all
the other islands put together: 'Each day their number is increasing,
with the help of their Patroness of Candelaria'. The evolution of the
church will be described shortly.

The capital of Palma, Sta. Cruz, had 800 houses by 1590; many of
its immigrant workers were labourers from Portugal and Flanders.
Torriani wrote that Hierro and Gomera could have supported more
people but the exactions of the owner made few willing to live there;
like land ownership, the subject of the common islander's reward for
agricultural labour is beyond the scope of this book (see Mercer 1973).
The capitals of the two small islands, Valverde (Amoco originally) and
San Sebastián, had respectively 250 and 200 houses. The Count's
Tower, on the shore of the second of these settlements, was now a
prison.

Finally, a note on the industry and commerce, other than upon the
export of slaves. Thomas Nicholas (Cioranescu 1963), an English
sugar-merchant who was in the islands from 1556–63, recorded a
dozen processing factories in the favoured zones of each of the two
main islands, with lesser activity in this trade on Palma and Gomera;
these *ingenios* would have been fed with raw cane by adjacent
plantations. A will made in Gran Canaria early in the colonial period
left 'a sugar factory with its slave house, workers' house . . . and 20
black and 3 white slaves' (Camacha). Associated with the factories

were enterprises building the ships which carried out the sugar. Another important export, notably to England, was wine (Morales). The orchil lichen—first coveted by Jean de Bethencourt, scraped off the rocks around Las Palmas by Rejon's soldiers in their spare time—was exported from all islands in huge quantites to different parts of Europe. It grew best in the wetter western islands but eventually became scarce everywhere, being finally collected off the last cliff faces by men lowered in slings.

Also soon in short supply, with more serious and lasting consequences, were the trees (Nicholas, Viera). The ancient islanders' flocks may or may not have damaged the woods. The narratives of the French conquerors showed that the trees then still extended to the shores. The Europeans began by uncontrolled burning for their plantations, by taking the best trees for making houses, by cutting them to fuel their sugar-boiling factories and the distilleries, to build ships and to make the pitch for caulking these. Secondly, the finest wood was exported: the *barbusano* laurel (*Apollonias barbujana*), the *palo blanco* olive (*Picconia excelsa*) and the pine. Thirdly, the animals taken from the islanders were amalgamated, by local decree, into flocks of a thousand each, under the care of several shepherds—in an attempt to keep control of them, since the islanders of course 'stole' them back when they could—and this led at once to over-grazing, with the impossibility of woodland regeneration. Finally, with little or no usable land, the poor, consisting of freed islanders and unsuccessful Europeans, were forced to become wood-sellers and charcoal burners, as well as the pitch-makers, encouraging the domestic consumption of wood. This deforestation occurred in all islands, according to local supply and demand for wood. Amongst the place-names are memorials to the vanished woods; for example, in Gran Canaria, Vega de los Mocanes, Bco. de los Acebuches, Monte del Lentiscal.

Amongst the consequences of the deforestation was the disappearance of the streams; the French conquerors had suggested water-driven mills could be set up even in *Fuerteventura*, whilst the early saw-mills of Tenerife were in fact powered in this way. Soil erosion soon followed. And, in the middle of the twentieth century, variably-rewarded attempts to re-afforest the dry, windswept and barren valleys and mountains (Pl. 9a).

THE ECCLESIASTICAL INVASION

The turn of the fifteenth century was a period of complexity, in Iberia, in many ways. In the religious sphere it saw the expulsion of the Jews in 1492; the fall of Granada in that year was followed by toleration of the Moors until, provoked, they revolted in 1501, to suffer in 1502 the first of the edicts against their religion and culture. The screws of religious intoleration tightened throughout the century until, in 1609, even the resident, converted Moors, or *moriscos*, were ejected from the Peninsula.

In the Canaries the scene was much more complicated and, in some ways, opposed in its evolution. The presence of Christian clerics before and during the conquests has already been illustrated. As the last three islands fell, so waves of ecclesiastical *colons* flooded across them, obtaining grants of land and upon them building hermitages, churches, monasteries and convents. Images for these were miraculously washed up, in the Candelaria tradition, at Garachico, Icod, Abona . . . others were located by climber-priests up trees, following reports of mysterious lights high in their branches. The final section, concerned to show that a proportion of island blood and culture survived, will illustrate Maire's note, in a 1682 translation, that 'The Great Canary, as well as Teneriffe, and the Palme, continued Idolaters some time after the Conquest'. By 1500 the Europeans of Tenerife were themselves complaining at the size of the religious community, presumably supported out of public funds. There was soon strife between the priests and the monks, with the Dominicans, later joined by Espinosa, forcibly taking control of the Candelaria shrine in 1530. The suppression in 1824 of the Canaries' 40 monasteries and 15 nunneries was closely followed by the return of the famous image to the sea, washed away in a great flood. All this religious machinery was brought to bear on the survivors of the pre-conquest people and, encouraged by threats and bribes, these were soon baptized and all superficially Christians.

However, whilst the old 'pagan' beliefs were being expunged, two further heresies were reaching the islands. From 1476 until 1593, as will be described, immense numbers of Africans were caught on the coast adjacent to the Canaries; these slaves were of course Moslems. Secondly, a number of the Jews expelled in 1492 from the Peninsula came to the Canary Islands. These Jews were allowed in for the same reason that, in 1609, upon the edict expelling even Christianized Moors from the Peninsula, the Canary *moriscos* were allowed to stay: the islands needed workers, both free and enslaved. In contradistinction to the three groups—the converted islanders, the Moslems and the Jews—the rest of the population referred to itself henceforth as 'Old Christians'.

Naturally it was not long before the Inquisition appeared—1499. In the next three centuries it burned 11 people in the flesh and a further 107 in effigy, reconciled 498 deviants and imposed penitence on 1,647 for various crimes. The chief miscreants were the *moriscos* or converted African slaves, these tending to escape back to the continent and there re-assume Islamic practices. In 1530, six who were drowned whilst fleeing were burnt in effigy. The Inquisition confiscated the property, if any, of such relapses. In 1524 20 Jews and other heretics, held responsible for a succession of plague, drought and famine, were the victims of an auto-da-fé. A Canary resident, Pedro Dorador, was found guilty of teaching Judaism in 1510.

The native islanders also came in for Inquisition attention. In 1505 a notable colony of Gomerans and Guanches living at Arguineguín (Gran Canaria) were denounced for not knowing 'the Ave Maria or Paternoster nor any prayer . . . nor which are feast days or vigils . . . and they eat meat on prohibited days'. In 1548 came the trial of Agustín Guanche, accused of 'going to Berveria (Barbary), the land of the Moors . . . renouncing our holy catholic faith . . . becoming a Moor and calling himself Barca'; possibly he was the Guanche burned in Las Palmas in 1557. The atmosphere of suspicion and denunciation was intense throughout the century.

CHAPTER TWENTY

Deportation and Slavery in the Fifteenth Century

It was seen in Chapter 12 that the Canary Islanders were already being caught and enslaved by Europeans in the middle of the fourteenth century, following the advance in ship design and navigation. Slavery was an institution in Iberia in the late Middle Ages, the subjects usually Moslems; these were either caught in wars and pirate actions or traded. Amongst Christians it was held that non-Christians taken in battle, *buena guerra* in Spain, might be legitimately enslaved. Nevertheless, the Canary Islanders were caught, throughout the fourteenth century, by private actions akin to piracy. Freed early from the Moorish conflict on their own island, the Mallorcan merchants led Iberia in the outfitting of the slaving vessels. The French conquests of 1402–5 began, equally unofficially, for personal gain, ending, to the profit of a state, under the tutelage of the Castillian Crown. During this 'war', many more islanders were turned into slaves, to work in the archipelago or in Europe.

Three-quarters of a century of shadowy history then followed for the Canaries. The Portuguese, having been the first Iberians to eject the Moors from the whole of their territory, soon raised slave-catching to a national occupation. Obtaining a monopoly in black Africa, they frequently carried out manhunts in the Canaries, on the way up or down. This brought protests from Castille, still occupied with the Moors at home and having only the archipelago and its adjacent African coast as a source of slaves. It seems most likely that, during the 75 years of partial control by Castille, the abduction of islanders for Peninsula slavery slowed down. The smaller islands were both worked out and in the hands of Castillian despots, these doubtless using all remaining islanders on their own lands; occasional assaults on the major and still-unconquered islands have been described.

Throughout the whole of this period there is only one recorded voice of protest. Juan de Baeza, the Franciscan missionary who actually worked amongst the islanders, attempting to improve their agriculture and post-conquest living standards, obtained a bull, in 1442, from Pope Eugene IV prohibiting slave-taking in the Canaries. It was ignored.

THE 'SECOND WARS'

Following their narrated submission, several islands rose and tried unsuccessfully to rid themselves of their Castillian masters. This repeated pattern was the result of the equally-inevitable tyranny to which they had been subjected. The risings were classed as 'war' so that the dissidents—many unborn during the earlier conflicts—could be legitimately turned into slaves. It was also necessary to hold that, by their revolt, they had then lost their Christian status, otherwise a defence against enslavement.

The first of these rebellions to be recorded occurred in Hierro, in the early years of Maciot de Bethencourt's governorship. The small island had been delegated to Captain Lázaro Vizcaino: the islanders assassinated him and, *en masse*, took to the mountains. Maciot sent reinforcements and ended the rising. Diego de Herrera, acquiring the conquered islands early in the 1450s, found that, due to a short interregnum, he had in turn to quell revolts of the native people on Hierro and Fuerteventura; the details of his retribution are unknown.

Actions which took place after the Crown began the conquests on its own account are better known than those early in the century. In 1488, as described, the Gomerans of Agana and Orone rose, killed Hernán Peraza outside the cave of the beautiful Iballa and then besieged his wife, Beatriz de Bobadilla, in the Torre del Conde. Pedro de Vera and 400 men relieved the Castillians but were unable to dislodge the rebels from their retreat in the heights of Garajonai. So the Gran Canaria governor ordered that the rest of the islanders should assemble for Peraza's funeral in the capital. These were then caught, in the church, and used, together with a promise of amnesty, to bring the fighting men out of the mountains.

All the people of the Agana and Orone regions over the age of 15 were sentenced to death; some were hanged, some torn apart by horses, others impaled or drowned. A number had their hands and feet cut off. Yet others, exiled to Lanzarote, were in fact less officially thrown in the sea on the way. In the course of these exactions, Vera learned that the 200 Gomerans whom he had deported to Gran Canaria two years earlier had not only encouraged the rising in their home island but were actually plotting to kill Vera himself . . . once back on Gran Canaria, Vera hanged all the men amongst them.

Drawn from both groups, about 100 women and children were sent to Spain, on Vera's orders, to be sold as slaves. Until recently little was known of the fate of islanders once they reached Iberia but modern studies of documents of sale of the period (Cortés, Marrero, Serra 1959a) have extended their sorry histories. The Gomerans, 'heretics and ill-disposed towards their lord', were delivered to Valencia and the adjacent Balearic Island of Ibiza; amongst them, for example, was

Isabel, aged 11, her purchaser able 'to sell or exchange her according to his wish'. However, back in the Canaries, the bishop, successor to Juan de Frías (d. 1485) took up their case with Vera, only to be told that, unless he shut up, he would find a red-hot skull-cap on his head instead of the one he usually wore. Incensed, the bishop complained to the Queen. At odds with the period, their Catholic majesties had by now decided against the principle of slavery even if they had done little against the practice. In 1477 Isabel had ordered the release of all Christianized islanders on the Peninsula and now Fernando applied this to the Gomerans, with the added injunction that Vera and Beatriz de Bobadilla should deposit half a million maravedis for repayment to the buyers. The Crown also noted how Peraza himself had enslaved the Christianized islanders, keeping them 'in chains as if they were Moors'. This also encouraged the Hierro people to ask the Crown for the right to live where they liked, granted in 1482; though 'free', they were always to have Peraza and his successors as tyrannical landlords, so that emigration was already starting.

Serra's opinion is that the released Gomeran women and children got no nearer home than Gran Canaria, being retained there by Vera, in absolute control in the Canaries whatever the Crown might decree in Spain. In this way Vera would also eventually replace the workers he had hanged a year earlier. Serra adds that it was after Vera's various exactions on Gomera that the depopulated island received its first large-scale immigration of European *colons*.

Palma also had its 'second war', very soon after the conquest. However, to keep Vera's period of control together, his enslavement of the Gran Canaria people — who never rebelled — will be described next, then going on to Lugo's activities on Palma and Tenerife.

GRAN CANARIA: DEPORTATION AS CROWN POLICY
Vera's 1480 attempt to transport a shipload of islanders to Spain, in the course of the conquest, had failed, but, once the last 'Te Deum' had rung out across the Tirajana bowl, he at once broke his promises and shipped 360 captives to Seville. It is known that many Telde people, including their leaders, were soon also held in this Peninsula city, so possibly they were amongst Vera's prisoners. The Gran Canaria children were distributed amongst the settlers, ostensibly so that they should be taught Christianity, in reality to be raised as slaves.

Vera projected his sale of the islanders as a 'policy' designed to avoid risings, frightening the Crown into accepting it. Thus it was decreed that the islanders in residence should be limited to Fernando Guanarteme, the old Gáldar leader turned collaborator, and his retinue of 40 individuals or families; he took up residence on the

Guayedra lands he had requested of the Crown.

One wonders how the aged *guanarteme*, greatly responsible for the capitulation of the islanders—even if their eventual defeat was inevitable—felt about their immediate deportation and enslavement. At any rate, in 1485 he went again to Seville, on his own account, visiting the islanders held in the city. As a result, the mayor was told by Fernando and Isabel to look after them better, since they had 'heard from Fernando the Guanarteme that the Canary people living in Seville have been receiving insults and ill-treatment from the inhabitants . . . who take away their women and children for slaves, under the pretext that they are not Christians and, even if they've accepted baptism, treat them as prisoners of war'. The islanders were to be allowed to choose the masters whom they wished to serve, husbands and wives were not to be separated; however, they were also to be stopped from carrying on pagan ceremonies in their dwellings and, instead, to be taught 'the Christian doctrine and good habits'.

Although the Crown still would not allow any islanders to return, even those who had become free, it is probable that Fernando Guanarteme, in 1485, encouraged them to make their way back clandestinely. In 1491 the Gran Canaria *regidores* protested that there were then more islanders back than there were settlers—in fact only about 150 exiles had returned—so that the gullible Crown threatened death to any more who went back; the actions taken against those returned islanders, upon this royal support, have to be imagined. The lack of a 'second war' in Gran Canaria was due to its *conquistadores* extreme and efficient repression.

In 1492 the modern St Michael—as the expanding Canary church saw Lugo—was raising his army for the invasions of Palma and Tenerife. Amongst his force were many Gran Canaria men both from the Peninsula and from the island, the latter including Fernando Guanarteme and his followers and the survivors of the Gomerans exiled by Vera to Gran Canaria. For most of these the expeditions held out more hope than life as slaves. The island *regidores* and settlers were pleased to see many of them go. And, as has been seen, a good number were soon killed in combat with their fellow Canary Islanders.

CANARY SLAVES ON MADEIRA
The fifteenth-century archives of Funchal have survived. The Portuguese began to colonize the empty islands in 1420. Sugar-cane cultivation began about 1450, the population then rising from 300 men (Ca da Mosto, 1455) to 16,000 inhabitants by 1600—with a further 2,000 slaves.

The slaving expeditions of the mid-fifteenth century brought both

African negroes and Canary Islanders to the Azores and Madeira. Visiting the latter, Ca da Mosto described a Gran Canaria man who would offer to take on any two others, simultaneously, at throwing oranges at 8–10 paces: each would have 12 and he would hit with all of his and his opponents with none . . . but there were no takers. In 1466, afraid of a rebellion by the large negro population, the emphasis was put on bringing in Canary Islanders; it will be seen how, a century later, the eastern Canaries similarly found themselves overpopulated with hostile Moorish slaves. Nevertheless, as the century passed, so catching or buying Canary Islanders was increasingly discouraged by the Portuguese Crown, gradually and reluctantly renouncing its claims to the archipelago, these finally quashed by the 1479 Alcaçovas treaty with Spain. So the Canary slaves on Madeira were probably mostly caught before the conquests of Vera and Lugo.

The men of the southerly islands were put to work in the sugar cane and to look after the Europeans' flocks. However, at once at home on the rugged mountain terrain, the Canary Islanders simply went their own ways, with the animals. The two races of Madeira slaves did in fact support each other. In 1474 they were all banned from having houses of their own — as they hid each other — being forced to live with their owners. In 1483 this edict was eased: slaves could get yearly licences on good conduct, to live by themselves. At this time, brandmarks had to be visible — on the shoulder. Also in 1483 the Regent ordered the capture, by their owners, of all slaves on the run; those still free after six months would belong to anyone who could catch them — but they were then to be got out of Madeira. Had this Portuguese governor heard of Vera's policy, also of that year?

In 1490 the Portuguese settlers had had enough — they perhaps lacked the experienced inhumanity of the *conquistadores* who were colonizing the Canaries. All from the southern islands were expelled except enslaved women, children under 10 and those who had proved themselves in the sugar industry. Free islanders who stayed would have their possessions shared out, be given 50 lashes and expelled; owners who kept their slaves would be fined their value, a third to go to the informant, two-thirds to the church.

The expulsions left many animals loose in the mountains. It is likely that the long-lived custom of letting flocks look after themselves in the Madeira heights stems from the transfer of this from the Canaries — the free-ranging goats, *guaniles*, were described in Chapter 9. Shepherding was henceforth given to Moorish slaves, more docile and, probably, less used to the terrain.

There were, however, further expulsion decrees in 1505, with crimes by the Canary people to incur the cutting off of ears and other discriminatory punishments. It is worth noting that the negroes and Moors were never expelled from Madeira — only the Canary Islanders.

PALMA: THE FIRST LAW-SUIT

The weakest of the three large islands, Palma had probably suffered most from the slavers during the century. Most of the territories did not fight against Lugo but, by agreeing to peace treaties, were conventionally *bandos de paces* and, as such, not enslaveable.

Lugo's first action on achieving full control of Palma was to ship off Tanausu and the Ecero people. These had certainly resisted the Spaniards and so were classifiable as *bandos de guerra*. They had only been caught by treachery and Tanausu, in protest and rather than become enslaved, went on a hunger strike and was soon dead.

But Lugo also caught and transported members of the 'peace bands'. There were two reactions. First, the intermediary Francisca Palmesa, having played somewhat the same role as Fernando Guanarteme on Gran Canaria, now in her turn went to Spain to defend the enslaved islanders; this she did by starting the first legal proceedings, to become standard after the defeat and equally-illegal enslavement — even on fifteenth-century principles — of the Guanche *bandos de paces*. Secondly, the Palma islanders soon rebelled against their treatment — Lugo's nephew, Juan, had been left as governor — this 'second war', happily for the leading *conquistador*, classing them all once and for ever as *bandos de guerra*. According to Bernáldez, a highly-placed ecclesiastic of the period, Lugo rounded up 1,200 men, women and children, together with 20,000 animals. The rebel leaders were executed. 'From that moment', wrote Viera, 'many noble settlers came to Palma'.

CHAPTER TWENTY ONE

Deportation and Slavery: Tenerife

There is evidence that peace treaties, parallel to those made with some Palma leaders, had been agreed, before the invasion of Tenerife, with the territories of Abona, Adeje and Anaga; and there was of course the long-standing pact with the Christianophile Guanches of Güimar. Lugo's first breach of faith came when, to compensate his crushing defeat at Acentejo, he had shipped off a contingent of his Güimar allies. A German traveller called Münzer saw these men, women and children in Valencia. On one ship, setting out with 101 Guanches, 14 had died during the short journey. They were described as tanned, the women tall and well-built. These idolaters and *bestiales in moribus* arrived naked but, went on Münzer, were soon put in clothes *que bestias in humano corpore facit homines et mansuetos*. Many were in chains, with foot irons; they were given the heaviest work, such as beam sawing.

The conquest of Tenerife once completed, Lugo treated all Guanches as equally enslavable. The earlier peace treaties and the practical help of the Güimar people were both ignored. In a later law-suit Lugo alone was said to have transported 1,000 *paces*, Guanches from the treaty territories; also to pay his debts he took over their 15,000 animals, though, as in abrupt clearances of humans everywhere, many animals were left to wander in the mountains. The 10 leaders were all taken to Spain, being shown to the court at Almazan . . . eight were never heard of again. The Adeje *mencey* does appear to have been allocated land in his island but the only other to return, the Anaga leader, was forced to live in exile in Gran Canaria; Lugo stopped him from taking his flock there but the *mencey* thereupon brought the Guanches' first successful legal action, regaining his animals . . . at least on paper. However, it can be seen that—compared say to the colonized American and Australian peoples—some Guanches very rapidly adapted to the new society at least to the extent of using its legal system in their own defence, clearly their only hope of justice. Amongst the reasons for this were not only the Guanches' spirit but also the comparatively-sympathetic attitude of Fernando and Isabel, their court relatively near to the Canaries. A well-developed centralized system of justice in pre-conquest times would have predisposed the Guanches to understand and use the Iberian machinery.

The mass baptism ceremonies did not save the 'New Christians' from slavery. Indeed, as Ortiz de Zárate recorded during his investigations in 1506, there was on one occasion connivance by the Canary bishop: he called 200 *paces*, resident in Abona and Adeje, to his church for baptism, these people then being caught by Lugo and sold in Barcelona and Valencia. The Crown's agent noted how Lugo had sold a free Guanche woman and, when her husband, Francisco el Manquillo, had persistently sought her release, he was killed one night on the road. Other documents show a common trick of the governor: 'Guantejina, Guanche slave, had been redeemed, but then Lugo sold him again' . . . 'having sold a son of Ben Tor to this *mencey*'s daughter . . . he took him again and sold him to Diego de Llanos, of Palma'. For Lugo, money came before everything else: Juan Delgado, a Gran Canaria islander, helped Lugo in all his invasions, being killed in the disastrous attack on Saca in Africa . . . once back in Tenerife, in 1502. Lugo sold his defenceless widow, a Guanche, and her children.

Lugo's actions are used as illustrations only because, as *adelantado*, he was the subject of a public enquiry. The behaviour of his officials and of the rest of the immigrants is also only known where it features in legal documents. Thus, in 1500, the lieutenant-governor—the second man in the land—raped the wife of the Adeje *mencey*. The Guanches raised such a protest that he was exiled for nine months to Taghaost, in a Spanish zone of influence on the African coast, returning as a mere *regidor*. Possibly, had nothing been done, this would have led to the standard 'second war'; violation of the women had been high amongst the causes which had led the men of the islands conquered earlier to their self-destroying rebellions.

THE TRANSPORTED GUANCHES
In the cities of E. Iberia the Tenerife people found themselves part of a well-established lowest-grade level of society composed primarily of black and secondarily of white Africans. The Guanches were sold at public auctions. A woman fetched most, her children about two-thirds as much; men, rare, were intermediate in value. Shipped off too fast even for baptism, the islanders arrived with their Guanche names; recalling the place-name summary in Chapter 6, half of these began with 'A', of which half were 'At-', such as Atturchayayne; a fifth with 'C' or 'Ch-'; many with 'G' or 'T'. As usual they soon took or were given 'Christian' names, especially those of royalty: Isabel, Catalina, Fernando, Juan. Probably, as in Müntzer's time, they were also at once fitted out with chains and clothes and put to the heaviest labours. The men soon became known, in the Spanish cities, for their physical dexterity, as they had been in Madeira.

If the negroes had little hope of freedom and the Moors had to wait
for ransom, the Guanches had friends interceding for them at court or
bringing legal proceedings to free them. Some are known to have
escaped. Others featured in wills, in some cases being freed in these.
Many, however, ended their lives in slavery, as many of their
descendants were to do too.

A SLAVE'S LIFE ON TENERIFE

All contracts relating to slaves automatically specified that the subject
was taken *de buena guerra*, in just war. The slave could be sold,
exchanged, used as security, as when in 1509 Lugo gave 1,200 sheep
and five Guanche shepherds to guarantee a debt. There was also sale
or return: nobody wanted a bad slave since his master was liable for his
debts and other actions. In the contracts, where negroes are often
described as 'a thief', 'a drunkard', 'possessed of the devil', the
Guanches are simply 'on the run'. At first these *insoumis* were worth
less than the others but as labour demand rose so their value became
as high as those in captivity. In 1510 a Gomera settler traded an
escaped Guanche, pitch-maker, for a black slave who, in Gran
Canaria, had killed another of his own race — perhaps the two slaves
had by then exchanged islands. A slave was worth less than a good
horse. Any legacies to a slave went to his master.

Male Guanche slaves were put to work as shepherds — watching over
their own flocks — and in agriculture. The sugar-cane industry
brought in negroes and gradually these came to outnumber the
Guanches, a finite source. The island women were kept for sexual
relations and as house servants. Such islanders as were free, perhaps
all Gran Canaria and Gomera men who had helped in the conquests,
also became shepherds, working for wages; they had to pay for any
animals 'lost' and to produce the skins of those which died. Both slaves
and wage-earners were made to spend the nights with the animals
(*hacer majada*); these had to be penned, leading to the development
of portable wooden corrals. In 1503 the Tenerife Council decreed that
the shepherds should 'at least' be given enough barley; this was of
course to make *gofio*. A few Guanches were both free and had
animals: they were banned from the good northern pastures and told
to go to the Güimar lands.

It was soon found that the individual Guanches were beyond
control. Lugo and the other *conquistadores* had expected this but the
Crown's policy had swung over since the conquest of Gran Canaria,
more than a decade earlier, so that the Adelantado's preference for
totally clearing Tenerife of Guanches could not be implemented.
Correspondingly, the greater part of the Council's decrees during the

first two decades of the century were aimed at controlling and punishing the remaining islanders. In 1499 Lugo ordered the settlers to form squads to hunt down the *insoumis* in the mountains; this also set a precedent for the colonial cycle, a later example being when the British colonials hunted down and exterminated the last Tasmanians. In 1500 male fugitives were to receive the sentence of death, females to get 100 lashes and expulsion from Tenerife. It seems likely that this 'expulsion' should be read as sale to another island or to the Peninsula, presumably the most dreaded punishment; this would have been a way of passing round the Crown's disapproval of the lucrative sale of islanders to mainland Spain. This impression is supported by a 1513 act of surety by the Guanche Juan Alonso: Gonzalo Yanes, one of the Daute Portuguese, has a Guanche slave called Luís, of the Taoro territory, whom for bad behaviour he has punished and wants to sell out of the island — but Alonso becomes his guarantor and he is not transported. It was also decreed that no Guanche could serve less than sixteen years as a slave — as will be seen, the islanders had found a way to buy each other out. In 1503 Lugo increased the general severity of the floggings by ordering them to be done by the public hangmen, against the opinions of some members of his Council; however, two years later the owners regained the right to carry out the floggings themselves. To underline the status of the Guanches, general crimes committed by them carried the penalty paid by ordinary Castillian citizens *plus* 100 lashes. Conversely, a free Guanche maltreated by a settler was simply told by Lugo that this was not a punishable action. In 1504 all free Guanches were ordered to take up employment for wages and to stop living in isolated places and 'in the old ways'.

If it had to put up with the Guanches, the Tenerife Council saw no reason for it to tolerate the Gomerans. Free, they were hated by the immigrants as 'vagabonds and thieves' who 'did not live like Christians' nor go to church 'in spite of premiums'. So in 1504 they were all given a month to leave — or eight days if they had no house — together with their families. The expulsion order, with the death penalty if flouted, covered *all* islands under Lugo's control: Tenerife, Palma, Hierro and their homeland, Gomera. However, able to look after themselves, the Gomerans appealed — probably successfully, since in 1511 and 1518 further official attempts were made to eject them.

Not deterred, in 1506 the Council did decide that all Guanche shepherds should be expelled but — with the measure kept secret from the slave and flock owners in the meantime — the authorities would first recruit replacement shepherds in Spain. However, by now America was exerting a greater appeal than the Canaries, no Spanish substitutes appeared and this idea also failed.

The reasons given for the attempted expulsion include a good example of *conquistador* justice: the Guanches had no way of life in Tenerife now they had no flocks of their own. Some had been on the run for as long as six years and 'as they are natives, and know the land, they can't be caught . . . and they say that the land and animals were their grandparents'. The few Guanches refused to work for the immigrants or to live in settlements — control techniques in use today in the last European colonies in Africa, just as was the 1507 decree that slaves should never leave their masters' estates. The free Guanches 'did not mix, follow their old customs and go about in *tamarcos*', their ancient dress, made of skins. The Council further bewailed the absolute solidarity amongst the Guanches: 'They hide and feed each other in the mountains . . . and would die rather than reveal their secrets . . . to find them out by torture is impossible even if they are cut to pieces (*los hagan pedazos*)'.

The official list of punishments grew with measures against those who harboured runaways: free Guanches would have to pay the slave's value to his owner, slaves would get 100 lashes and 'expulsion'. Animal stealing would bring 100 lashes and, on the second offence, the ears cut off — as on Madeira — and again expulsion, presumed to mean sale abroad. A man who caught a runaway slave could keep him. Once caught again, the slave was held in chains; in 1521 a Guanche, Juan González, sawyer, stood surety for the removal of the chains of a slave girl, Eluira.

In 1511 the Guanches were given three weeks to register in La Laguna, move into settlements and appear at Mass. Subsequently they were forced to return, on fixed dates, to the capital, to give details of their means of subsistence. Two years later the Council estimated at 600 the Guanches in the island, saying that many had come back clandestinely; a third of these islanders were described as 'fighting men' and, 15 years after the conquest, referred to as 'our enemies'. In 1514 the Guanches were reminded that they were not to bear arms, a decree later limited to those who lived in the mountains. In 1518 curfews were decreed for all Guanches. Apparently totally circumscribed in time, place and activities, yet the islanders remained effectively beyond control. The decade saw the last two attempts to expel them all. Lugo kept the reins — or rather whips — of government until his death in 1525, in spite of his proven crimes and of strong opposition. In 1535 the settlers asked the Inquisition to deal with the *insoumis*, so far the latest record of Guanches still on the run in the heights.

FREEDOM

There were three legal roads to freedom, *ahorramiento*. Through a law-suit or petition to the Crown; by payment; by release by the owner, usually through a will. A freed man, *horro*, had to have an identity card to prove his status.

In 1498, two years after the Taoro capitulation, a law-suit was started by Rodrigo de Betanzos on behalf of the enslaved *bandos de paces* of Adeje, Abona and Güimar. The Crown sent the governor of Gran Canaria, Lope Sánchez de Valenzuela, to investigate. Lugo claimed there had been no *paces*; evidence of hostility included not going to Mass and living in the mountains. Sánchez freed a number of Guanches and, next year, Lugo's instructions to hunt down the *insoumis* noticeably excluded the people of *paz* territories, including Anaga.

This success led to petitions and legal actions from Gomera, Gran Canaria and Palma as well as further cases from Tenerife; the slaves concerned were in the islands as well as on the Peninsula. The owners tried various tactics. Official connections were used to obstruct proceedings. Francisca Palmesa, the Palma woman mentioned earlier, was offered 70,000 maravedis by Lugo and 60,000 maravedis by Inés Peraza to stop her action. The Duke of Medina-Sidonia hastily took his slaves outside the area allotted to the Crown's investigators on the Peninsula. In 1500, Enrique Canario, the ancient leader of the Icod territory, was being held, out of reach of the Court, with irons on his feet. So, soon, the Court widened its geographical scope. But, even where the case was won, the settlers' power within the archipelago was absolute: in 1500 Beatriz Canaria was simply given back to her owner — who flogged her almost to death.

Such law-suits continued for almost two decades. The islanders were represented by the Poor People's Procurator. Those who, like Leonor de Morales and Andrés of Güimar in 1512, went to the Peninsula to start the proceedings on behalf of their enslaved relatives and friends, had to have safe-conducts from the Crown when they went back; Lugo took little notice of these, as when he imprisoned Enrique of Anaga in 1508. The last known royal decree, obtained in 1519 by Juan de Armas, was that the free Guanches could live where they liked. Doubtless the result of such publicity was to create a bad image of the Guanches in the Peninsula mind: the University of Seville decided not to take any students from the Canaries in case they had 'native blood' . . . colonial discrimination was still at the stage of overt expression.

The second form of *ahorramiento* was for one islander to buy another and then officially release him. Thus, in 1509 at La Laguna, Pedro Guanche, native and resident of Tenerife, freed Rodrigo

Guanche, his brother, native of the island 'for having become a Christian and for his well-being'. It was common practice for a black slave to be acquired and given in exchange. Many Guanches left their property, in their wills, specifically for the redemption of one of their fellows—though not *to* him, since the property would then have passed directly to his master, as noted. The law instituting 16 years as the minimum period of slavery was passed at a time when the value of runaways was low, allowing easy redemption by purchase . . . the settlers loathed the way the new *horro* reappeared with impunity amongst them. The latest known redemption document, of a Palma slave, is dated 1557.

Lastly, there was freedom under a will of the owner—usually after a further term of service, for the heir. Guillén Castellano, a Gran Canaria native who fought with Lugo in Tenerife and was the only islander amongst the first Laguna *regidores*, died in 1513 and left 15 slaves of different ethnic origins: each was given a sentence of a further one to seven years, then to be freed. The will of Lope Hernández de Guerra, the man who strengthened the Spaniards' resolve late in the Tenerife conquest, also an original *regidor*: 'Ysabel and Maçías are to serve my wife all the days of her life and then be freed . . . the two others are to be inherited by my children with the other goods' (c. 1509). Juana de Placeres' will, 1509: the four slaves 'born in her house' are to serve her heirs for 15 years and then to be freed unless they have been disloyal—when they are to remain slaves for ever. Another will, 1508, gives a Guanche his freedom after three years . . . on payment of 10,000 maravedis. Lugo left 25 slaves, in 1525; the will's conditions appear unknown still.

Conscience, hypocrisy and the church were blended in some legacies. Any concessions to the slaves were always 'because he is a Christian'. Some were left to the monastic orders, the monks at length to release them and find them a way of life. A common condition was that the freed islander had to give a silver coin to provide a mass for the soul of his dead master.

NEGRO AND MORISCO SLAVES

Although this book is primarily concerned with the evolution of the original Canary people, to understand their integration into the European-style society of the sixteenth century it is necessary to consider, at least in summary form, the way in which their function as slaves was soon taken over by the two other ethnic groups, the negroes and the Moors. The earliest of these in fact came from the Peninsula with the Iberian settlers.

Subsequently there were brought in negroes from Senegal and

Guinea. Some of the slaving boats would have been on their way to the West Indies, direct or by way of Iberia. The man-hunts by the eastern Canary Spanish also caught black people, probably enslaved, on the adjacent coast, as shown by the documents of sale. The sugar-cane plantations were the negroes' place of work. Some escaped from Madeira, reached the Canaries and were caught there. A few were usually on the run in the highlands together with the unsubmitted islanders.

There were also of course half-caste slaves, *prietos*. The parents would be a black slave-woman and a white settler. The *prieto* child belonged to the woman's owner and was usually sold at birth, sometimes to the father, to compensate for the woman's lost working time. If the slave died in childbirth, then the father had to compensate the owner.

In the Bco. de Silva, by Telde, on Gran Canaria, there are two inscriptions engraved on a lava-flow. According to Kraus, one is in Shluh Berber, spoken in S. Morocco, and is an invocation to a god; the other, in the Hassania dialect of the Arabic-speaking tribes on the African coast adjacent to the Canaries, says 'man of the Erguibat', this the largest of those tribes. Between 1476 and 1593, immense numbers of 'Moors' were captured and brought into the Canaries.

Diego de Herrera, having passed the conquest of the three largest islands to the Crown, did manage to establish a base at the much-disputed Sta. Cruz de Mar Pequeña, its site probably on the coast of Morocco's most southerly province, Tarfaya (Fig. 1). The treaties with the Portuguese gave the Spaniards the right — by Iberian law at least — to carry out manhunts on the whole coast. Herrera made 46 raids and filled his two eastern islands with *moro* slaves, or *moriscos* as they were called once they were Christianized. As the last of the Canaries were conquered, so *moriscos* were sold to the new settlers. Soon they were catching their own, well organized into slave-raiding cooperatives and positively aided by the Crown. If by 1500 this had come round to defending the native islanders, it was simultaneously most enthusiastic about this hunting of African Moslems . . . as a twentieth-century Spanish writer put it, 'For the greater glory of God and the honour of Christianity'. Around the turn of the century, with Herrera long dead, Lugo was the most active commander on the coast, shipping captured *moros* to Spain to pay his debts, as well as to the islands (Mercer 1976). In 1525 Charles V went as far as to waive his *quinto* tax on imported *moros*, by way of encouragement. The raids continued regularly until the middle of the century.

The flocks of the nascent bourgeoisie of La Laguna pastured the northerly Taborno massif, in the care of shepherds from Las Mercedes. These wore cloaks until very recently, being perhaps the last in the Canaries to do so: in W. Morocco there is a village called Tabornost, its name coming from the *burnous* (*bornos*, 'cloak' in Arabic). Some have derived the post-conquest shepherd cloak from the skin garments worn by the ancient people but there seems no real link.

The *moros* brought problems as well as their cloaks to the Canaries. On the run with the other slaves, they added a dimension by taking Spanish ships and going back to Africa; around 1520 the desperate Tenerife Council decided that all vessels should be capable of being immobilized, by removal of a key part, when not in use. In 1528 the Inquisition was looking into the case of 'Maria Morisca, a white slave belonging to Pedro Descalona'.

Sta. Cruz de Mar Pequeña was lost by the Spanish in 1524 and Sta. Cruz de Cabo de Gué, near Agadir, by the Portuguese in 1541. In 1569, thoroughly planned counter-raids on the Canaries were begun by the Moroccans and Algerians. The Old Christians of the two eastern islands suddenly became aware they were outnumbered by there by hostile *morisco* slaves. The Maghrebi forces looted and burnt the Spanish settlements, capturing large numbers of Europeans for slaves. *Moriscos* of recent arrival left in the attackers' ships. Many Spanish moved to the bigger islands for safety.

It was this onslaught which caused Torriani to be commissioned, in 1590, to survey and advise on the fortification of the archipelago. The Castillo de Guanapay (Pl. 14a), the refuge of the Lanzarote people, was already in use by then. The Italian noted that three-quarters of the population of Fuerteventura were *moriscos* or their descendants; 13 villages were entirely populated by them. One settlement is today still called Tarfaya. The lives, speech and marked cultural contribution of these Africans have been examined in the author's work on Fuerteventura (1973). There are also material relics, such as the small bowl found in pieces by the author near a hut on the Africa-facing coast (Fig. 26). Torriani noted a characteristic of the eastern islands which survives today: the country people have a strong sense of fatalism, surely of Islamic origin, and also mark each pause in a conversation with '*Si Dios quiere*', if it is the will of God . . . or Allah. When Torriani asked a *morisco* if he was going to Mass on Sunday, the reply was 'If I'm forced to do so'.

The last Spanish raid on the African coast — in spite of the Crown's prohibition, the result of the Maghreb's rise in retributive power in the Mediterranean — was in 1593. The Africans' final onslaught on the Canaries came in 1618, when a thousand people were caught on Lanzarote and Gomera.

In 1609 came Philip III's decree that all *moriscos* should be expelled from Spain. The slave-owners of the Canaries obtained exemption on

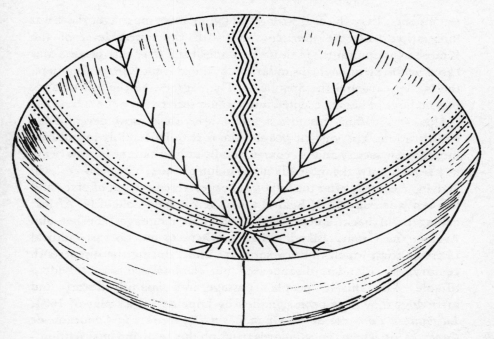

Figure 26   *Moorish-style bowl, Fuerteventura (125mm across)*

the grounds that the Africans were needed for the heavy work. On the
Peninsula most *morisco* families had been there for centuries, were
free and felt at home, so they wished to stay—in the Canaries they
were despised 'New Christians', enslaved and would have preferred to
leave for their home-land.

THE DISAPPEARANCE OF THE ANCIENT CANARY ISLANDERS
By 1600 it was normal for travellers to record that the pre-conquest
people had died out. These were by now all called 'Guanches', since
Tenerife had become the most important island, with the Teide
peak—the highest ground easily accessible to Europeans—of great
interest to early scientists. One of the last islanders to have lived during
the conquests was a Palma man, aged 80, seen by Girolamo Benzoni
in 1541; setting yet another precedent, continuing today in say the
degeneration of the last native Brazilian peoples as their lands are
taken away from them, the Palma man was permanently drunk.

The steady supply of negro and *moro* slaves during the sixteenth
century had allowed the slow but continuous *ahorramiento* of the
island people. The mountain dwellers increased, each *horro* building
himself a hut, starting a flock, constructing and cultivating a few level
terraces out of the sloping hillside. Others stayed in the main

settlements. In each case, strongly aided by inter-marriage, there was integration with the *moriscos* and with the lowest level of the European immigrants. It must be underlined that this process was eased by the physiological similarities of the ancient Canary Islanders, the N. Africans and the Spaniards. The negroes, on the other hand, had no hope of being accepted into Canary society.

However, within this lowest social level there now developed a stratification. The ancient people, the first to be forcibly introduced into the new society and, of course, totally at home in the islands, were as a result always the most advanced in integration. The *moriscos*, still arriving a century after the fall of Tenerife, were both out of place and less easily de-culturized. Behind them, across the whole of N. Africa, calling them back, spread Islam and their languages, Berber and Arabic; the Canary Islanders had nowhere to go, no vast cultural reservoir from which to draw support. Thus, during the seventeenth century, the islanders disappeared but the *morisco* was still identifiable. The ancient people's passage into Spanish history and mythology may have been signalled by Lope de Vega's play of 1621: *La Famosa Comedia de los Guanches de Tenerife y la Conquista de Canarias'*, in which the Spaniards triumph due to divine intervention.

However, island slavery was by no means on the decline, quite the reverse. Yet the slaves are never mentioned by contemporary accounts of say trade or society, suggesting an awareness that something about the institution was shameful. Sánchez has studied baptismal records of Sta. Cruz de Tenerife at the end of the century: entries for slaves and their children were astonishingly high, the peak reached in 1686 with 43 per cent of all baptisms. And, in a society dominated by the church, all Europeans would have had their children baptized but probably not so all the slaves. In 1678 Tenerife had 49,000 inhabitants. An island birthrate of say 25 per 1,000 (the Canaries still has the highest proportion in Spain, 18:1,000) would give some 1,250 births; most would live long enough to be christened and, according to the proportion of babies to adults in the 43 per cent slave baptisms, in 1678 these last would have totalled 500–850 individuals. Such a yearly addition implies a large slave population — and in 1735 it was recorded that the Tenerife owners were deliberately getting their slave-women pregnant in order to increase the supply of labour.

The proportion of negroes is unknown. Some doubtless left the Canaries as soon as they could, others withdrew to form all-black and ultimately abandoned communities in remote regions. Viera (1772) records negro families *at* Tirajana but by Stone's time (1887) they are free and in the mountains *above* Tirajana; the author found that, in the village, the sugar-cane plantations are now just a distant memory. The determination of the recent anthropologists to deny the negro element in the present population, evident both historically and to the observer, has been discussed.

The Spanish hatred of the Moors — better called Arabs and Berbers, as their lands do not coincide with Morocco — goes back to the conflicts of the Middle Ages. It also stems from the intertwining of the two groups in Spain during the Arab-Berber occupation, since this resulted in a gradation of the Spanish people between N. African and European in physiology. The fall of Granada in 1492 did not end the intermarriage on the Peninsula since, there too, slaves were steadily imported during the next century; only in 1609, as noted, were all distinguishable *moriscos* ejected, no matter how long they had been there. After that, the more 'Moorish' the appearance of a Spaniard — most easily assessed on degrees of brown in skin-colour — the greater the prejudice by other, whiter Spaniards. Now, in the Canaries the *moriscos* were never expelled — and perhaps nowhere have more determined efforts since been made to avoid the social stigma of *moro* ancestry. A single still-current example must suffice: in the desert conditions of Fuerteventura, the peasant women developed a special anti-tan outfit, seen by the author a decade ago: a bonnet with huge side-flaps (Fig. 27), long gloves with no palms, stockings with no soles, worn in 40°C when working the fields. The idea for the stockings may of course have come from the islands' gaiters, used from before the conquest into the last century. To call someone a *moro* is the height of

Figure 27   *Recent anti-tan bonnet, Fuerteventura*

insult in the Canaries. And, as a result of the continued enslavement and forced breeding of *moriscos* in the archipelago — Spain only abolished slavery in 1830 — in the eighteenth century it suddenly became preferable and fashionable for the Canaries' working classes to claim . . . pre-conquest ancestry.

CHAPTER TWENTY TWO

Limited Survival

America, *el dorado*, soon exercised a much greater attraction to the *peninsulares* and their capital than did Granada and the Canaries. The archipelago's gold—slaves and animals—had been rapidly worked out. The five centuries since the founding of the Las Palmas fortress soon settled into a cycle composed of long periods of stagnation broken up by brief phases of economic success and, also cyclical but on a minor scale, successions of droughts, famines and plagues.

The financial booms were based on one or two products and, as with all monoculture economies, the collapse of the market always brought disastrous consequences. The orchil lichen soon became so rare that the ships went elsewhere, for example to the uninhabited Salvage Islands, just north of the Canaries (Fig. 2). The sugar-cane industry found it could not compete with that of the West Indies. About 1750 came the production of soda, needed by the European textile and glass factories of the nascent Industrial Revolution; the Canary Islander set about burning the archipelago's soda-plants (*Mesembryanthemum crystallinum, Gasoul nodiflorum*), just as the Hebridean poor, their land more recently taken from them, were being forced to burn seaweeds to make kelp. Early in the nineteenth century a laboratory process was discovered which produced the soda more cheaply—and various peasant communities on the margins of industrializing Europe were reduced to starvation. Next, in the Canaries, came cochineal: from 1825 the islanders duly prepared extensive plantations of their *Opuntia* cactus and spread the insect over them. By 1850 half a million dry kilos of cochineal bodies were being exported—and, from 1862, the market dwindled due to the discovery of synthetic colourings. The fragile Canary economy again collapsed. About 1900 there came the planting of the banana on the well-watered northern coasts and of the tomato on the irrigable southern lands. Competition from poorer economies together with the archipelago's dropping water-table may soon affect these two products. However, during the current century, tourism has taken over first place in the Canary economy.

As elsewhere, the orientation of the labours of the Canary poor towards growing or collecting products for sale, through middlemen, to an outside capitalist market has had two effects: it has kept them poor — the island profits from each boom were retained by the landowners and export agents — and it accelerated the destruction of their ancient ways of life. Correspondingly, the archipelago has become less husbanded than exploited.

Alongside the poverty and its associated cycle there have been four other factors in the stagnation of the islands. First, the doctrines of the church, at once teaching acceptance of their situation to the conquered and enslaved peasantry, a part already fatalistic in orientation. Secondly, a great many immigrants' obsession with nobility and hierarchy, still seen in island attitudes today: no *hidalgo* ever soiled his hands by working, so that the Canary labour force has long carried the dead weight of a numerous gentry.

Thirdly, the Canaries, together with the ex-Spanish Sahara, have always been the dumping ground or place of exile for administrators and military personnel not wanted on the Peninsula. These have either become local tyrants or else simply sat out their terms of office. Perhaps the only exception was Francisco Franco, captain-general of the army in the Canaries in 1936 (the author, born there a couple of years earlier, spent the Civil War in Las Palmas). Fourthly, the general indifference of the central government. Out of these last two grievances have come the use of the word *godo*, Goth (Pl. 15b), to describe the Peninsula Spaniard; the term has been brought to the Canaries by returning emigrants to S. America, its origin there in similar circumstances. And, indeed, Canary discontent with centralization has brought into being autonomy and independence demands such as preceded the breakaway of Spain's American colonies in the nineteenth century. The re-growth of island self-awareness together with one of the new movements will be described in Appendix One, in particular because this group claims to represent an indigenous Canary people descended from the pre-conquest islanders.

Returning now to these two final chapters, the aim is to demonstrate not merely the physical and cultural survival of the ancient people as a notable ingredient in the composition of the present islanders and their society — since by now the existence of much evidence of this must have been made clear — but to bring together all these different contributions by the ancient people.

The evidence falls into two groups. The lesser, given in the present chapter, consists of those aspects which, though they have died out during the five centuries since the conquests, lasted beyond these for long enough to be separately recorded and, in doing so, to add their weight to the greater group, its elements surviving to the time of writing. Also, the aspects which have died out are of interest for their own sakes; many have not yet been discussed since there was no evidence for them in the islands' prehistory nor were they mentioned in the conquest chronicles—or, in one or two cases, the subjects needed too detailed a treatment to be included in the background or intruded in the narrative. The order followed in this and the next chapter will be that used in Chapters 3–11, on the people's prehistory.

An islander's Hispanicization process depended on the degree to which he was within reach of the settlers and of their secular and religious authorities. In the first, widespread phase he would be re-named, clothed, put to live and work as the lowest order of the new society. The reader will judge for himself the potentials of the old and new cultures for allowing the people satisfying lives. A single facet might be considered, as an example—a comparison of the present means of self-expression open to Gran Canaria women against the possibilities current in the period before the conquest. Then, the women made elegant pottery with a wide range of ornamentation; they decorated their caves and huts; they painted their bodies with intricate personal designs and made all their own clothing. Custom and fashion played a part but they were of local origin, in harmony with the community. Now there is little room for expression, with household and personal possessions imported and following the dictates of the universal culture of industrial society.

DANCE, MUSIC, SONG AND STORY

Had the *conquistadores* and their chroniclers had a more friendly approach to the islanders they might have shared in and recorded their ancient festivals. Their main form of entertainment was to dance and to sing. Notes made by post-conquest travellers usually describe the dances and songs as sad, slow, rhythmic, monotonous. Was this the full pre-conquest range or were these the last expressions of a conquered and oppressed people?

On Gran Canaria the islanders met in open houses, wrote Abreu; their favourite dance had quick short steps, still current in his time as *el canario*. Amongst the Guanches the most popular dance was the *guaracha*, this said to have survived until an unknown date, under the Castillian names of *tanganillo* and *saltona*, in the south of Tenerife. Here caution is needed, as the subject enters the *folklórico* of modern Spain; *el baile canario*, Canary dance, was brought in almost entirely by the early European settlers, as was *el traje canario*, Canary dress, and all the rest of the tourist scene. The very use of the work *canario* reflects the notable disassociation of the past from the present, discussed in the final chapter.

The people of Hierro and Gomera regularly danced the *tajaraste* until the middle of this century. The inhabitants of the former came together at feasts, *guatiboa*, sitting in a circle and eating roasted lambs, *jubaques*; to slow plaintive tunes 'they danced in a ring, joining hands . . . and now and then jumping up in pairs'. This was probably the *tajaraste*, in a feast still current in Abreu's time. Three hundred years later, Verneau watched the dance on Hierro: the people formed two parallel lines, faced each other, took each other's hands and then walked and leaped backwards and forwards—endlessly. Herrera, writing in the 1950s on Gomera, however places the dancers in a single file, men in front of women, describing how the line moved forward with measured steps and jumps, including half-turns of the body. Until specialized comparison is made with the rhythms and dances of the N. African interior it can only be noted that the *tajaraste* is in line with the ancient Berber origin for the islanders.

There is only one certain musical instrument, referred to once only: a shaker, consisting of a pot containing hard objects (Gómez Escudero, 1485). Siemens (1969) stretches both definitions and imagination to the limit in his paper, the only feasible idea being that the boomerang-shaped sticks found on Palma may have been clapped together, in pairs; he notes that they are used in this way by the ancient Egyptians and the present Australian aborigines. Early writers reported the flute, usually forwards-running, occasionally transverse, above all played by shepherds; this instrument was however probably of European origin. Pérez Vidal said the flutes had five holes and that, by the time he wrote, 1963, only old men recalled the ancient tunes, presumably early post-conquest in entry too.

However, several chroniclers concur that, whilst dancing, the ancient people kept the rhythm going by singing, clapping their hands and stamping their feet. By Verneau's time the *tajaraste* was backed by drum and flute. Herrera, on Gomera, refers to a drum and huge castanets, *chacaras*; their origins, like the *carcabat* hand-clappers of the W. Sahara negroes, may lie in black Africa, through the early sugar-plantation slaves. Certainly both drum and castanets are post-conquest in appearance in the Canaries.

All that is known of the festivals of the Palma people is that they met at their territory's sacred pillar of stones, singing and dancing around it. Régulo describes how until early this century the islanders would join together for communal tasks and afterwards hold a party at which they danced and sang ballads.

This brings up the songs. On Gran Canaria, either laments or love sonnets, set to grave and plaintive tunes. Verneau said he heard a winnowing song, gloomy and repetitive, of pre-conquest origin. The Gomerans led the archipelago in 'laments of eight, nine or ten syllables, weeping as they sang, as do their descendants', wrote Torriani. Darias records an Hierro song:

Mimerahana	What are you doing here?
Zina zinuha	What's that you're carrying there?
Ahemen aten, haran, hua	Milk, water, bread, what do they matter
Su Agarfa finere nuza	If you won't look at me, Agarfa.

Island mythology and early history would have been transmitted in Régulo's 'ballads', but little attempt seems to have been made to seek and record the last vestiges. Berthelot found that Doramas' resistance to the Spanish was still very much alive in the Moya area of Gran Canaria: he had lived in a clearing in the forest now called after him and 'the peasants in the valley show it off with pride, because the tradition of his great deeds, his heroism and his superhuman strength are still preserved amongst them'. The known legends, perhaps only known still thanks to their role as place-names, seem always to concern islander-*conquistador* confrontations, rather than prehistoric events: the story of Iballa (Gomera), Ferinto's Leap (Hierro), Silva's Precipice (Gran Canaria). Some decades ago, Diego was in contact with old shepherds, in Tenerife, who told witch stories to while away the time in the high pastures — such men, some perhaps still available, may well represent the end of yet another stage in the loss of the ancient culture.

WORSHIP

The immigrant church eliminated some of the pre-conquest beliefs, took over others. For a time the people of Hierro called Christ by the name of their male god, Eraoranhan, and Mary by that of their female deity, Moreiba.

The summer festival, *beñesmen*, went on after the conquest, especially in Tenerife. Originally in late July or August, the early Catholic priests seem to have adjusted it to their own midsummer feast of San Juan, this probably leading to the unevidenced idea that the ancient people celebrated the summer solstice. However, most are known to have had a lunar calendar and there was certainly some worship of the heavenly bodies — but the current general interest in primitive astronomy has not yet reached the Canaries. Diego (1968a) asked an old shepherdess, high up in Chipude on Gomera, when she moved her flock to new pastures, the reply being 'In the first month' — this turned out to be April-May, suggesting a calendar opening in the spring.

Another aspect not yet followed up is the evidence for tree worship. The Guanches venerated the *tagoror* dragon tree at Orotova, seeing it as a protective spirit. Used by the Spainards as a boundary post when dividing up the land amongst themselves in 1496, it fell in 1867; its well-authenticated measurements were 75ft high, 78ft around the trunk. Mention has been made of the discovery, by the early priests, of Christian images in the branches of pine trees in Tenerife; others were found in Palma (El Paso) and Gran Canaria (Teror). This practice by the church may show that the islanders already associated trees with the supernatural.

Figure 28   *The sacred water-tree, Hierro*

This is a convenient point to describe the most famous tree of all, mixture of the divine and the practical, of tree and water cults: the Garoë or Holy Tree of Hierro (Pl. 10a, Fig. 28). Its very existence was denied by Bacon and by Corneille but in 1610 the island council decided that 'the Sacred Tree having fallen and the trunk and branches blocking the holes in which the water used to collect, the place must be put in order'. Its miraculous nature lay in its water-producing property, in a very dry island.

The Garoë was a laurel or *til* (*Ocotea foetens*), said to be 50ft tall. Torriani wrote that four men could barely get their arms around it. It stood at about 1,000m in the Tigulahe ravine, in the Lomos highlands above Valverde. One possible origin for the name of Hierro is *hero*, 'spring' in the pre-conquest tongue; by the nineteenth century this had become *heres*, cistern (Berthelot). Nichols (1556, in Cioranescu): 'This iland hath no kind of freshwater, but onely in the middle . . . a great tree with leaves lyke an olive . . . a great sesterne at the foot . . . This tree is continually covered with clowdes . . . the leaves . . . keep up a gentle dripping . . . this water sufficeth the iland for all neccesitie, as well the cattell as for the inhabitants'. Torriani noted that the clouds *rose* from the valley below — warmer, their vapour would condense on the cool shiny leaves of the Garoë. The Italian also remarked that all three western islands had *tiles de agua*, water-laurels, only they were less impressive; the same condensation occurred on the 'holm oak'. Bethencourt's MS also referred to Hierro 'trees' producing water, 'the best one could find to drink'; Berthelot said there were cisterns in many valleys, confirming that the Garoë was not the only water-tree. However, Torriani was impressed by the sacred laurel, understanding how it had come to be venerated.

The Garoë's fall in the 1610 hurricane was soon followed by doubts that it had existed. In 1629 the Canary bishop certified that he had seen the site and the dry root. At a public enquiry in 1753, four witnesses, aged 80, 85, 90 and 94, said that their fathers, all between 90 and 100 at death, had each collected some of the dead roots to burn during storms, to calm these, and also to make into crosses. There is an island song about the Garoë, of unknown origin.

As Pl. 10a shows, a laurel seedling has recently been planted on the site, above the many cisterns. Oddly, the author found these full of water, even without the Garoë . . . could that particularly fine laurel have simply been living over a spring? In this way its water-producing powers would have seemed miraculous; simultaneously, its resulting great size would have produced above-average condensation. Of course, to have publicized the continuance of water in the cisterns after the Garoë's disappearance would have been to have destroyed the myth.

Two vestiges of the practical side of pre-conquest life are of interest. Berthelot noted that in the remote dry pasturages, the shepherds still made condensation-collecting holes, *guazimos*, in the trunks of the *mocan* tree (*Visnea mocanera*), above the first branches; Darias said pines were also hollowed out. At the village of Tiñor, the author recently saw planks laid beneath the pines: the condensation from low cloud on each tree drips on these, runs down and fills a bucket each night, the people's only water-supply. It is clear why, divine or not, the Garoë was venerated.

BURIAL

'This witness saw . . . a league from Telde . . . in one of the old burial caves . . . a man who had recently died . . . with a mat below him and another on top . . . who seemed to be wearing a *tamarco*' — this and similar evidence, 20 years after the fall of Gran Canaria, shocked the Inquisition. How long these clandestine old-style burials went on is unknown but in the seventeenth century the Güimar people — the last in the archipelago to publicly claim to be pure islanders — fiercely defended their ancestral vaults against outsiders. The description has been given (Chapter 7) of the seventeenth century visitor who, after doctoring some of the Güimar people, was taken as a favour to see the burial caves. More recently, Berthelot suggested a veneration for the dead above average for a Catholic society; on Hierro, for example, on 2 November, food offerings and skins of wine were placed on the tombs in the Franciscan convent — a practice likely to have been encouraged to an unknown degree by the monks, however.

Diego has recorded (1976, 1968a) two traces of the old burial customs. The work *mirlado*, ancient Castillian now obsolete on the Peninsula, is still used in Tenerife to signify a shrivelled, dried-up or mummy-like person. The shepherds of the remote Valle de Santiago (W. Tenerife) were in 1951 still making pieces of *Cneorum pulverulentum* into crosses to protect them against 'infected air' . . . it will be recalled, from Chapter 7, that the seeds of this plant were believed to slow putrefaction and so had been widely used in mummification.

DAILY LIFE

In 1851 the Rev. T. Debarry, on a health cure in the Canaries, was entertained to a dish of *gofio* by a family living near La Laguna: 'It is . . . given with milk . . . to try to promote the good looks of females about to enter into wedlock by making them as fat as possible'. This custom, then, survived from its antecedents amongst the Berbers of N. Africa until at least four centuries into the European phase of island society.

The ancient Canary skin-clothing was of course rapidly superseded, the islanders adopting a wide and sometimes bizzare range of styles from the different conquerors and settlers, as can be seen in Verneau's illustrations. In spite of Pérez Vidal (1963), the long-lived cloaks — one figures in a contract of service of 1510, on Tenerife — are more likely to have African and European antecedents. Spinning and weaving, with other crafts, would have come in with the first settlers. Gaspar Fructuoso noted that Palma's 'native' women were no good at weaving, incidentally at least another sign of their distinguishable survival (1590).

More interesting is the existence of a pre-conquest word, *tenique*, for the stones sewn in the corners of the cape to keep it down in the high wind, avoiding its wearer being blown over and perhaps killed. Diego (1968a) adds that the weighted cape was also turned into a flailing weapon, carrying on to propose that skin-encased stones on thongs were used in this way too—but he produces no convincing evidence for either use or period.

Verneau has an excellent drawing of a Mogán (Gran Canaria) shepherd wearing baggy shorts which at a distance look like a skirt— these do recall the ancient shorts. At this time, the Frenchman records, the eastern islanders still made the *mahos*, the skin shoes which gave them or stemmed from their own name within the archipelago; the shoes were of goatskin, the hairy side outwards. Until not long before, the men had worn locally-knitted woollen gaiters, perhaps continuing those of skin found on the mummies and in the early histories.

One other point relates to appearance. Torriani noted that the pre-conquest common men of Gran Canaria had their heads shaved, the nobles growing their hair long. Though he did not link the two, he also remarked that, in his day, about 1590, the ordinary man on Lanzarote had his hair shaved off. This may also account for the baldness of the Hierro men in the etching of the Sacred Tree (Fig. 28), though this could be current artistic convention. Elsewhere he said that sharp stones, *tausas*, were still used for shaving on Gran Canaria.

During Verneau's nineteenth-century visit to Hierro, a 'ball' was spontaneously organized to entertain him, in one of the villages. Though the wood and thistle technique for making fire was perhaps by then generally obsolete, provision for lighting consisted of a heap of thinly-split sticks of pine. An old man, still as a statue, held one up, alight, in his hand; as the *hacha* neared its end, another old man lit a second and then the first man then sat down. Also about the end of the last century, Stone's guide to a burial cave at Icod (Tenerife) used split pine torches. In 1977, camping in a Teide lava-field, the author found a neat bundle of these sticks still just held together by a rotten string. Verneau also saw a lamp of fired clay 'of pre-conquest type' in use in Tenerife; the fuel was animal fat and the wick of dry grass.

WOMEN'S WORK

Again it was the untiring Verneau who recorded the method he saw used to make butter, in S. Tenerife. A skin half-full of milk was suspended by a long cord from the branch of a tree and then two women sent it to and fro between them until separation took place. Verneau considered the method to date from before the conquest.

'We rode on to La Atalaya . . . the inhabitants are dark, wild-looking people, entirely occupied in forming utensils of earthenware, more Etruscan than Spanish in their appearance' — a note by Debarry during his adventures in the interior of Gran Canaria around 1850. By this time pot-making had become concentrated in a few villages on each island and, although still made by women, was correspondingly a specialized task; the longest-lived potteries were listed in Chapter 10.

There are no records of the pottery made between the time of the conquests and the twentieth century. Pots are still being made at some of the places noted but the vessels seen by the author in no way resemble those of the ancient islanders. In particular a study was made (1973) of the methods of the last potter at Sta. Inés (Fuerteventura), retired but willing to talk about her work. Her techniques, already described, could have stemmed from those of the ancient islanders; most of her vessels did not, except for the undecorated milking pot, called by her a *tofio*, the óld Mahoh name. This pot, together with her strong Cromagnoid features (1973, plate on p. 144) would have been enough to show the survival of the old islanders.

STONE WEAPONS

'They Throw Stones with a force almost as great as a Bullet, and now use Stones in all their fights as they did anciently', recorded Sprat's traveller in 1667. Although there is a single mention of the recent use of the sling amongst shepherds (Pérez Vidal 1963), this was probably an immigrant weapon. The last major battles fought by the islanders with staffs and stones were in 1740. Twice within a month the Fuerteventura peasants overwhelmingly routed raids into the interior by English pirates, on the earlier occasion driving ahead of them a line of camels as protection against the first and only volley of musket fire. In total, 20 marauders were caught and 80 killed . . . had the history of the conquests by George Glas (1764) been available, these English might have been less casual in their incursions.

CHAPTER TWENTY THREE

Survival to the Present

This chapter will show how the old islanders and their culture have survived to the present — though neither exist in pure form, of course. The strongest proportions will be found amongst the rural and, to a lesser degree, urban working classes. It must be hoped that the contents of this chapter will not fall into the hands of the culture-destroying tourist, to be used as a mere game-list of 'curiosities' to be hunted down, stared at, photographed and purchased — making the people feel 'primitive' in doing so. Though it is not of course by their material possessions that societies should be judged.

PHYSICAL ANTHROPOLOGY

It is likely that many more women than men survived the conquests, together with their children of each sex. These women would have been taken as wives by the *conquistadores* and other early *colons*. There are several recorded examples of the marriages of well-known Europeans to the daughters of island leaders. Maciot de Bethencourt set the precedent with Teguise, Guadarfrá's daughter; one of Fernando Guanarteme's daughters married a Spanish noble, another a descendant of Maciot and Teguise; Ben Como's daughter became the wife of the *conquistador* García del Castillo. Names were changed by baptism, marriage — and to avoid slavery and discrimination. Some kept their origins clear: Catalina la Guancha was proceded against, at La Laguna in 1672, for demoniacal practices, with similar names recorded later still. Children of mixed islander-European parentage were declared Spanish. Even the Inquisition accepted, in the sixteenth century, that it was impossible to draw up a list of those with pre-conquest ancestry.

The swing to desirability of native ancestry in the 1600s was held by Berthelot to be still current late in the nineteenth century. Verneau, also writing then, was of the opposite view. The author's impression — on an aspect worthy of deeper study — is that the rural people now look back with admiration and sympathy at the ancient islanders but, referring to them as 'they', '*los canarios*', '*los guanches*', leave it to the listener to assume there is no relationship. The reasons for this are likely to range from their depressed past to the official history of the islands taught in schools. This leads on, again, to the issue of island consciousness, discussed in Appendix One. Table 39 shows population growth since the conquest. The official population estimate in 1978 is almost 1.5 million inhabitants.

Census	1678	1742	1802	1860	1900–20	1950
Fuerteventura	4	6	12	11	11(1910)	14
Lanzarote	4	7	16	16	19(1910)	29
Gran Canaria	21	34	55	69	183(1920)	332
Tenerife	49	60	70	94	138(1900)	318
Gomera	4	6	8	11	23(1920)	28
Palma	14	18	29	31	c50(1920)	64
Hierro	3	4	4	5	8(1920)	8
Total	99	135	194	237	432	793

Table 39: *Population growth (thousands)*

To the question upon whereabouts in the archipelago the ancient people survived in greatest purity, the travellers of the last few hundred years have given a unanimous answer: in the south of Tenerife, in particular Güimar, territory of Añaterve the collaborator. Berthelot added a secondary survival zone up the west coast to Santiago; his criteria were speech, including 'cries of joy', surnames, dances, fire-making, milking goats, making butter, milling grain and so on. The many ecstatic descriptions of 'living Guanches' by past travellers will not be given here since, as stated early in the book, such isolated notes add little and, above all, these observers had a misconception of the physiques of the ancient islanders, the error still retained by the modern tourist guide-book. Sprat's 1667 account said the village of Güimar was 'inhabited for the most part by such as derive themselves from the old Guanchios . . . they are generally very poor, yet the poorest thinks himself too good to marry a Spaniard'. This lasted until at least the eighteenth century. The continuing claim was partially kept up by its connection with the Candelaria shrine; however, Serra (1959a) says that enthusiastic local participation in this cult is no longer to be associated with Guanche ancestry but is now simply due to having the famous shrine, with its replacement image, in the village.

Finally the most important evidence, the work of the twentieth-century anthropologists. All have demonstrated the survival of the ancient people. In Part Three the author raised objections and made suggestions on various aspects. Parts Five and Six will have shown the inadequate attention paid by these modern studies to the large-scale clearances, immigrations and inter-island transportations which resulted from the conquests. Each island should be treated in the light of its own peculiar history, pieced together from all the various sources. As an example, none is more complex than Tenerife in terms of population movement.

First, the Taoro league people on the fertile north coast were greatly killed in battle and by plague or were subsequently deported, the region then being populated not only by the Europeans but also by the many free Gran Canaria men who had fought with them; possibly the tame and less desirable southern territories provided both slaves and wives for the rapidly evolving north; Lugo is also known to have brought in Palma people as plantation slaves; the free Gomerans were on the island in quantity sufficient to merit the repeated expulsion edicts. The reader may recall that Schwidetsky found that a comparison of ancient and modern physiology on Tenerife indicated that the Mediterranean pole has taken over the north coast since the conquest. Two reasons can now be proposed. First, the Cromagnoid people of the Taoro league zone, decimated, were replaced by slaves and serfs from the southern, more Mediterranean region, their inhabitants having either collaborated or surrendered with little loss of life. Second, the incoming Gran Canaria men were clearly from the Gáldar-Telde population centres—and these were their island's Mediterranean concentrations. However, any simple reconstructions are to be treated with caution in view of the lack of accurate data on the population movements. The anthropologists have also ignored the enormous influx of white African *moriscos*, statistically significant in the two main islands and even outnumbering the other ethnic groups on Lanzarote and Fuerteventura. As noted, these waves of gradually-assimilated Berbers and Arabs are not part of the official history of the Canaries. There is also the overall problem of the physical overlap of the pre-conquest islanders, N. Africans and Spaniards. However, though the exact extent of their survival may be beyond untangling, as those early anthropologists, the Inquisition, accepted, one aspect is clear: the ancient islanders have contributed a strong element to the present country people and as Schwidetsky noted, to the poorer populations of the towns.

SPEECH

In a unique note, a group of eighteenth-century French travellers, led by Verdun de la Crenne, remarked of 'the last Guanches' of Güimar: 'They use their ancient tongue amongst themselves though all understand Spanish well'. There is only a single record of a European importation being translated into the pre-conquest speech, Atmaycequayarirari, 'Mother of he who possesses the world', the Virgin

British Museum Society

Mary (Abreu). It is not known when the islanders' Berber-related tongue ceased to be spoken. Many common words continue in use, above all amongst the shepherds (Pl. 16): *baifo* (kid), *jaira* (sheep), *guanil* (free-roaming animal). Pérez Vidal (1963) listed the many words still used on Hierro for animal colours; for example, *ambracafiranca* for cinnamon with white patches all over the body. Many place-names continued unchanged, throughout the archipelago.

Gomera's whistled language has also survived. Sprat's informant of 1667 appears to have referred to Tenerife: 'They wistle so loud as to be heard five miles off . . . to be in the same room . . . were enough to indanger breaking the Tympanum of the ear . . . he . . . could not hear perfectly for fifteen days after'. However, this note omits an essential detail, the purpose of the whistling. Verneau, on Hierro, heard the villagers being called together by whistling, for the party in his honour; a large sea-shell was also blown as a signal. On Gomera, without any doubt, the whistling has the status of language: on one occasion, Verneau's guide whistled his profession ahead to the next village, so that by his arrival many invalids had assembled for treatment. From the time of the French conquerors through to the present, it is Gomera which has been known for the whistled speech.

BELIEF

Although the author has not witnessed it, the Fiesta de las Ramas is said to be still held at Agaete (Gran Canaria). In the last century this consisted of a procession down to the sea where the people beat the water with branches, clearly a continuation of the Gáldar region's pre-conquest drought-breaking ceremony. It is not obvious how this was fitted into the conquerors' religion; throughout the last 500 years, catastrophes such as drought, locusts and disease have brought forth village processions carrying Catholic images and led by the parish priest.

The last traces of the worship in high places seems to have been in N. Gomera. Verneau recorded an Agulo custom which followed Mass on 25 April, the day of the village's patron, St. Mark: beating tambours and playing guitars, the people would go to visit the ancient rock-shrines, there to sing and get drunk. Not that getting drunk is a pre-conquest survival: on Tenerife 'to this day they drink no wine' wrote Sprat's 1667 informant.

The *fiesta* in honour of the Candelaria shrine still takes place on 2 February. For a couple of hundred years after the conquest, the last Guanches tenaciously claimed the honour of carrying the image in the procession. In the nineteenth century, the Güimar people, dressed in skins and with long lances, used to act out its finding on the shore about 1400.

SPORT

An ancient pastime which is part of many feast days is the wrestling match, now called *lucha canaria*. 'Those duels were generally fought on public festivals or such like occasions', recorded Abreu, 'which drew together a great concourse of people, when the combatants had an opportunity to display their dexterity, strength and valour. These spectacles made a great impression on the minds of the youth, exciting in them a spirit of emulation to excel in gallant feats'. This description refers to the duels with stones and staves on pre-conquest Gran Canaria, described in Chapter 11.

A wrestling match was once held to decide a pasturage dispute between the Gáldar and Telde territories; it took place in private, being won by the renowned Adargoma, but afterwards, agreement being reached on the grazings, each contestant generously said the other had won. The islanders' 'heroic' quality once came out in a wrestling match: a defeated contestant, desperate to prove his valour, flung himself over a precipice . . . the winner, not to be outdone, then did so too.

On Gomera, said Abreu, 'when the men had any quarrel . . . to be decided by combat, they laid aside their cloaks, tied a kind of bandage around their waists, and bound their foreheads with a sort of painted turban'. Berthelot watched a wrestling match at Güimar, noting that the spectators remained silent throughout. Now at least, the *lucha canaria*, with its peculiar rules, can be seen in all islands.

Other feast-day sports have ended or become blended into those of the European settlers. The art of stone-throwing may now be lost. Of the two eastern islands, Abreu said their 'principal diversions' were leaping and jumping: 'two men took a staff . . . held as high above their heads as they could reach . . . some could at three jumps leap over three poles placed in that manner behind each other'. Running was popular in the two main islands. At Arico (Tenerife) there was a lifting stone of great weight. On Gran Canaria, tree-trunk tossing was a favourite competition — and the most demonstrative would climb a precipice carrying a trunk and place it prominently for all to see.

SECULAR STRUCTURES

The troglodyte village of Artenara had 1,000 inhabitants in Viera's time (1772). Atalaya, the village of potters visited by Debarry around 1850, was in 'a deep ravine, the head of which is composed of a rubbley kind of stone, in which are formed cavern cottages, tier above tier, so thick and numerous, that the place can only be described as a human warren'. During the author's childhood in the island, it was forbidden to photograph this settlement — but in fact it was just the largest and most accessible and many others still occur all over the Canaries. As described in Chapter 8, many still-occupied caves in Gran Canaria are not natural but have been expertly quarried in the soft ash tuff. It is common for piped water and electricity to be now laid on to the occupied caves. Many are quite adequate dwellings, with above-average insulation from heat and cold.

Diego (1960b) described a cave-dwelling in use by shepherds which, he reasonably felt, may be very close in living style to those of the pre-conquest period. The cave is in the remote Dehesa pastures of W. Hierro (Fig. 23), in the Mña. de las Cuevas. Entered by a door, inside there are stone beds, seats and shelves, also a hearth; outside, another hearth. All the household goods are made of juniper wood: a pot 11cm deep, with a strong short handle, recalling those in the Tenerife museum (Fig. 19n); large dishes for mixing up *gofio*, to 50cm across; long spoons with limpet-shell bowls. In the middle of the floor stands a one-legged table or shelf (1m 50cm high), the *sebadera*; its name derives from the grease covering the leg to prevent the rats climbing up. The present writer saw *sebaderas*, outside other occupied caves nearby, in use as stands for drying cheeses. Not far away is the Corral del Capitán, the animal pen where, five centuries ago, the islanders stabbed their tyrannical governor, Captain Lázaro Vizcaino.

Another survival in the Dehesa of Hierro can be described here: the existence of the post of 'shepherd's mayor', its function only to settle pastoral problems. Diego plausibly sees this as a vestige of the ancient *tagoror* meetings (Pl. 10b) at which, together with worship and feasting, the region was administered.

The evolution of the commonest rural huts seems beyond assessment, since it is now difficult to distinguish the simpler pre-conquest buildings, round or oval, from those, including animal pens, made by the surviving islanders, the Africans and the poorer Europeans. Those recognizably prehistoric by their distinctive features — for example, being sunk in the ground or cross-shaped in plan — are not now in use.

Espinosa (1590) mentioned that, in the Güimar lands, each house had a seat outside it where a visitor sat and waited to be seen by the occupants. In Fuerteventura, almost 400 years later, the shepherds who visited the author's farmhouse high in the central cordillera would stop at a distance and clap their hands or whistle to attract attention — to go up to the door was considered bad manners. A few years later the author saw this custom again in the adjacent Sahara: to respect privacy, a tent had to be approached from behind, the visitor then stopping short and signalling his presence.

DAILY LIFE

Diego's major study (1968a) of transhumance in Tenerife showed that the Güimar shepherds continued to use the old migration routes and pastures, moving up to the Llano de Maja (Pl. 8a) in the summer and returning to the coast in the winter; the last of these men have been mentioned in connection with the ending of oral traditions (Chapter 22). The pre-conquest domesticated animals also have their descendants—today's Palma goats are a striking example. Surviving veterinary practices are bleeding and greasing, with a *Cneorum* decoction in place of quinine. The handed-down medical treatment of humans has been little studied but at least on Fuerteventura there are herbs and animal grease still in use (Mercer 1973).

The transhumance to the sea, now primarily to collect shellfish, has continued at least on Fuerteventura; the use of euphorbia juice to poison the fish in the rockpools is still known there. Fishing with lights at night went on until at least the last century.

'Their food is Barly roasted, and then ground with little Mills . . . and mixt with Milk and Honey . . . they carry it on their backs in Goat-skins' (Sprat 1667, upon Tenerife). One of Verneau's pictures shows this *gofio* satchel, or *zurrón*, on Gran Canaria (Mogán). The Rev. Debarry and his womenfolk, amongst Tenerife's first tourists (1851) did not enjoy their *comida típica*: 'A very large pan, filled with *goffio* . . . looking mightily like bird-lime, was placed before the swarthy family, and each, as he felt disposed, plunged his fingers into it, and carried away a piece of this unsavoury looking stuff. It is considered very nourishing . . .'. The author has eaten *gofio* recently in exactly the same way in a mountain house in Fuerteventura. Such isolated dwellings retain their rotary querns but few if any now use them, taking their grain to the nearest power-mill or, increasingly, buying their *gofio*, now commonly wheat or maize, already roasted and ground.

Diego (1960a) has the surprising information that, on all except the two eastern islands, fern roots are still roasted and milled into *gofio* flour. In the last century it actually formed the staple in N.E. Palma, the island also best known for its pre-conquest consumption of this food, but in other islands such as Gomera it was only eaten in famines (Verneau). Barilla-seed *gofio*, already described, was a regular food in the last century, being eaten again—doubtless with many other ancient foods—in the *años de hambre* which followed the 1936–9 Civil War (Diego 1947).

WOODEN TOOLS

Hierro mythology has it that, at the end of the reconquest of the island, in 1455, by Inés Peraza and Diego de Herrera, the last un-captured islander, Ferinto, leaped a great ravine in his unavailing attempts to escape his pursuers; the place is still called El Salto de Ferinto. In the seventeenth century, the Royal Society of London's editor (Sprat) said his informant saw the Tenerife men 'leap from Rock to Rock, from a very prodigious height . . . sometimes making ten fathom deep in one leap. The manner is this: First they Tertiate their lance (. . . about the bigness of a half Pike), that is, they poise it in their hand, then they aim the point of it at any piece of a rock, upon which they intend to alight (sometimes not half a foot broad). At their going off they clap their feet close to the Lance, and so carry their bodies in the Air. The point of the Lance first comes to the place, which breaks the force of their fall; then they slide gently down by the Staffe and pitch with their feet upon the very place they first designed . . . Their Novices sometimes break their necks in learning'. The Mogán shepherd in Verneau's drawing has a 4m staff with an unusual leather grip.   CAMDEN P.L.

Late in 1977, at the very end of his field-work, the author was standing on the Balos outcrop (Pl. 5a) examining the faint engravings, amidst the multitude of modern imitations, names and other defacements. The jets going in and out of Gando airport, on the nearby coast, regularly superimposed themselves on the roar of the dense traffic along the *carretera* between Las Palmas and the vast southern tourism complexes such as Maspalomas. With remarkable lack of self-consciousness, not seeing themselves as anachronisms, a flock of about 100 many-coloured goats, some with bells around their necks, gradually made their way through the pale green *balos* plants and up the ravine. There was an occasional bleat, the water-worn cobbles were rolled about, the bells tinkled as the animals jumped or stood on their hind legs to get at the upper branches of the shrubs. Their shepherd came across to talk. He was tall and tanned, middle-aged. On his back he wore a *zurrón* or *gofio*-satchel, of white goat-skin. In his hand he carried a new travelling-pole, about 2m 50cm long with a powerful steel spike on the tip. He insisted that the most important engravings were on the up-*barranco* end of the outcrop. Once round there he pointed out the ancient Saharan alphabet in-scription on which is superimposed one of the grid-shaped signs: 'Those,' he said, with intense enthusiasm, 'are from the beginning of the world'.

Archipelago Consciousness: Autonomy and Independence Demands

At present there is a pro-independence extremist movement, the 'Movimiento para la Autodeterminación y Independencia del Archipielago Canario', or MPAIAC (Pl. 15b, referred to as em-pie-yac, in English imitation of the Castillian pronunciation). Since it is becoming notorious for its terrorist activities, the reader may well hear of its existence and claims. This appendix will summarize the evolution of the Canary home-rule groups and then the nature and aims of MPAIAC, itself a pawn in the political manoeuvres of the various countries around or interested in the W. Mediterranean.

Early in the nineteenth century, following decades of particularly acute hardship and of economic stagnation, the Canaries saw the American colonies obtain their independence. The French revolution was still a recent event. Autonomy was therefore discussed in the islands; a publication called *El Guanche* was founded. However, the dissidents neither looked back to the ancient people for inspiration nor, indeed, were they peasants. As in S. America, they were primarily of the settler class and their aims were economic and administrative autonomy. Their demands led, in 1852, to the granting of 'free port' status to the Canaries. Many foreign observers of the late nineteenth century, such as Stone and Verneau, noted the live resentment of the *hidalgo* class towards the *peninsulares*. As remarked in Chapter 22, once the rift was entrenched in the minds of the Canary bourgeoisie, each and every new arrival from mainland Spain — mostly bureaucrats and soldiers but, recently, also company executives — was likely to be received with hostility.

On the other hand, the Canaries' rural and urban poor, primarily composed of the descendants of the ancient islanders and of the more recently arrived black and white Africans, in social groups stable for many centuries, have throughout nurtured a resentment towards the distinctive settler-class, these keeping it alive by their jealously guarded status in Canary society. Slavery had perhaps ended by 1750 but the 'free' country people were and have remained serfs within the *latifundismo* system: the inactive landowner receives half the yield from each of the plots, individually inadequate for a tolerable living, which he allows the peasants to work. *Latifundismo*, by no means limited to Spain, was of course an import of the *conquistadores*.

Emigration began as fast as the Europeans gained control of each island. At present 3% of the proprietors control 75% of the irrigable land; at the other extreme, 90% of owners have 13% of this land. The steady emigration — preferred to emulating the French and rising in revolt — has drained the Canaries of the most enterprising working-class islanders . . . in turn making it easier for the oppressive system to continue. The position has always been made the more acute by the birth rate, as noted the highest in Spain.

In 1898 came the second phase of colonial dissidence: the independence of Cuba and the Philippines. This brought fresh autonomy demands in the Canaries, an island movement occupying La Laguna for three days in 1909 and, 400 years after Lugo's assaults, Peninsula troops had to be sent to quell the rebellion. The result of this defiance of the *godo* government was however an increase in autonomy for the island councils, the Cabildos.

The Franco dictatorship, totally centralized, brought the Canaries back under the control of the Peninsula, directly or effectively abolishing such autonomy as the archipelago had acquired. At the end of the 1950s — and this time with the spectacle of many African colonies, Spanish and otherwise, freeing themselves from European domination — the first home-rule group of the current phase began in the Canaries. Obviously enough, this was equally the expression of the discontent felt throughout Spain under the totalitarian regime. Clear groupings, such as the Canary archipelago and the Basque nation, were natural foci for home-rule movements claiming that problems of all kinds would be solved with autonomy or independence.

It is not intended to do more here than summarize the events of the subsequent 20 years, at their most complex at the time of writing (and a study of the progress of autonomy throughout Spain is in preparation). Numerous movements have been formed in the islands, gradually drawing more on the working class but still with a degree of middle class and intellectual support; there is a right-wing group based in Central America. All were proscribed by the fascist government of 1936–75 and, no less, by the Republican leadership in exile. There have been sporadic demonstrations, leading to violent clashes and prison sentences. However, the majority of the Canary people have not supported these movements and, until recently, they were very little known outside the archipelago.

Archipelago problems in the 1970s
The Canaries' mounting troubles have brought island consciousness to perhaps its highest pitch since the fifteenth-century invasions. The heavily-exploited archipelago now holds 1.5m people, with the highest

birth-rate in Spain. Unemployment (11%) and inflation (30%) are each above peninsula rates. So too is analphabetism (16%).

The backward and exploitative nature of agriculture has been described. The major industries are each under foreign or peninsula control: fish-canning, tobacco and, above all, tourism — perhaps a fifth of the money spent by foreign visitors remains in the Canaries. The essential fishing industry is so poorly equipped that nine-tenths of the fish caught in Canary waters are taken by foreign vessels. The national economic crisis, as Spain joined the downward trend of the industrialized states in the 1970s, has played its part in the depression of the Canaries.

The problems are increasingly blamed on the *godos*, now often referred to as *españoles*; these now get up to 100% pay supplements to work in the archipelago, further irritating their Canary associates. As an example of the perennial tension between *canarios* and *peninsulares*, early in 1977 the Civil Governor sent the national Policia Armada, with machine guns, to force the Policia Municipal to allow building to continue on a Las Palmas site not approved by the municipal authorities.

The most serious recent confrontation came in December 1977. The Suárez government's answer to student unrest at La Laguna, originally over university regulations, was to fly in 600 riot police from Zaragoza and Cordoba. These shot a student within the university buildings and, at the official mourning, some invited participants were assaulted and others forced to eat their crêpe armbands. The islanders were insulted as '*canarios*'. The peninsula police then ran amok (as in a Basque town in mid-1978), firing off smoke-bombs and rubber bullets, setting light to dwellings and attacking those who tried to put out these fires. In an action, then, reminiscent of 1909 and of the clearly not-so-distant days of Franco, La Laguna was occupied and the rebellion of 200 students suppressed. Canary autonomy and even independence movements gain support from such over-reaction by the central authority.

MPAIAC: liberation movement without a people

The present home-rule activists fall into two groups. The moderate, pro-autonomy movements now find their demands coming within the national debate and government proposals for devolving a still-untested degree of power to the dozen or so regions which make up Spain. Correspondingly, these Canary movements find many of their supporters now content to leave the matter to the newly-legalized left-wing political parties. In the June 1977 general elections, the main self-determination party, *Pueblo Canario Unido*, obtained only 6% of the island vote; UCD, which won the elections, gained 18 Canary seats, PSOE, the socialists, four seats; abstention, however, ran at 39% in Tenerife province and 30% in that of Gran Canaria, against the national average of 22%.

The only active pro-independence group is the *Movimiento para la Autodeterminación y Independencia del Archipiélago Canario*, or MPAIAC. This extremist movement is the invention of one man, Antonio Cubillo, a lawyer born in La Laguna of Tenerife-Galician parents. Cubillo was imprisoned for his part in the *Movimiento Autonomista Canario* and, following its end in 1963, he formed MPAIAC. Its manifesto states that the Canaries and its people are part of Africa, continuing:

> The government of Madrid . . . is trying to convince . . . the OAU and the UN that the Guanche people has disappeared as a national entity . . . the opposition to Spain exists in our country not only because of historical reasons but also in the name of ethnical, political, economic, geographical and cultural differences which make the Canarians a self-contained unity different from the Spaniards.

Upon independence:
1) The Canaries would become the 'Aguayo Guanche' (Pl. 15b) or Guanche Republic, African in orientation and federal in organization. Its flag would be three vertical bands, white, blue and yellow, with a circle of seven stars on the middle section, representing the seven equal-status islands on a blue sea.
2) Each island would be autonomous. Each would be divided into *menceyatos* or regions, with their own elected *menceys* (the Guanche word for 'leader') and their assistants or *achimenceys*. The villages within each *menceyato* would elect its *guanarteme* (the ancient Gran Canaria word for 'leader'), the mayor. The government of each island would be through meetings of all these officials in Supreme Tagorors (the Guanche assemblies). These would be led by a president or *quebehi* ('highness', used to a leader by the Guanches) designated by the *menceys*.
3) The federal, legislative body would be the National Tagoror, composed of two chambers: the upper house or Sabor (the ancient council of nobles on Gran Canaria), holding the members of each Supreme Tagoror, and the lower house or Taoro (the territory which long resisted the *conquistadores* of Tenerife, its name said to have meant 'the plain' in Guanche), this composed of *guayres* (Gran Canaria nobles) or directly-elected representatives of the islanders.
4) Both the ancient tongue and Spanish would be official languages. The pre-conquest cultural traits would be stimulated.

These then are the aspects of the ancient people and their way of life which Cubillo incorporated in the MPAIAC manifesto. Study of the rest of the document shows the Guanche Republic would be a strongly socialist state. Amongst the measures promised are land reform, action to curb the domination of foreign and peninsula capital, workers' co-operatives, the ending of facilities for the US, South Africa and other ideologically-opposed countries. There is no space to give MPAIAC proposals in detail; many are certainly measures needed in the Canaries. Nevertheless, in spite of the fertile conditions the group made no real impact in the islands—it has claimed many demonstrations in which it has merely participated—or on the Madrid government.

In November 1976, the frustrated MPAIAC turned to terrorism. Indiscriminate 'destabilization' has meant over a hundred bomb attacks by the 'Fuerzas Armadas Guanches'. Targets have included large peninsula-based department stores; the La Laguna house of the captain-general of the army in the Canaries; an army recruiting centre and a naval base; the South African airline office. In April 1978, international tour operators were threatened with bombings against their offices and hotels unless they paid a 'tourist tax' to MPAIAC; it was rumoured that, in July, troops were sent to the tiny islands of Graciosa and Lobos to avert their occupation, with tourists as hostages, by MPAIAC. In Madrid, the movement damaged lorries of Pescanova SA, a massive peninsula organization dominating the Canary fishing industry. It was also MPAIAC which, in March 1977, by placing a bomb in Gando airport (Gran Canaria)—to damage the tourist industry—diverted to Los Rodeos (Tenerife) the two large jets which there crashed into each other. The world's biggest air-disaster brought MPAIAC temporarily into the front ranks of international terrorism. Late in 1977, during a visit of Juan Carlos to Las Palmas, the writer saw graffiti reading 'Guanche Republic—out with the *godo* monarch—self-determination' whilst on the pedestal of the nearby statute of Columbus was sprayed the pun 'Colonialista'.

The Canaries in international strategies

Many islanders fear that the archipelago is about to become a key-piece in several conflicts at once, the secretary of the Canary branch of the Spanish communist party referring to it as the Cyprus of the Atlantic. The US sees the islands as monitoring and launching platforms for intervention in Africa; there is already a NASA telecommunications station and, under construction, a nuclear submarine base. The Spanish right favours entry into NATO and, with or without this, the extension of US installations in the islands; a large, new and unused airfield in southern Tenerife is held available. The

Canaries' harbours and airfields are among the most modern in Africa. Correspondingly, the USSR has approved MPAIAC, avowedly Marxist and against the US presence; the Russian fishing fleet, along with the Japanese, takes the bulk of the Canary catch. The more the Canaries are threatened the more the present government is likely to welcome the US.

The second level of confrontation brings in the African states and their roles in the Sahara conflict (Mercer 1976, 1979a). Coincident with Franco's death, in 1975 Spain handed over the Spanish Sahara and the Saharaui people to Morocco and Mauritania, in exchange for economic and other benefits. This led to the current war between the occupying neo-colonial powers and the Saharauis (Polisario). The former are backed by the US, France and, of course, the present Spanish government (until late in 1978), the latter by Algeria, Libya and USSR — to put it very simply.

Algeria has been the supporter of MPAIAC. According to Salvador Sagaseta, leader of yet another home-rule group of the sixties (*FLN Canaria*) and long exiled in Sweden, Cubillo gave the movement an African-ethnicity basis (distorting history and anthropological studies) in order to draw on the only possible support. Algeria installed MPAIAC alongside the numerous movements proscribed by African governments of opposed ideology. In 1968 Algeria persuaded the OAU Liberation Committee to recognize MPAIAC provisionally. In 1976, to bring pressure on Spain and the US over the Sahara invasion, it gave financial support and radio time to Cubillo's group. 'The Voice of the Free Canaries' included lessons by Cubillo in the Guanche tongue, put together by him out of the known pre-conquest words mixed with elements of current Maghreb speech; he once managed to convince a leading European newspaper that Guanche was 'persecuted' by the Spanish authorities. However, this alliance of Canary pawn and African knight was to last only until the middle of 1978.

The fifteenth-century *conquistadores* of the Canaries were once disturbed by the news that the archipelago was being claimed by the King of Fez; for those who have studied the bases of the Moroccan submission, in 1975, to the International Court of Justice hearing over the Western Sahara, there would be a feeling of *déjà-vu* were Morocco to now claim the Canaries too. A poster in Las Palmas in 1977 showed Hassan II and Juan Carlos sitting in a US military boot with the words 'The Canary people are with the Democratic Arab Republic of the Sahara'. The US backs Hassan on all issues in order to strengthen the conservative Maghreb front, because of its need for its Moroccan bases — to be extended to the Sahara if Hassan could win the war there — and to safeguard various investments in the region. Cubillo indeed tried Morocco for support before going to Algeria, but was rejected. Morocco's counter to Algeria's pressure on Spain, by its support for MPAIAC, is to threaten to turn the screw on Ceuta, Melilla and the Chafarinas Islands, an issue otherwise tactically shelved by Hassan.

However, since 1976 Morocco has been carrying out complex, often clandestine activities in the Canaries, partially in direct connection with the adjacent Sahara war and partially to counter Algeria-MPAIAC action in the archipelago—the Maghreb conflict carried to the Canaries, potentially. As the described poster stated, there is indeed a degree of sympathy in the Canaries for the Saharauis, if unloved at least with a century's interaction with the archipelago, unlike the Moroccans; there is also a superficially-shared interest in the polemical fishing agreement between Spain and Morocco, discussed below. As long ago as 1968 Cubillo tried to link his concept of the Canaries to the then-Spanish Sahara in a federal union; the Saharauis, if ready for any public support, including from MPAIAC, have never even acknowledged Cubillo's movement, let alone his dream of federation. The Cape Verd—Guinée-Bissau project of union could be seen as a precedent—but to the immense cultural gulf between the Canaries and the Sahara one has only to add the pro-colonialism difference in economic development for it to be seen that the Saharauis could never consider the scheme.

Morocco's archipelago manoeuvres have included trying to round up all Saharauis there, in order to deport them to their annexed territory; early in 1978 a plot to this end was revealed, involving the Spanish police and the Moroccan and Mauritanian consuls in the Canaries. It has been said that there are Moroccan secret police operating in the islands. A wider and more ominously long-term strategem of 'the King of Fez' began in 1976: Moroccan immigration into the Canaries was encouraged, an estimated 100–150 of Hassan's subjects entering the islands each month, and the Moroccan consulate was then opened. Groups of Moroccans are now a conspicuous sight at island *fiestas*. Moroccan investment, with official stimulus and Lebanese nationals as a front, has reached important proportions in the Canary economy; there has been fear of Moroccan take-overs of island enterprises. Some archipelago capital crossed to Morocco. Many island firms supply Hassan's troops in the occupied Sahara with provisions also uniforms. The long-standing movement of arms from the Canaries to the desert may now be accompanied by mercenaries recruited by Morocco. The Western Sahara's phosphate mine, usually at a standstill due to Polisario guerrilla action, has tried to keep on many Canary employees, in spite of the general Spanish withdrawal; more recently the Canaries have heard that Hassan is looking for building workers to put up 2000 houses at Cape Bojador, though, as long as the war continues, the much-publicized investment in the desert will remain one of the king's many mirages. Hassan not only needs the Canary labour force — he hoped that the use of Spanish nationals in the Sahara would encourage the Spanish government to continue backing the annexation.

The Canary and Sahara fishing grounds shared out by Madrid and Rabat

Nevertheless, on the main Canaries-Morocco issue, Hassan is in maximum conflict with the islanders. The Saharan bank, now probably the world's best fishing zone, has been a source of livelihood for many islanders since the *conquista*, providing around 75% of the Canaries' catch. The 1975 Tripartite Agreement between Spain, Morocco and Mauritania placed limits on Canary fishing off the continent's coast: 800 vessels in the annexed Sahara waters, 200 vessels in the existing Mauritanian zone. Such a treaty was inevitable once the Sahara was decolonized, no matter to whom it were passed. But in February 1977 a further treaty was signed between Spain and Morocco — and this was unnecessarily unfavourable to the Canary fishermen. Under last-minute pressure from Hassan and in spite of the Spanish left, the Cortes ratified the deal in 1978. With the Suárez government limply repeating its regular face-saver that this only reflected its 1975 transfer of 'administrative power' but not of 'sovereignty', Hassan was once again able to claim Spanish endorsement of his annexation of the Sahara. There have been intermittent strikes and demonstrations in the Canaries ever since.

The 1977 treaty — to say no more here of the lobby behind the Tripartite Agreement — was drawn up in the interests of the controllers of the largest Spanish boat-building and fishing concerns (including Pescanova SA). Essentially, Morocco is to be lent 3000–4000m pesetas of public money to buy boats, set up a processing industry, improve its port facilities and open a training school; the vessels, plant and expertise will of course be provided by the big Spanish companies. This agreement should be compared to the total lack of support in the past by the government for the small, primitively-equipped Canary vessels and their associated enterprises. It is estimated that 15,000 islanders will be put out of work. Some Spanish boat-owners, however, are said to look forward to using cheap, less-unionized Moroccan crews, if needs be under Hassan's flag, and the Canary strikers have already been warned that, if they persist, their firms may move to Morocco.

The basic issue has not been allowed to surface for public debate: the demarcation of Canary, Saharan and Moroccan territorial waters.

Spain and Morocco have, during the 1970s, laid claim to 200-mile and 70-mile limits respectively, obviously conflicting in the Canary and annexed-Saharan waters; in 1977, Morocco was prospecting for oil within the claimed Canary zone. Simultaneously, and although Hassan and even Adolfo Suárez prefer to ignore it, Sahara guerrillas have been destroying vessels and capturing crews fishing off their shores. Islanders, such as the eight from the fishing boat *Las Palomas*, have been held in the desert for long periods, to bring pressure on the Spanish government; better known is the parallel capture of French *co-opérants* working in Mauritania, though in their case Giscard d'Estaing simply used it as an excuse to increase his country's intervention in the desert war. The Saharauis are not leaving the Canaries to MPAIAC. The island fishermen thus find themselves caught between the Moroccan *dijnn* and the blue men.

1978: Incipient stabilization in the Canaries?

By 1978, faced with MPAIAC terrorism on land, Saharaui harassment on the seas and African demands for 'decolonization' at the OAU, many Canary people had begun to see themselves as manning a frontier post. The government at last took action. The newly-appointed captain-general is known for energy and capability; the defence minister's visit has brought increased fortification. Following a meeting of the Spanish and Moroccan kings, the infiltration of the latter's subjects may have been stopped (at the price of the fishing agreement's ratification?). It was announced that the Canary fishing fleet would be given government aid. All shades of opinion in the Cortes were at least agreed on the unshakeably-Spanish nature of the Canaries.

The year had opened with 'pre-autonomy status' being accorded the archipelago, placing it alongside other Spanish 'regions'. The islanders' petition had begun: 'The traditional aspiration of the Canary people to self-government has now become an urgent necessity'. If welcomed in the Canaries, it was primarily seen in Madrid as a manoeuvre to weaken the MPAIAC and OAU case. Each island is to have a degree of autonomy, with a general assembly consisting in the main of 12 delegates from each of the most heavily peopled islands, Tenerife and Gran Canaria, five each from Palma and Lanzarote, three from Fuerteventura, two from Gomera and one from Hierro. In April the interim Canary Junta was formed, with maximum disagreements based on a dozen political divisions. A first action was to declare, well-meaningly if unrealistically, the general neutrality of the archipelago at all levels of the current international confrontations.

In April came an assassination attempt against Cubillo, in Algiers, by two Spaniards; the MPAIAC leader was very seriously wounded, only just surviving. His assailants were surprisingly caught before they could leave the country, being tried and sentenced, one to death, the other to 20 years' imprisonment. A wave of arrests of MPAIAC activists then at once followed in the Canaries, up to a hundred being detained, together with dynamite and weapons. The Spanish government denied complicity in the assassination attempt.

Ultimate responsibility for the attack on Cubillo did not emerge even from the trial. The official Algerian line was that the Spanish government was responsible, perhaps through a barely-distinguishable right-wing group. If causing political damage—since it increased African sympathy for Cubillo—this would certainly explain the simultaneous campaign against MPAIAC in the Canaries. The Spanish left-wing GRAPO (*Grupo de Resistencia Anti-fascista Primer Octubre*)—whose communiqués Cubillo had read in his broadcasts— said the stabbing was planned by members of the Spanish secret service, based in Bordeaux, following a failed attempt to lure Cubillo there with a promise of weapons. More imaginative reconstructions are that FRAP (*Frente Republicano Anti-fascista y Patriótico*), also Spanish and left-wing, tried to eliminate Cubillo since he was, in fact, a CIA agent—and others have even suggested the attack was organized by the Algerian secret service, presumably to increase African pressure on Spain over the Sahara. The Canaries themselves now hold such anti-MPAIAC bodies as the *Liga Anti-terrorista, the Servicio de Inteligencia Canario*, the *Falange Negra Exterminadora*.

Cubillo's fortunes appear also to have swung, in 1978, at the OAU. During the first half of the year, the Liberation Committee, heads of state and ministers all discussed the Canaries. Attitudes reflected the several spheres of conflict: fears of US, French and NATO expansion into Africa, the all-Africa progressive versus conservative confrontation, the perennial Moroccan-Algerian hostility and the current Saharan war. The fortunes of MPAIAC reached a peak during the first few months of 1978: in the Canaries someone scrawled on a wall 'Classes in Arabic'. In February, opposed only by Morocco and Mauritania, the OAU repeated its 'decolonization' demand and formed a commission (Algeria, Libya, Nigeria, Guinea, Senegal) to examine the issue. The Liberation Committee recommended material aid to MPAIAC. The movement was encouraged to press for recognition by the UN decolonization committee. Even the Socialist International conference, meeting at Dakar in May, decided to send a mission to study the situation in the Canaries. The Spanish government refused to admit an official OAU fact-finding delegation, instead inviting various African states to send representatives to visit the islands and itself sending around a mission to explain its views; some governments, mindful of Spain's ties with the US and of its behaviour towards the Saharauis, felt they preferred to hear the direct views of the Canary islanders.

More discreet diplomacy was also practised by Spain. In January the leader of the socialist party (Felipe González, PSOE) persuaded Algeria to stop Cubillo's broadcasts; the party's steadfast support for the Saharauis was underlined, including its opposition to the sales of arms to Morocco and to the use of the Canaries by French planes on their way to intervene in the war. Algeria and Libya were also reminded by the Count of Barcelona, that Spain had never yet recognized Israel. By June, Moroccan and Mauritanian opposition to OAU pressure on the Canaries was supported at the OAU by their allies there over the Sahara: Senegal, Gabon and the Ivory Coast. The Central African Republic, Mauritius and Tunisia now also followed Hassan's pro-Spanish line. By the time of the Khartoum summit in July, the crystallization of the 'moderate' front, accepting fresh intervention in Africa by their ancient colonial masters, appeared to have taken the interest out of the comparatively-minor issue of the Canaries — though not officially abandoned, it was shelved. And, in September, Algiers held its XVth International Fair: all the main African liberation movements were officially present . . . but there was no sign of MPAIAC. Simultaneously, the Spanish government party (UCD) took an important step towards supporting the Algerian-backed Saharauis: partially this was due to the release of the previously mentioned Canary fishermen but an unpublicized part of the deal seems likely to have been Algeria's abandonment of MPAIAC. It is to be expected that the rest of the African countries will now come to see that MPAIAC is a liberation movement without a people.

In summary, it is a fact that the present Canary Islanders of all classes, though to a large extent supporting increased autonomy as a help towards removing the bureaucratic and economic obstacles to revitalizing the archipelago — if this is still possible on such over-exploited and over-populated islands — are almost unanimously against independence. It remains to be seen whether the extremists and the cynical interplay of world politics continue nevertheless with their various forms of pressure on the Spanish government and the Canary people. Though the ancient islanders were brutally conquered and colonized by the fifteenth-century Spaniards, though there is much African blood, dating from before and after the conquests, in the present islanders, it is their wishes rather than MPAIAC and OAU political dogma and manoeuvres which should take precedence.

APPENDIX TWO
Radiocarbon Datings

Incomplete publication by the excavators has meant that this table is
not in accordance with archaeological practice. In most, perhaps all
cases, the ages given have assumed an assay date of 1950. The half-
lives used were not published. The dates are presumably all un-
corrected. The corrections would be to deduct up to 50 years from
those later than 500 AD; make no change between 500 AD–0; add up
to 40 years to 0–1000 BC. The table is laid out from east to west by
island, the earliest sites first within each division.

Site	Date AD	Lab. Ref.	Sample Assayed
GRAN CANARIA			
Cuevas del Rey			
(Tejeda)	285±60	GRO-1191	Wood
Acusa	430±45	GRO-1127	,,
,,	570±60	GRO-1188	Mummy skin
,,	647 ?	?	'Funeral cave'
Guayadeque	540±60	GRO-1189	Mummy skin
,,	730±60	GRO-1190	Wood
Cascajo de las Nieves			
(Agaete)	737? 783?	?	Coffin wood
Agaete	1000±40	GRO-1872	Wood
La Guancha			
(Gáldar)	1075±60	GRO-1192	,,
TENERIFE			
La Arena			
(Bco. Hondo)	*540BC±60*	CSIC-189	Charcoal
,,	*20BC±60*	CSIC-188	,,
,,	150±60	CSIC-187	,,
Roque Blanco	570±120	T-195B	Human bone
,,	720±80	T-195A	,, ,,
La Enladrillada			
(Tegueste)	735±50	?	'Funeral cave'
,,	800±50	?	,, ,,
Hoya Brunco			
(La Guancha)	910±110	?	Human bone
,,	930±110	?	,, ,,
,,	1170±100	?	,, ,,
La Palmita			
(Tejina)	910±110	?	Pine bier plank

PALMA

Belmaco	800±70	CSIC-257	?
,,	880±70	CSIC-256	?
,,	970±50	CSIC-255	?
,,	1020±70	CSIC-254	?
El Humo	1250±70	CSIC-193	?
,,	1280±70	CSIC-191	?
,,	1350±70	CSIC-194	?
,,	1580±70	CSIC-190	?
,,	1690±70	CSIC-192	?

HIERRO

Hoyo de los Muertos

(Guarazoca)	750±60	CSIC-145	Vegetable layer
,,	900±60	CSIC-144	Human bone

Bibliography

References follow to original source material, ancient and modern, together with the most valuable syntheses and discussion papers. The main periodicals, with abbreviations used below, are:

Almogaren (*A*), *Anuario de Estudios Atlánticos* (*AEA*), *Excavaciones Arqueológicas en España* (*EAE*), *Fontes Rerum Canariarum* (*FRC*), *Homenaje a E. Serra Rafols* (*HSR*), Monographs of the Instituto de Estudios Canarios (IEC), *El Museo Canario* (*MC*), 1963 *Panafrican Prehistory Congress, Proceedings of Fifth Session* (*PPC*), *Revista de Historia* (*Canaria*) (*RH*).

Abercromby, J., 'The prehistoric pottery of the Canary Islands', *J. Roy. Anthrop. Inst.*, 44 (1914)

Abreu y Galindo, J., *Historia de las siete Islas de Canarias* (1632). *In* Glas

Alcina Franch, J., 'Las pintaderas de Gran Canaria', *AEA* 2 (1956)

Alcina Franch, J., 'El vaso con mango-vertedero en el Viejo Mundo y en América', *AEA* 4 (1958)

Alcina Franch, J., 'La figura perniabierta en el Viejo Mundo y en América', *AEA* 8 (1962)

Alcobé, S., 'Grupos sanguíneos en nómadas del Sáhara Occidental', *Inst. Bernadino Sahagún* 1 (1945)

Alimen, H., *The Prehistory of Africa* (London 1957)

Allison, G. B., 'Blood groups and African prehistory', *Actes II Cong. Panaf. Préh.* (Algiers 1952)

Almagro Basch, M., *Prehistoria del Norte de Africa y del Sáhara Español* (Barcelona 1946)

Almagro Basch, M., *El Estado Actual de la Investigación de la Prehistoria del Norte de Africa y del Sáhara*, Monograph, Instituto de Estudios Africanos (Madrid 1968)

Alvarez Delgado, J., 'Antropónimos de Canarias' *AEA* 2 (1956)

Alvarez Delgado, J., 'La conquista de Tenerife' *RH* (1959)

Alvarez Delgado, J., 'El episodio de Iballa', *AEA* 5 (1959)

Alvarez Delgado, J., 'Primera conquista y cristianización de Gomera', *AEA* 6 (1960)

Alvarez Delgado, J., *Inscripciones líbicas en Canarias* (Tenerife 1964)

Anon., *Conquista de la Isla de Gran Canaria*, ed. Bonnet, B., Serra Rafols, E., *FRC* 1 (1933)

Anthonioz, R., 'Les Imraguens', *Bull. I.F.A.N.* 30 (1968)

Arco Aguilar, M. del, 'El enterramiento canario prehispánico', *AEA* 22 (1976)

Ashizawa, K., 'Repartition Mondiale des Dermatoglyphes Palmaires', *L'Anthrop.* 76 (1976)

Azurara, Gomes Eannes de, *The Chronicle of the Discovery and Conquest of Guinea*, trans. and ed. Beazley, C. R., Prestage, E., (London 1896)

Bacallado, J. J., 'Distribución y evolución de la avifauna Canaria', *see* Kunkel

Balout, L., 'Le problème du peuplement préhistorique de l'archipel Canarien', *AEA* 15 (1969)

Balout, L., 'Canarias y Africa en los tiempos prehistóricos', *AEA* 17 (1971)

Bannerman, D. A., *The Canary Islands* (London 1922)

Bardon, L., Bouyssonie, J. & A., 'Outils écaillés par percussion', *Rev. Ecole Anthrop. Paris* 16 (1906)

Barker-Webb, P., Berthelot, S., *Histoire Naturelle des Iles Canaries* (Paris 1835–49)

Beltrán Martínez, A., *Los Grabados del Barranco de Balos (Gran Canaria)* (Gran Canaria 1971)

Beltrán Martínez, A., Alzola, J. M., *La Cueva Pintada de Galdar* (Zaragoza 1974)

Benítez Padilla, S., 'Origen de las hachas de jadeïta', *PPC* (1966)

Berthelot, S., Barker-Webb, P., *Histoire Naturelle des Iles Canaries* (Paris 1835–49)

Berthelot, S., 'Les Guanches', *Mem. Soc. Ethn.* (1841, 1845)

Berthelot, S., *La Conquête des Canaries* (Tenerife 1849)

Berthelot, S., 'Nouvelle découverte d'inscriptions lapidaires à l'Ile de Fer', *Bull. Soc. Geog.* (1876)

Berthelot, S., *Antiquitées Canariennes* (Paris 1879)

Boccaccio, G., *De Canaria* (Florence 1827). Contains Recco's MS

Bosch Millares, J., 'La medicina canaria en la época prehispánica', *AEA* 7 (1961)

Bosch Millares, J., 'Paleopatología craneana de los primitivos pobladores de Canarias', *AEA* 15 (1969)

Bosch Millares, J., 'Paleopatología ósea en los indígenas prehispánicos de Canarias', *AEA* 17 (1971)

Boutier, P., Verrier, J. le, *Le Canarien* (1402–5). For La Salle's version *see* Serra (1959b), for Bethencourt's *see* Major

Bramwell, D. and Z. I., *Wild Flowers of the Canary Islands* (Tenerife 1974a)

Bramwell, D., 'Los Bosques de Canarias', *MC* (1974b)

Bramwell, D., 'The Endemic Flora of the Canary Islands', *see* Kunkel (1976)

Bravo, A. M., Las Casas, M. T. de, 'Grupos sanguíneos en La Palma', *Acta Médica de Tenerife* 10 (1958)

Cabildo de Tenerife, *Acuerdos, 1497–1525, FRC* 4, 5, 13, 16 (1949–68)

Ca da Mosto, A. de, *Voyages*, trans. and ed. Crone, G. R. (1937)

Camacha y Perez Galdós, G., 'El cultivo de la Caña de Azucar en Gran Canaria', *AEA* 7 (1961)

Camps, G., 'Tableau chronologique de la Préhistoire Récente du Nord de l'afrique', *Bull. Soc. Préh. Fr.* 71 (1974)

Caro Baroja, J., *Estudios Saharianos* (Madrid 1955)

Castillo Ruíz de la Vergara, P. A., *Descripción de las Islas Canarias* (1737), ed. Santiago Rodríguez, M., (Gran Canaria 1954)

Castro Alfín, D., 'El poblado de La Atalayita, Fuerteventura', *MC* (1972)

Charon, M., *et al*, 'Occupation Holocène de la Région du Cap-Juby', *Bull. Mem. Soc. Anthrop. Paris* 10 (1973)

Chil y Naranjo, G., *Estudios Históricos de las Islas Canarias* (Gran Canaria 1876–80)

Cioranescu, A., ed., *Thomas Nichols, IEC* (1963)

Cioranescu, A., 'Los primeros pobladores de Sta Cruz de Tenerife', *AEA* (1975)

Classe, A., 'La Fonética del Silbo Gomero', *RH* (1959)

Comisión de Arqueología del Museo Canario (CAMC), 'Inventario de yacimientos rupestres de Gran Canaria', *MC* (1974)

Coon, C. S., *The Living Races of Man* (London 1966)

Cortés Alonso, V., 'La conquista de las Islas Canarias a través de la venta de esclavos en Valencia', *AEA* 1 (1955)

Cortés Alonso, V., *La esclavitud en Valencia 1479–1516* (Madrid 1964)

Cortés Alonso, V., 'Los cautivos canarios', *HSR* (1970)

Crawford, O. G. S., *The Eye Goddess* (London 1957)

Cro-Magnon Symposium (Gran Canaria, Tenerife), 'Proceedings', *AEA* 15 (1969)

Cruz Jiménez, M., *et al*, *Carta Arqueológica de Tenerife* (Tenerife 1973)

Darias y Padrón, D. D., *La Isla del Hierro* (Tenerife 1929)

Debarry, T., *Notes of a residence in the Canary Isles* (London 1851)

Diego Cuscoy, L., 'Noticias sobre el gofio de "Vidrio"', *RH* (1947)

Diego Cuscoy, L., 'El Ajuar de las Cuevas Sepulcrales de las Canarias Occidentales', *II Cong. Nac. Arq.* (Madrid 1951)

Diego Cuscoy, L., 'La cueva sepulcral del Bco de Jagua, en el Rosario (Tenerife)', *RH* (1957)

Diego Cuscoy, L., 'Los grabados rupestres de Tigalete Hondo (Mazo, La Palma)', *RH* (1958)

Diego Cuscoy, L. *et al*, *La Cueva Sepulcral del Roque Blanco* (Tenerife 1960a)

Diego Cuscoy, L., 'Una Cueva de pastores en La Dehesa', *MC* (1960b)

Diego Cuscoy, L., 'Armas de madera y vestido del aborigen de las Islas Canarias', *AEA* 7 (1961a)

Diego Cuscoy, L., 'Ajuar doméstico guanche', *RH* (1961b)

Diego Cuscoy, L., 'Una cueva sepulcral del Bco. del Agua de Díos, en Tegueste (Tenerife)', *EAE* 23 (1964a)

Diego Cuscoy, L., 'Tres cuevas sepulcrales guanches (Tenerife)', *EAE* 37 (1964b)

Diego Cuscoy, L., 'Notas sobre El Julan (Hierro)', *PPC* (1966)

Diego Cuscoy, L., *Los Guanches, vida y cultura* (Tenerife 1968a)

Diego Cuscoy, L., *Armas de los primitivos canarios* (Tenerife 1968b)

Diego Cuscoy, L., 'La covacha del Roque de la Campana (Mazo, La Palma), *HSR* (1970)

Diego Cuscoy, L. *Gánigo* (Tenerife 1971)

Diego Cuscoy, L., *Guía, Museo Arqueológico de Tenerife* (Tenerife 1973)

Diego Cuscoy, L., 'Escondrijo del Risco de los Guanches', *MC* 35 (1974)

Diego Cuscoy, L., Galand, L., 'Nouveaux documents des Isles Canaries', *L'Anthrop.* 79 (1975)

Diego Cuscoy, L. 'Un fragmento de los Apuntes de J. de Anchieta y Alarcón (Necrópolis y Momias)', *AEA* 22 (1976)

Dug Godoy, I., 'Excavaciones en el poblado prehispánico de Zonzamas (Lanzarote)', *MC* (1972)

Dug Godoy, I., 'Idolos y adornos de Tejía (Lanzarote)', *MC* (1974)

Espinosa, A. de, *The Guanches of Tenerife (1594)*, ed. Markham, C., (London 1907)

Falkenburger, F., 'Nueva clasificación craneológica de los antiguos habitantes de Canarias', *Act. Mem. Soc. Esp. Ant. Etn. Preh.* 17 (1942)

Fernandes, V., *Das Ilhas do Mar Oceano* (Portugal 1507)

Fernandes, V., *Description de la Côte Occidental d'Afrique*, ed. Monod, T., *et al* (Bissau 1951)

Fernández, J. M., 'La fauna entomológica canaria', *PPC* (1966)

Fernandopullé, D., 'Climatic characteristics of the Canary Islands', *see* Kunkel (1976)

Fischer, E., 'Sind die alten Kanarier ausgestorben?', *Zeitschrift für Ethn.* 62 (1930)

Font Tullot, I., 'El clima de las Islas Canarias', *AEA* 5 (1959)

Frutuoso, G., *Las Islas Canarias*, ed. Serra Rafols, E., *et al*, *FRC* 12 (1965)

Fusté, M., 'La excavación de la Cueva del Morro (Guía, Gran Canaria)', *MC* (1958a)

Fusté, M., 'Antropología de Gran Canaria', *MC* (1958b)

Fusté, M., 'Contribution a l'Anthropologie de la Grand Canarie', *L'Anthrop.* 63 (1959)

Fusté, M., *Estudio Antropológico de los Esqueletos inhumados en túmulos de la región de Gáldar (Gran canaria)*, *MC* (1961)

Fusté, M., 'Diferencias antropogeográficas en las poblaciones de Gran Canaria', *AEA* 8 (1962)

Fusté, M., *et al*, 'La distribución de los tipos de haptoglobinas en la población de Canarias', *MC* (1965a)

Fusté, M., 'Physical Anthropology of the Canary Islanders', *Am. J. Phys. Anthrop.* 23 (1965b)

Fusté, M., 'Nuevas aportaciones a la Antropología de las Islas Canarias', *PPC* (1966a)

Fusté, M., 'L'Anthropologie des populations préhistoriques des Iles Canaries', *PPC* (1966b)

García y Bellido, A., 'Anforas antiguas de Canarias', *HSR* (1970)

García Marquéz, F., 'Almogarems y goros', *AEA* 14 (1968)

Garralda Benajes, MD, 'Cuentas de collar prehistóricas en Gran Canaria', *MC* (1966)

Glas, G., *The Discovery and Conquest of the Canary Islands* (London 1764)

González Antón, R., 'La Cerámica Prehispánica de Tenerife', *RH* (1971)

González Antón, R., *La Cerámica de Gran Canaria* (Tenerife 1973)

González Yanes, E., Marrero Rodríguez, M., ed., *Protocolos del Escribano Hernán Guerra, La Laguna, 1508–10*, *FRC* 7 (1954)

Guasch, J., *et al*, 'Los factores hemáticos en España', *Medicina Clínica* 18 (1952)

Guímera Ravina, A., 'La Cueva Sepulcral del Roque de la Tierra, Roques de Anaga, Tenerife', *AEA* 19 (1973)

Hausen, H., 'A pre-Canarian basement complex, remains of an ancient African Borderland', *PPC* (1966)

Hernández, P., 'Eran monoteístas nuestros aborígenes?', *II Cong. nac. de Arq.* (Madrid 1952a)

Hernández, P., 'Neolitismo de los aborígenes canarios', *II Cong. Nac de Arq.* (Madrid 1952b)

Hernández Pérez, M. S., 'Contribución a la carta arqueológica de La Palma', *AEA* 18 (1972)

Hernández Pérez, M. S., *La Palma Prehispánica* (Gran Canaria 1977)

Herrera, E., *La Gomera* (Tenerife 1965)

Hooton, E. A., *The Ancient Inhabitants of the Canary Islands* (Cambridge, Mass., 1925)

Huetz de Lemps, A., *Le climât des Iles Canaries*, S.E.D.E.S., Tome 54, Univ. de Paris (1969)

Jiménez de Gregoria, F., 'La población de las Islas Canarias, 1750–1800', *AEA* 14 (1968)

Jiménez Sánchez, S., Schwidetsky, I., 'Haar- und Augenfarbe in der Provinz Gran Canaria', *Homo* 9 (1958a)

Jiménez Sánchez, S., 'Cerámica Gran Canaria de factura Neolítica', *AEA* (1958b)

Jiménez Sánchez, S., 'El Complejo Arqueológico en Tauro Alto, en Mogán (Gran Canaria), *EAE* 39 (1964)

Jiménez Sánchez, S., 'Yacimientos arqueológicos de Guía de Gran Canaria', *AEA* 11 (1965a)

Jiménez Sánchez, S., 'El Yacimiento del Junquillo, Rosita del Vicario (Bco. de la Torre, Fuerteventura)', *RH* (1965b)

Jiménez Sánchez, S., 'Pinturas rupestres antropomorfas en Gran Canaria', *PPC* (1966a)

Jiménez Sánchez, S., 'Exponentes megalíticos cultuales de los canarios aborígenes', *PPC* (1966b)

Jiménez Sánchez, S., 'Estaciones Arqueológicas de Canarios Aborígenes', *AEA* 12 (1966c)

Jiménez Sánchez, S., 'Nuevas notas de Prehistoria Canaria', *AEA* 16 (1970a)

Jiménez Sánchez, S., 'Nuevos pictogramas y grabados parietales' *RH* (1970b)

Johnson, R. H., *et al*, 'Blood groups of the Aït Haddidu Berbers of Morocco', *Hum. Biol.* 35 (1963)

Kämmer, F., 'The influence of man on the vegetation of the island of Hierro', *see* Kunkel

Klemmer, K., 'The Amphibia and Reptilia of the Canary Islands', *see* Kunkel

Kraus, H. H., 'Zwei prähistorische Felsinschriften in den Bco. de Silva (Telde) von Gran Canaria' *MC* 1964)

Kunkel, G., ed., *Biogeography and Ecology in the Canary Islands* (The Hague 1976)

Lorenzo Perera, M. J., 'Un enterramiento individual en la Cueva de Chajora, Guía de Isora (Tenerife)', *AEA* 22 (1976)

Lorenzo Perera, M. J., *et al*, 'Una cueva sepulcral en la ladera de Chabaso

(Igueste de Candelaria, Tenerife), *AEA* 22 (1976)

Lotte, Lt., 'Coûtumes des Imraguens', *J. Soc. Af.* 7 (1937)

Maire, Sieur le, *Voyages aux Iles Canaries, Cap-verd, Sénégal* (Paris 1695)

Major, R. H., trans. and ed., *The Canarian* (London 1872)

Marcy, G., 'El verdadero destino de las 'pintaderas' de Canarias', *RH* (1942)

Marín y Cubas, T., *Historia de las Siete Islas Canarias* (Madrid 1687)

Marrero Rodríguez, M., *La esclavitud en Tenerife, IEC* (1966)

Marrero Rodríguez, M., 'Los Procuradores de los naturales canarios', *HSR* (1970)

Martínez de la Peña, D., 'Un episodio de la Conquista de Canarias en una famosa pintura renacentista de los Países Bajos', *AEA* 16 (1970)

Mauny, R., *Gravures, peintures et inscriptions rupestres de l'Ouest Africain* (Dakar 1954)

Mauny, R., *Les Navigations Mediévales sur les Côtes Sahariennes antérieures à la découverte Portugaise (1434)*, (Lisbon 1960)

Meco, J., 'Paleontología del Neógeno y Cuatenario marino del Sáhara Español', *MC* (1974)

Mercer, J., *Canary Islands: Fuerteventura* (Newton Abbot 1973)

Mercer, J., *Spanish Sahara* (London 1976)

Mercer, J., 'The Canary Islanders', *World Minorities* (Minority Rights Group, London 1977)

Mercer, J., *The Sahrawis of Western Sahara* (Minority Rights Group, London, 1979a)

Mercer, J., 'The Canary Islanders in Western Mediterranean Politics', *African Affairs* (April, 1979b)

Mies, G., 'Untersuchung einiger Lederarbeiten der Ureinwohner der Kanarischen Inseln', *MC* (1960)

Moal, G. le, 'Les Habitations semi-souterraines en Afrique de l'Ouest', *J. Soc. Af.* 30 (1960)

Monod, T., *Gravures, peintures et inscriptions rupestres du Sahara Occidental, Bull. C.E.A.O.F.*, A, 7 (1938)

Morales Lezcano, V., *Relaciones mercantiles entre Inglaterra y los Archipiélagos del Atlántico Ibérico 1503–1783)*, IEC (1970)

Museo Canario, *Guía* (1958)

Naranjo Suarez, J., 'Un nuevo ídolo aborigen en los Altos de Mogán', *MC* (1970)

Navy Hydrographer, *African Pilot: West Africa* (London 1967)

Nuez Caballero, S. de la, 'Palabras prehispánicas canarias recogidas por Pérez Galdós', *AEA* 12 (1966)

Núñez de la Peña, J., *Conquista y antigüedades de Canarias* (Madrid 1976)

Ortiz de Zárate, *Reformación del Repartimiento de Tenerife en 1506, FRC* 6 (1953)

Ortuño, F., 'Tipos de vegetación de Canarias', *AEA* 1 (1955)

Parejo, M., 'El sistema ABO en la población actual de las Islas Canarias', *PPC* (1966)

Pellicer, M., 'Panoramas y perspectivas de la arqueología canaria', *RH* 1968

Pellicer, M., 'Elementos culturales de la Prehistoria Canaria', *RH* (1971)

Pellicer, M., Acosta, P., 'La Cueva del Bco. de la Arena', *AEA* 17 (1971)

Pellicer, M., Acosta, P., 'Excavaciones Arqueológicas en la cueva de la Arena (Bco. Hondo, Tenerife), *AEA* 22 (1976)

Pérez de Barradas, J., *Estado actual de las investigaciones prehistoricas sobre Canarias* (Madrid 1938)

Pérez González, R., 'La Laguna', *Est. Geog.* 32 (1971)

Pérez Vidal, J., 'La cestería en Canarias', *RH* (1961)

Pérez Vidal, J., 'La ganadería canaria', *AEA* 9 (1963)

Pérez Vidal, J., 'La vivienda canaria' *AEA* 13 (1967)

Pericot, L., 'Prehistoria Canaria', *AEA* 1 (1955)

Pitard, C. J., Proust, L., *Les Iles Canaries* (Paris 1908)

Pons, J., Fusté, M., 'Las líneas dermopapilares y el complejo racial de Gran Canaria', *MC* (1963)

Pons, J., 'Sobre la antropología canaria', *AEA* 15 (1969)

Posnansky, M., McIntosh, R., 'New Radiocarbon dates for North and West Africa', *J. Af. Hist.* 17 (1976)

Powers, R., 'Dental anomalies in Guanche skulls', *Man* 59 (1959)

Pre-Columbus Transatlantic Relations, First International Symposium (Canary Islands 1970), 'Proceedings', *AEA* 17 (1971)

Recco, Niccoloso da, *Expedition Chronicle (1341)*, *see* Boccacio

Régulo Pérez, J., 'El habla de La Palma', *RH* (1968)

Riley, J., *Loss of the American Brig 'Commerce'* (London 1817)

Río Ayala, J. del, 'Un radical F en algunos topónimos de Canarias', *PPC* (1966)

Röben, P., 'Limnetic fauna of the Canary Islands', *see* Kunkel (1976)

Robert, D., 'Pôteries Récentes des Iles Canaries', *J. Soc. Af.* 30 (1960)

Roberts, D. F., *et al*, 'Blood groups and the affinities of the Canary Islanders', *Man* N.S.1 (1966)

Robin, J., 'Moors and Canary Islanders on the coast of the Western Sahara', *Geog. J.* 125 (1955)

Rohen J., 'Histologische Untersuchungen an Augen altkanarischer Mumien', *Homo* 10 (1959)

Rosenfeld, A., 'Prehistoric pottery from Lanzarote', *MC* (1963)

Rösing, I. S., 'ABO-Blutgruppen und Rh-Faktoren auf Teneriffa' *Homo* 18 (1967)

Rumeu de Armas, A., *España en el Africa Atlántida* (Madrid 1956)

Sánchez Herrero, J., 'La población de las Islas Canarias en la segunda mitad del siglo XVII (1676–88', *AEA* 21 (1975)

Schmincke, H. U., 'The Geology of the Canary Islands', *see* Kunkel (1976)

Schwartzfischer, F., Liebrich, K., 'Serologische Untersuchungen an prähistorischen Bevölkerungen, insbesondere an altkanarischen Mumien', *Homo* 14 (1963)

Schwidetsky, I., 'Anthropologische Beobachtungen auf Teneriffa', *Homo* 7 (1956)

Schwidetsky, I., 'In welchem Alter starben die alten Kanarier? (Teneriffa)', *Homo* 8 (1957)

Schwidetsky, I., 'In welchem Alter starben die Altkanarier? (Gran Canaria)', *Homo* 9 (1958)

Schwidetsky, I., 'Faktoren des Schädelbaus bei der vorspanischen Bevölkerung der Kanarischen Inseln', *Homo* 10 (1959)

Schwidetsky, I., *La población prehispánica de las Islas Canarias* (Tenerife 1963)

Schwidetsky, I., 'Anthropologische Untersuchungen auf den Kanarischen Inseln: Herkunftskreise und Fingerbeermuster, Provinz Teneriffa', *Homo* 15 (1964)

Schwidetsky, I., 'Etude d'Anthropologie sociale sur la Population pre-espagnole des Iles Canaries', *PPC* (1966)

Schwidetsky, I., 'Groupes sanguins et histoire des populations aux Iles Canaries', *HSR* (1970)

Schwidetsky, I., 'Die vorspanische und die heutige Bevölkerung der Kanarischen Inseln', *Homo* 22 (1971)

Schwidetsky, I., 'Anthropologische Untersuchung auf den Kanarischen Inseln: Herkunftskreise und Fingerbeermuster, Provinz Gran Canaria', *Homo* 23 (1972)

Schwidetsky, I., *Investigaciones Antropológicas en las Islas Canarias* (Tenerife 1975)

Schwidetsky, I., 'The Prehispanic Population of the Canary Islands', *see* Kunkel (1976)

Sedeño, A., *La Conquista de Gran Canaria (1484)* (Gran Canaria 1936)

Serra Rafols, E., 'Las datas de Tenerife', *Act. Mem. Soc. Esp. Ant. Etn. Preh.* 19 (1944)

Serra Rafols, E., 'La navegación primitiva en los mares de Canarias', *RH* (1957)

Serra Rafols, E., 'Los Ultimos Canarios', *RH* (1959a)

Serra Rafols, E., Cioranescu, A., ed., *Le Canarien* (Tenerife 1959b)

Serra Rafols, E., 'El Redescubrimiento de las Islas Canarias en el siglo catorce', *RH* (1961)

Serra Rafols, E., 'Les relations possibles des cultures canariennes avec celles de l'W. Africain', *PPC* (1966)

Serra Rafols, E., 'La navegación primitiva en el Atlántico Africano', *AEA* 17 (1971)

Sevillano Colom, F., 'Mallorca y Canarias', *Hispania* 120 (1972)

Siemens Hernández, L., 'Instrumentos de sonido entre los habitantes prehispánicos de las Islas Canarias', *AEA* 15 (1969)

Siemens Hernández, L., Barreto de Siemens, H., 'Los Esclavos Aborígenes canarios en Madeira (1455–1505)', *AEA* 20 (1974)

Sosa, L. de, *El Adelantado Don Alonso de Lugo y su Residencia*, ed. Rosa Olivera, L. de la, Serra Rafols, E., *FRC* 3 (1949)

Souville, G., 'Relations entre l'Afrique du Nord et les Canaries au Neolithique', *AEA* 15 (1969)

Sprat, T., ed., *Relation of the Pico Teneriffe* (London 1667)

Stone, O., *Tenerife and its six satellites* (London 1887)

Tamagnini, E., 'Os antigos habitantes des Canarias', *Rev. Fac. Ciencias Univ. Coimbra* 2, No. 3 (1932)

Tarradell, M., 'Los diversos horizontes de la prehistoria canaria', *AEA* 15 (1969)

Torriani, L., *Descripción de las Islas Canarias (1590)*, ed. Cioranescu, A. (Tenerife 1959)

Valera, D. de, *La Crónica de los Reyes Católicos (1480–*3), *FRC* 2 (1934)

Vaufrey, R., 'L'âge des spirales de l'art rupestre nord-africain', *Bull. Soc. Préh. Fr.* 33 (1936)

Verlinden, C., *L'Esclavage dans l'Europe Mediévale: Péninsule Iberique-France* (Brugge 1955)

Verlinden, C., 'Lanzorotto Molocello et la découverte Portugaise des Canaries', *Rev. Belg. Philol. Hist.* 36, No. 4 (1958)

Verneau, R., 'Semites aux Iles Canaries', *Bull. Soc. Anthrop.* (1882)

Verneau, R., 'Une mission scientifique dans l'archipel canarien', *Arch. Missions Sc. Litt.* 2nd S., 13 (1887)

Verneau, R., 'Habitations, sepultures et lieux sacrés des anciens canariens', *Rev. d'Ethnog.* 8 (1889)

Verneau, R., *Cinq années de séjour aux Isles Canaries* (Paris 1891)

Viana, A. de, *Antigüedades de las Islas Canarias* (1604)

Viera y Clavijo, J. de, *Historia General de las Islas Canarias* (Madrid 1772)

Wölfel, D. J., 'La curia romana y la corona de España en la defensa de los aborígenes canarios', *Anthropos* 25 (1930)

Wölfel, D. J., *Leonardo Torriani, Die Kanarischen Inseln und ihre Urbewohner* (Leipzig 1940)

Zeuner, F. E., 'Líneas Costeras del Pleistoceno en las Islas Canarias' *AEA* 4 (1958a)

Zeuner, F. E., 'Domesticated animals from Guayadeque', *MC* (1958b)

Zeuner, F. E., 'Prehistoric Idols from Gran Canaria', *Man* (1960)

Zeuner, F. E., 'Prehistoric Hand Adzes from Gran Canaria', *Man* (1961)

Zeuner, F. E., *A History of Domesticated Animals* (London 1963)

Zeuner, F. E., 'The Cultural Problems of the Canary Islands', *PPC* (1966)

Zeuner, F. E., Bravo, T., 'The first fossil mammal (rat) from the Canary Islands', *PPC* (1966)

Index

British Museum Society

The British Museum Society